Richard Brookhiser

Alexander Hamilton
American

A Touchstone Book
Published by Simon & Schuster
New York   London   Sydney

TOUCHSTONE
Rockefeller Center
1230 Avenue of the Americas
New York, NY 10020

First Touchstone Edition 2000

TOUCHSTONE and colophon are registered trademarks
of Simon & Schuster, Inc.

Designed by Carla Bolte

Manufactured in the United States of America

20   19   18   17   16   15   14   13   12   11

The Library of Congress has cataloged the Free Press edition as follows:

Brookhiser, Richard.
    Alexander Hamilton, American / Richard Brookhiser.
        p.   cm.
    Includes bibliographical references (p.   ) and index.
    1. Hamilton, Alexander, 1757–1804.   2. Statesmen—United States—
    Biography.   3. United States—Politics and government—1783–1809.
    I. Title.
    E302.6.H2B76   1999   98-46846
    973.4'092—dc21   CIP
    [b]

ISBN-13: 978-0-684-83919-6
ISBN-10:   0-684-83919-9
ISBN-13: 978-0-684-86331-3 (Pbk)
ISBN-10:   0-684-86331-6 (Pbk)

Illustration credits: 2. Monmouth County Historical Association, Gift of the Descendants of David Leavitt, 1937; 3. The Museum of the City of New York; 4. Collection of The New-York Historical Society; 6. Schaffer Library, Union College, Schenectady, NY [for Hamilton]; Independence National Historical Park Collection [for Jefferson]; 7. The Historical Society of Pennsylvania; 8. The Bank of New York; 9. UPI/Corbis-Bettmann; 10. Collection of The New-York Historical Society; 11. Portrait File, Miriam and Ira D. Wallach Division of Art, Prints and Photographs, The New York Public Library; 12. Collection of The New-York Historical Society; 13. Portrait File, Miriam and Ira D. Wallach Division of Art, Prints and Photographs, The New York Public Library; 14. Collection of the New Jersey Historical Society; 15. Chase Manhattan Bank Archives; 16. The Maryland Historical Society, Baltimore, Maryland; 17. The Parish of Trinity Church in the City of New York; 18. National Park Service, Manhattan Sites, Hamilton Grange National Memorial; 19. Collection of The New-York Historical Society; 20. Courtesy of Donaldson, Lufkin & Jenrette Collection of Americana.

FOR WILLIAM RUSHER

Acknowledgments

I WOULD LIKE TO THANK Robert J. Berk, William Cissel, Forrest McDonald, North Peterson, and Dorothy Twohig for help and encouragement.

I would also like to thank my editors, Adam Bellow and Bruce Nichols, and my agent, Michael Carlisle.

Contents

Alexander Hamilton
American

Note on Money

DURING THE LATE eighteenth century, the British Empire used the old British system in which 12 pence equaled a shilling and 20 shillings equaled a pound. But in the Thirteen Colonies, money of any sort was rare. The most common coin was the Spanish piece of eight, commonly called the Spanish dollar. After the Revolution, the United States adopted the decimal system it has today, with 100 cents to the dollar. New York State declared the pound equal to $2.50; a shilling equaled 12 ½ cents. The British pound (the pound sterling) was more valuable, worth over $3.

Conversion is guesswork. A decent guess is that the dollar in Hamilton's lifetime (except for the period of wild inflation during the Revolution) would be worth approximately thirteen dollars today.

Introduction

FROM THE BEGINNING, the Fourth of July has been an occasion for interpreting, defining, and imagining America as well as commemorating it. On July 4, 1789, in New York City, the nation's capital, the main oration of the day, and the most important interpretation, was given by a local politician and lawyer, Alexander Hamilton.

He spoke in St. Paul's Chapel, an Episcopal church on Broadway, which still stands, like a toy at the feet of the World Trade Center. His speech was a eulogy for the Revolutionary hero General Nathanael Greene. The republic was already old enough to have buried heroes who were not martyrs in battle: Greene had died of sunstroke on the Georgia plantation he had been given as a reward for liberating the state in the last year of fighting. Hamilton knew his subject well: Greene had spotted him as a promising artillery captain in the early days of the war.

Hamilton had gone on to be a colonel on George Washington's staff for four years. He had served in the New York State Assembly and in Congress. He had been a delegate to the Constitutional Convention and one of the Constitution's ablest and most prolific advocates in the newspapers. In his spare time, he had passed the New York bar exam and established himself as a lawyer. In two months, he would become the first secretary of the treasury. He was thirty-two years old.

Hamilton had wavy chestnut brown hair, a classical nose, and deep-set violet eyes. People called him "little"—Fisher Ames, who admired him, called him a "great little man"; John Adams, who did not, called him "the little man."[1] He was five feet seven, not short by the standards

I

of the day (Adams was three inches shorter). But he was slim when many men, including Adams, were stout. Strengthening the impression of littleness was something youthful about him, younger even than his years: lively, open, impetuous. The most famous portrait of him, by John Trumbull (the engraving on the $10 bill is taken from it), shows the hair, the features, and the stature. But the portrait his family liked best, by James Sharples, also shows an anticipatory crinkling at the corners of his eyes and lips. He looks as if he is eager to say something, probably something smart.

As an orator, Hamilton was not a spellbinder. His method, which could be just as effective, was to find the first principles of his topic, and tirelessly, even relentlessly, work out their consequences. "There is no skimming over the surface of a subject with him," wrote William Pierce, a fellow delegate to the Constitutional Convention who had listened to him speak, sometimes for hours at a stretch; "he must sink to the bottom to see what foundation it rests on." The foundation of his eulogy of Greene was a meditation on character and opportunity. "[T]hose great revolutions which occasionally convulse society," he told the former revolutionaries assembled in St. Paul's Chapel, "compensate for the evils they produce" by "bring[ing] to light talents and virtues which might otherwise have languished in obscurity, or only shot forth a few scattered and wandering rays. Nathanael Greene, descended from reputable parents, but not placed by birth in [an] elevated rank . . . must, in all probability, have contented himself with [a] humble lot . . . scarcely conscious of the resources of his own mind, had not the violated rights of his country called him to act a part on a more splendid and more ample theater."[2]

This was certainly true of Greene, a son of Quakers, who learned about warfare from reading books in a Boston bookstore. But the revolution showed that the resources of his mind were spectacularly suited to the real thing, for in his last campaign, though he lost all the battles he fought, he managed to maneuver the British away from their base and to final defeat at Yorktown.

But Hamilton's analysis of how convulsions churn society, bringing talents from obscurity to an ample theater, was even more suited to himself. Nathanael Greene came from nowhere special; Alexander Hamilton came from nowhere. Greene was born in Rhode Island, a future state, albeit a small one. Hamilton was born and raised in the sugar islands of the West Indies, and did not come to America until he was fifteen. Greene had "reputable parents," and worked in the family business managing a forge before war called. Hamilton was put out to work as a clerk in a merchant house when he was nine. Greene's parents were married. Hamilton was illegitimate—a "whore" child,[3] as he was called in a court document—and his father deserted his family the year Hamilton went to work. Many of the leaders of the American Revolution were rich, powerful men—Washington, Thomas Jefferson, John Hancock. None had come from so far back as Hamilton.

But the Revolution was over. How then could the experience of Greene, or Hamilton, be repeated? What made Hamilton's rise in the world more than an episode, or a detail in a dramatic life, is that he had thought of ways to bring light to the talents of other men as well as himself: an interlocking system of law, finance, and work that would enable his countrymen to become conscious of their resources. He did not outline his plans to his Fourth of July audience; there were not many details yet to outline. But he had been thinking of the problem for years, and the rest of his life, especially his term as treasury secretary, would be devoted to it. Most men who make it provide for their families, thank fortune, and maybe give to charity. Some raise the drawbridge behind them. Hamilton, who had already come from the Caribbean to the pulpit at St. Paul's, and would go on to more glittering prizes yet, wanted to generalize his experience. That is why he is a great man, and a great American. Americans like to think of themselves as self-made, even though few of us are. Hamilton was, and wanted to give others the opportunities to become so.

This is not what most people today know about Alexander Hamilton. He is by no means a forgotten man, but his reputation, though vivid, is skewed. He survives in our memory as a collection of sensational details—his birth ("the bastard brat of a Scotch pedlar," as John Adams put it);[4] a very public adultery, the first American political sex scandal; his death in a duel, shot by the vice president of the

United States. These are interesting facts, but hardly inspiring, or even coherent.

He is also remembered as the money guy, the chief financial officer who took over the nation's books when they were in bad shape, and balanced them. Americans speak disdainfully of the other republics in the hemisphere as banana republics—poor, therefore chaotic, therefore prey to dictators and radicals. Had Hamilton not done his job so well, the United States might have become a maple republic. That is certainly important, but nobody loves his accountant. "The discussion of such matters," as Aristotle observed, "is not unworthy of philosophy, but to be engaged in them practically is illiberal and irksome."[5] There is a statue of Hamilton in front of the Treasury Department in Washington, D.C., and millions of tourists pass it on their way to the White House next door. But it is not a destination. Hamilton, we feel, belongs where he is, on the $10 bill, not on Mt. Rushmore.

There is a deeper layer of his reputation that is less flattering. According to this view, although Hamilton signed the Constitution, he did not believe in it, or the liberties it secured. He put up with republican government because he had to, while laboring to transform it, or even subvert it. At heart, he was an aristocrat and a plutocrat, who favored rule by an elite of the rich. James Madison, a colleague and coauthor who became an enemy, said as much in a left-handed tribute long after Hamilton had died. "If his Theory of Government deviated from the Republican Standard, he had the candor to avow it, and the greater merit of cooperating [in] a system which was not his choice."[6] For the sake of Hamilton's achievements, we are willing to ignore his political preferences, in the same grudging spirit in which he swallowed America's preferences. But he is not one of us.

The most lurid version of this view makes Hamilton a corrupter, as well as an alien, a serpent in the American Eden, forcing on us the dominion of big money or big government or both. When Thomas Jefferson, another enemy, reached the presidency on the ruins of Hamilton's party and political hopes, he complained that he was in fact the loser. "When this government was first established, it was possible to have kept it going on true principles but . . . the ideas of Hamilton destroyed that hope in the bud. We can pay off his debts in fifteen years: but we can never get rid of his financial system." The poet and economist Ezra Pound put it more bluntly: "[A]s for Hamilton . . . he was the Prime snot in ALL American history."[7] When I bought a nineteenth-century biography of Hamilton, by Henry Cabot Lodge, in a used bookstore, I found on the first page a penciled note: "Remember, in reading this book, that Lodge is greatly prejudiced in favor of Hamilton." You wouldn't find a warning label in a secondhand copy of Dumas Malone's *Jefferson and the Rights of Man.*

Historians and biographers are not immune to extreme views. The partisan spirit of American politics during the second half of Hamilton's career—one historian called the 1790s the "age of passion"—continues to inflect accounts of it two centuries later. "I am sorry to say," wrote Dumas Malone in 1951, that "Hamilton comes out of my investigations worse than I had expected. . . . I cannot escape the conviction that he, more than any other major American statesman of his time, lusted for personal as well as national power." This is more politely expressed than the slogans and editorials of Jefferson's supporters—or of Jefferson himself, who in one outburst characterized Hamilton's career as "a tissue of machinations against the liberty of his country"—but it is the same message. Present-day Jeffersonians still see the triumph of Jefferson's party as the victory of truth and justice, and although their man has taken some hits in recent decades, chiefly on the issue of slavery, this hasn't turned any of them into Federalists. Modern Hamiltonians meanwhile write as if they were still sourly waiting for the rural vote of the election of 1800 to come in. Until that happens, they abuse the winners. "It is difficult to resist the conclusion," wrote one latter-day Federalist, "that the twentieth-century statesman whom . . . Thomas Jefferson" at the height of the French Revolution "would have admired most is Pol Pot."[8] (This fan of Hamilton didn't try very hard to resist the conclusion.) Since the Hamiltonians are less numerous, Hamilton suffers both from the general tone of historical dispute, and from being outvoted.

This may account for the number of grassy-knoll–type theories that cluster around his life. Writers doubt his own account of his birthday; they wonder whether he had an affair with his sister-in-law; they accuse him of being a crook; they find secret hair triggers on his pistols, and argue that he intended to murder Aaron Burr in their final duel. (The fact that Hamilton's shot hit a tree branch, and that Burr's hit and killed Hamilton, presents an obvious difficulty to this theory, though not one beyond the ingenuity of its proponents.) These are arguments encountered in serious books or articles; on the Internet and its forerunners, Hamilton is variously described as gay, as a love child of George Washington, and as part black.

Many of these distractions and detractions contain slivers of truth. Hamilton's private life impinged on his public career. His origins shaped his view of the world, by defining what he wanted himself and others to get away from. His love affair was a public event (made public by Hamilton) with political repercussions. His death was another public event, prepared by his political situation: he had been trading partisan shots with the man who killed him for twelve years before they traded real ones. Hamilton was concerned with many other aspects of public life besides money, but he did see getting and spending as one of the chief ways that men work out their destiny in the world, and as a key to national happiness and strength. Getting the nation's finances right was not illiberal or irksome to him, but a vital matter for America and Americans. He was the friend of the rich (certain kinds of rich: he didn't have much use for land speculators, or plantation owners). But he was also the friend of workingmen, and for part of his career, at least, workingmen knew it. He was a friend of the poorest Americans, its slaves, whom he wanted to free; the fairy tale of his black ancestry makes some emotional sense.

The charge of aristocracy is more complicated. In one of his last letters, he wrote that democracy was America's "disease," and a "poison." Such sentiments were not unique to him. All of the founders wanted a government of checks and balances, not plebiscites. "The evils we experience flow from an excess of democracy," said Elbridge Gerry, later made vice president by the Democratic party. Hamilton supported popular elections and popular sovereignty in a variety of contexts. At the same time, he clung to forthrightly antidemocratic rhetoric after it had become unfashionable; losing a series of elections did not make him more hopeful about the wisdom of voters. The counterpoint—like an insistent bass line—to Hamilton's political professions was his political behavior. He repeatedly took his case to the people he sometimes condemned. He was "the most frank of men," wrote his friend Ames; "indiscreet, vain and opinionated," wrote another friend, Gouverneur Morris.[9] From his teens on, he poured his opinions and indiscretions into a torrent of political journalism, greater in volume than that produced by any other founder, including Benjamin Franklin, who was a printer; he founded a newspaper—the *New York Evening Post*—which still exists. Though he deplored the people's judgment when it went against him, he always appealed to it.

Scholars are right to be passionate about the careers of Hamilton and his contemporaries: they set the course for the rest of American history, and it is at least arguable that the course has not been entirely correct. The winners may not have won all the arguments. Even the crazy theories and the daydreams of popular mythology show an element of good judgment. They are the tribute that stupidity pays to greatness. We do not project our hopes and fears onto ciphers and timeservers.

This book examines Alexander Hamilton by telling his story and by probing his world. The next six chapters, and the last, survey the high points of his career, which begins at age fifteen (he was precocious as well as smart). "St. Croix/Manhattan" covers his youth and his second chance in America. "War" shows him on George Washington's staff. In "Laws," he argues his first cases as a lawyer, and helps rewrite the nation's fundamental law. "Treasury Secretary" examines Hamilton's first three years in that job, the period of his greatest creativity: economics as soul craft. "Fighting" presents the steady crescendo of political opposition. In "Losing," Hamilton encounters opposition from political allies and problems arising from his own misjudgments. The last chapter begins with a coda of retirement—though only by Hamilton's standards, for he founded a newspaper and argued a landmark case concerning the freedom of the press. Along the way, Hamilton worked with or against other founders who were either great, or significant: Washington, Madison, Jefferson, Adams;

Philip Schuyler, George Clinton, Timothy Pickering, Aaron Burr. We see him in different situations—war and peace, victory and defeat, on the national stage and embroiled in newspaper wrangles—and in different moods—steady and penetrating as a searchlight; noisy and destructive as firecrackers; dark and depressed.

The next-to-last chapters step outside the narrative to look at three themes that run through his life: "Words," "Rights," and "Passions." The torrent of his words is set in the context of the journalism of his day. The American press never had higher highs or lower lows than it did at the end of the eighteenth century. *The Federalist Papers* appeared in the daily papers; so did the story of Jefferson's dalliance with Sally Hemings. Hamilton's theories of rights are at odds with modern rights talk. His thinking was preconstitutional, appealing to common law, the law of nations, and the law of nature. He gave as much thought to the rights of governments as to those of individuals. Often standing in opposition to Hamilton's reasoning and his notions of rights are the passions of men. The passions that resonated in his career were ambition, licentiousness, and honor. Ambition was a subject of anxious debate in early America: How much was good? What was the right kind? Licentiousness—allowing one's desires to overcome one's responsibilities—was a political as well as a personal matter. Protecting America's honor was one of the goals of his system, but defending personal honor was too often done on the dueling ground.

The thread that runs through every chapter, and every aspect of Hamilton's life, is his identity as an American. Like that of many Americans after him, this identity was adopted. Hamilton's immigrant origin was no bar to his advancement, though his enemies held it in reserve, along with his illegitimacy and obscurity, to throw at him in moments of anger: "brat of a Scotch pedlar" was as much an insult as "bastard." Like other foreign or half-foreign leaders, from Catherine the Great to Churchill (and Hitler), Hamilton was a nationalist figure. When a native-born American of the period spoke of his country, he often meant his home state. ("It is a painful situation to be 300 miles from one's country," wrote Jefferson in Philadelphia after finishing the Declaration of Independence.)[10] Hamilton always and only meant the United

States. He looked forward to the time when his fellow citizens would consider themselves "a race of Americans," and he either minimized America's regional differences or worked to wear them down. He foresaw the material shape of the country far more clearly than any other founder.

But there were times when foresight failed, and the identity did not fit, and he gave way to shame or despair. "I can never adopt the reasonings of some *American* politicians," he wrote scornfully when he was still a new American. "Every day proves to me more and more," he wrote more than two decades later, "that this American world was not made for me."[11] The one American activity he never quite mastered, though he spent years on it, was politics. Certain of his rivals—Clinton, Burr, Madison, and especially Jefferson—understood it better, which is why they beat him. His failure to be more like them is partly his fault, and partly to his credit. Hamilton characteristically accused his enemies of flattering the people—an art he was incapable of practicing. At their best, the best of them did more than that. But they also flattered.

A secondary thread is Hamilton's identity as a New Yorker. New York gets short shrift in our memories of the founding, falling between the glory that was Boston and the grandeur that was Virginia. But Hamilton's life, the life of a quintessential New Yorker, restores it to center stage. He went to college, joined the army, and practiced law there. His last house stands in Harlem; his grave is at the top of Wall Street. New York's style—intense, commercial, go-getting—reflected his vision of America; New York politics—brawling and byzantine, stirred by mobs and newspapers and controlled by a handful of rich families—shaped his options and his agendas.

Hamilton did so much, it is hard to keep track, so another thread of even a distilled look at him must recover the careers that have passed out of popular recollection. Hamilton's fondness for things military provoked suspicion from those who feared him as a Caesar—yet so little was he a Caesar that twice during his years in the army he personally tried to save Congress from hostile soldiers, both British and American. Hamilton's feel for geopolitics won the praise of an old European fox, Talleyrand. Even more strangely, Hamilton's career as a lawyer has fallen into obscurity. He was both an excellent (and well-paid) trial lawyer and one of the greatest American constitutional lawyers—not surprisingly, since he helped write the Constitution. If John Marshall was the father of judicial review, Hamilton was the grandfather. Years after Hamilton died, Marshall said that, next to him, he felt like a candle "beside the sun at noonday."[12] He deserves a statue in front of the Supreme Court almost as much as his statue at the Treasury Department.

Hamilton's career as a journalist poses a special problem for this writer. Most biographers have the comfort of knowing that they are better than their subjects in at least one thing: Napoleon might be a greater general, or Beethoven a better composer, but their biographers are better biographers. It is sobering to reflect that Hamilton was a better journalist than I am. His biographers are a distinguished group, and they can show literary talents that he did not possess. But then, none of us has written a *Federalist* paper.

One of Hamilton's favorite authors was the historian Plutarch; during the war, he copied passages from the *Lives of the Noble Grecians and Romans* into the pay book of his artillery company. This was not an eccentric preference—Plutarch was a fixture in American libraries. Early Americans read his *Lives* for the same reason Plutarch wrote them: to be improved by moral biography, by lives examined in moral terms. "The virtues of these great men," Plutarch explained, "serv[e] me as a sort of looking-glass, in which I may see how to adjust and adorn my own life. . . . My method . . . is, by the study of history, and by the familiarity acquired in writing, to habituate my memory to receive and retain images of the best and worthiest characters."[13] Plutarch also wrote of his subjects' vices, which he sought to learn from. Both virtues and vices—many virtues, some vices—appear in Hamilton's character.

But Hamilton's life is a mirror for politics as well as morality—for public as well as private life. We cannot always find the specific policies of today reflected in it: though some issues he dealt with remain current—trade, taxes—others have faded: there will never be a second discussion of the Louisiana Purchase. Hamilton's positions fit no current political model. Modern conservatives would distrust his trust in government; modern liberals would find him lacking in compassion (one reason he wanted federal taxes was to make the poor work). But Hamilton's methods and his goals are always news. How to appeal to citizens and what they need in order to fulfill themselves will be matters of concern, and dispute, as long as America lasts.

Moments of founding appear to later times to be bathed in a timeless glow: the face of Janus looks both ways, and all things seem possible, including great things. Then the moment passes, and founders become politicians once again. They were politicians all along, of course, but afterward their nature becomes inescapable. Founding fathers, unless they die (like Greene) just after the moment of victory, are also sons; they are us. Alexander Hamilton did what we do; he just did it earlier. Because he was a great man, he generally did it better. His life, and the lives of his peers, can guide and caution us.

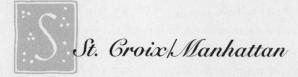

Chapter One

St. Croix/Manhattan

IN THE LATE eighteenth century, Bryan Edwards, a Jamaican author, inserted this description into a reference work on the West Indies. "The nights" in summer "are transcendantally beautiful. The clearness of the heavens, the serenity of the air, and the soft tranquility in which Nature reposes contribute to harmonize the mind, and produce the most calm and delightful sensations. The moon too in these climates displays far greater radiance than in Europe: the smallest print is legible by her light; and in the moon's absence her function is not ill-supplied by the brightness of the milky-way, and that glorious planet Venus, which appears here like a little moon . . . cast[ing] a shade from trees."[1]

When Alexander Hamilton was born, the Caribbean was as enchanting as it is now. It was also richer, thanks to sugar. At the end of the Seven Years' War in 1763, when the British victors considered restoring some of their conquests to France, they seriously debated whether to return Canada, or the island of Guadeloupe. One sugar island weighed evenly in the balance with half of North America. Some West Indian planters made fortunes. They lived high in the islands, and when they returned to the old country. "Such eating and drinking I never saw," wrote a visitor to Jamaica. "Such loads of all sorts of high, rich and seasoned things and really gallons of wine and mixed liquors. They eat a late breakfast as if they had never eaten before. It is as disgusting as it is astonishing." "There was no such thing as a [seat in Parliament] to be had now," an English lord wrote in 1767; rich West Indians "had secured them all at the rate of 3,000 pounds at least, but many at four thousand pounds, and two or three that he knew at five thousand pounds."[2]

If war, disease, and hurricanes spared them, sugar planters could do well indeed. But there was little else to do in the West Indies. The sugar islands were floating agricultural factories, with few small farms, and small service populations in their ports. When young George Washington of Virginia (hardly an egalitarian society) took a trip to Barbados in 1751, he was struck by the material disparity he saw there. "There are few who may be called middling people. They are either very rich or very poor."[3]

Beneath the poor whites were the slaves. Sugar farming was labor intensive; on plantations, slaves outnumbered their white masters by twenty to one. Their life was harsh. In 1755, Denmark decreed that masters in the Danish Virgin Islands could not punish their slaves by mutilating them, or putting them on the rack, though they might shackle and flog them. In spite of this lenience, the slaves of St. Croix planned a revolt in 1759. The free black man who revealed the plot ahead of time committed suicide, after which his body was hung, then burned at the stake. Slaves found riding or walking the streets of Christiansted, the main town, after eight o'clock at night were given 150 lashes at the fort, "at no expense to the owner." Edwards, describing the British island of Nevis as a "beautiful little spot," added that the population was 600 whites and 10,000 blacks: "a disproportion which necessarily converts all such white men as are not exempted by age and decrepitude into a well-regulated militia."[4] In the Second Amendment to the United States Constitution, the "well-regulated militia" would be a force for freedom. In the West Indies, it was a force for keeping the labor force in line.

Hamilton, who grew up in Nevis and St. Croix, never wrote a fond word about the Caribbean, and never made the slightest effort to return for a visit as an adult. The prosperity of the West Indies existed chiefly in its balance sheets, and made little use of human capital apart from muscle. With its barren riches and its lack of opportunity, it was a place to leave behind, and a model for what a happy country should avoid.

Hamilton's early life and the lives of his family were set in the small islands—the Leeward and the Virgin Islands—that rim the northeast corner of the Caribbean. Hamilton's mother, Rachel Faucett, was born on Nevis, but went to St. Croix, a twenty-hour sail with the trade winds, as a teenager. She followed one of her sisters, who had married a St. Croix planter named James Lytton. About 1745, Rachel married another planter, John Lavien, and a year later she bore him a son. Like many whites in the Caribbean, the families were a mix of nationalities, who had settled without regard to the islands' formal owners: the Faucetts were Huguenots and the Lyttons English; Lavien was probably German.

Hamilton family tradition held that Rachel had "witnessed . . . family quarrels"[5] as a girl. If so, she found a new set of them in her marriage to Lavien. They settled on a cotton plantation he owned, ironically named Contentment, but in 1750, he had her jailed in the town fort in Christiansted—the same place where curfew-breaking slaves were lashed—for refusing to live with him. When she got out, she returned to the British West Indies, where she met James Hamilton.

James Hamilton, the fourth son of a Scottish laird, had come to the Caribbean to make his fortune as a merchant. Fifty years later, Alexander Hamilton wrote a friend that "I have better pretensions than most of those who in this Country plume themselves on Ancestry." This was an unusually defensive tone for him: Hamilton characteristically expected people to endorse his ideas and his actions because he had shown how right they were, not because he had a good pedigree. He went on to admit that his birth was "not free from blemish,"[6] for Rachel had two sons with James Hamilton—James Junior and Alexander—without getting a divorce from John Lavien.

Illegitimacy may not have had quite the stigma in that century that it acquired under the Victorians in the next, but it was still shameful. A dozen years later, when Benjamin Franklin arranged for his illegitimate son William to be named royal governor of New Jersey, John Adams called it an "Insult to the Morals of America." Rachel and James Senior seem to have tried to avoid the stigma: Alexander believed that his mother had gotten a second marriage, and the records of a christening on the Dutch island of St. Eustatius mention the presence of James Hamilton and "Rachel Hamilton his wife." In the Danish Virgin Islands, however, Rachel was still Rachel Lavien—until 1759, when John Lavien divorced her for her "ungodly mode of life."[7] Since Rachel was the party at fault, Danish law did not allow her to remarry. Presumably, James Senior discovered this state of affairs when he moved with his family to St. Croix in 1765. A year later, he left them, never to return.

To support herself, Rachel opened a provision store in Christiansted. Alexander went to work as a clerk in a merchant house; his older brother worked for a carpenter. In 1768, Alexander and Rachel came down with a fever. The son recovered; the mother died.

These, and a few other dry details, reflected in scattered church and legal documents, are virtually all we know of Hamilton's earliest childhood. They leave several puzzles. One is the year of his birth. Hamilton indicated, and descendants of his who wrote biographies of him stated flatly, that he was born in 1757, which would mean that he began working in a merchant house at the age of nine. But in settling Rachel's estate in 1768, the probate court listed her illegitimate sons' ages as fifteen and thirteen, which would mean that Alexander had been born in 1755. Biographers in thrall to documents tend to accept 1755; defenders of the later date point out that the clerk was not perfect, for he misspelled the name Lavien. The desire to add two years to Alexander's age may also reflect an impulse, encouraged by the practice of assigning schoolchildren to grades, to discount the abilities of the gifted. Without being a Mozart, Alexander Hamilton was a very bright boy—and he was hardly unique. Benjamin Franklin was apprenticed to a printer at the age of twelve, and published his first journalism when he was sixteen. The future theologian Jonathan Edwards wrote an eloquent and observant essay on flying spiders when he was twelve, and entered Yale College a year later. One of the supporters of an "older" Hamilton inconsistently argues that his responsibilities as a clerk were not that great.[8] If they were not, then it is all the more likely that a younger boy could have fulfilled them. Recognizing that even a younger Hamilton would not have been miraculous, and believing that a man is more likely to know his own birthday than a clerk in a probate court, I will accept 1757.

A more important question is the character of his parents. Since Hamilton's relations with women played an important role in his public career, it would be interesting to know more about his mother. Hamilton described her to his children as a woman of "superior intellect," "elevated and generous sentiments," and "unusual elegance of person and manner." John Lavien accused her in his divorce papers of "whoring with everyone."[9] Neither man was an objective witness. What is clear is that Rachel was a good businesswoman; when she died, the accounts of her store were in order, and she had only a few short-term debts.

It is also clear that James Hamilton, Sr., was a bum. He had other qualities—his surviving letter shows charm, and his decision to move from Scotland to the Caribbean suggests that he had a stock of youthful enterprise, or at least hope—but he was a bum nevertheless, and this would have been clear to his sons. When he left his family, he did not disappear, but went back to the Leeward Islands, where he lived a long and uneventful life. He and his famous son made sporadic efforts to keep in touch. In 1783, Alexander wrote to his older brother, who had asked him for money: "But what has become of our dear father? . . . Perhaps, alas! he is no more, and I shall not have the pleasing opportunity of contributing to render the close of his life more happy than the progress of it." Ten years later, James wrote the secretary of the treasury from St. Vincent that he would take "the first ship that sails for Philadelphia." But two years after that, Alexander wrote a friend that though he had "pressed" his father to come, James had decided not to, on account of his health. Perhaps he was reluctant to be so directly helped by the son he had abandoned. In 1799, the old man died. Afterward, Alexander wrote that his father had "too much pride and too large a portion of indolence—but his character was otherwise beyond reproach."[10] This was more generous than accurate. Pride and indolence are faults (Alexander inherited the first, though not the second). But they were not James's only faults. If he had vanished, his lover and his children could have consoled themselves with romantic, even tragic, speculations about his character and his fate. But he simply moved over a few islands. James Hamilton walked away from a complicated situation, and made it plain that that was what he had done. When Alexander Hamilton became a husband and father, he dedicated himself (sometimes with very mixed results) to behaving differently.

Rachel left a modest estate—nine slaves, thirteen silver spoons, and thirty-four books. James Junior and Alexander received none of it. John Lavien appeared before the probate court and claimed everything for his and Rachel's legitimate son. The Lytton family, into which Rachel's sister had married, gave the Hamilton boys some help, buying back the thirty-four books at an auction. But the Lyttons were coming to grief too. Two of Alexander's Lytton cousins had left the island as bankrupts; a third killed himself. James Lytton, their father, died a month later. Alexander was practically alone in a small world.

A year later, age twelve, he wrote his first letter that survives, to Edward Stevens, an older boy who had been sent to New York to attend King's College, now Columbia University. "[T]o confess my weakness, Ned, my Ambition is so prevalent that I contemn the grov'ling and condition of a Clerk or the like, to which my Fortune &c. condemns me and would willingly risk my life tho' not my Character to exalt my Station. . . . Im no Philosopher, you see, and may be justly said to Build Castles in the Air. . . . yet Neddy we have seen such Schemes successfull when the Projector is Constant I shall Conclude saying I wish there was a War."[11] St. Croix was a bigger island than Nevis, with more than twice the population—24,000, of which 2,000 were white—and as a merchant's clerk, Alexander could observe its traffic with a wider world. But in the normal course of things, a local boy without a family could not expect to see the world, still less to exalt his station. Neddy Stevens might get away; not him.

Three factors altered the course of things. In 1771, the Reverend Hugh Knox, a Scotch-Irish Presbyterian minister, moved to Christiansted and noticed the ambitious boy. Knox was interested in education, and he had plans to teach the local slaves. He himself had been educated at the College of New Jersey in Princeton, at that time the finest school in the Thirteen Colonies. Jonathan Edwards had served briefly as president; Knox had studied with Edwards's son-in-law, Aaron Burr. Knox could introduce Alexander to two new worlds—learning, and North America.

Hamilton's employer, Nicholas Cruger, had even more extensive connections on the mainland, which would propel Alexander in that direction. The Crugers, originally a German family, had been New York merchants for three generations. Nicholas's uncle had been the first president of the New York Chamber of Commerce. Nicholas and his three brothers were dispatched by the family to different centers of business: St. Croix, Jamaica, Curaçao, and Bristol, England. (The brother who went to Bristol ultimately became mayor, and a member of Parliament.) In Christiansted, Nicholas Cruger owned ships, warehouses, a general store, and a counting house, where Hamilton worked, on Kongensgade, or King Street. Cruger and other New Yorkers began trading in St. Croix at mid-century for its sugar, delivering it to the refineries of old New York families like the Roosevelts. In return, they brought the islanders the staples that were not produced locally. One of Cruger's handbills advertised Albany white pine, pork, codfish, Madeira, and mules from Puerto Rico. Cruger was not a regular slave-trader, though in 1771 he did auction three hundred "first class slaves . . . just in from Africa." In Virgin Islands dialect today, the phrase "the City," when used without qualification, means New York, or America (the two are assumed to be interchangeable).[12] There was no United States when Hamilton was Cruger's clerk, but Cruger's hometown had already become a pivot for the Virgin Islands' dealings with North America, and the world.

The third factor in Hamilton's change of fortune was the impression his abilities made on these men. In the fall of 1771, Cruger left St. Croix for four months on account of bad health, leaving his fourteen-year-old clerk to mind the store. In the letters he sent out during this period, Hamilton passed judgment on loads of flour ("realy very bad"), apples ("in every respect very indifferent"), and the captain of a ship the Crugers had hired ("I think he seems rather to want experience in such Voyages"). He suggested that Nicholas's brother in Curaçao mount guns on the ship to protect it from the Spanish coast guard, and fretted when this was not done. "I begd Mr. Teleman Cruger to put some force upon her. How he came to neglect it I don't know."[13]

In 1772 Hamilton got to read himself in print. On the last day of August, a hurricane raked the island, killing thirty people and sweeping ships a hundred yards inland. Alexander wrote to his father describing the disaster; some local adult saw the letter, and in early October it appeared ("by a Youth of this Island") in the *Royal Danish-American Gazette.* It opened with staccato description: "The roaring of the sea and wind—fiery meteors flying about it in the air—the prodigious glare of almost perpetual lightning—the crash of the falling houses." Pious reflections followed, perhaps inspired by the Reverend Mr. Knox: "That which, in a calm and unruffled temper, we call a natural cause, seemed then like the correction of the Deity. . . . The father and benefactor were forgot [while] a consciousness of our guilt filled us with despair." These were interesting thoughts to be addressed to a father, no benefactor, who had forgotten to return home. The last sentence, like a flash, prefigured the mature Hamilton: "Our General," he wrote, of the Danish governor of the island, "has issued several very salutary and humane regulations, and both in his publick and private measures, has shewn himself *the Man.*"[14] All his adult life, he would make confident judgments of the performance of superiors and subordinates. He was doing it at the age of fifteen.

His authority for doing so sprang from his own passion to perform well—he never criticized from the role of a detached analyst or a kibbitzer. Years later, Hamilton told one of his sons that clerking for Cruger had taught him "method" and "facility," and that his years in the King Street counting house had been "the most useful of his education."[15] But method and facility would have been of little account without his will to see the job done right, by himself if necessary.

Later that month, the young author was put on a ship and sent to the mainland. Other foreigners who would come to America during the Revolutionary period, like Thomas Paine and the Marquis de Lafayette, were citizens of superpowers, who saw the new country as a haven of virtuous simplicity. Hamilton's trajectory was different: he was coming from the fringes to the center.

. . .

Hamilton's move to the mainland was a joint project of Cruger and Knox. The plan was to send him to the College of New Jersey at Princeton, after he had done the necessary academic catching up. Hamilton studied at a grammar school in Elizabethtown, New Jersey, reading in his room until midnight, and in the morning before school began, in a nearby cemetery.

Dr. John Witherspoon, the Scottish minister who had succeeded Aaron Burr as president at Princeton, made the college a republican seminary. But Hamilton was not destined to be one of his disciples. When Hercules Mulligan, a New York merchant tailor who knew the Crugers, took him to meet Witherspoon, the teenager "stated that he wished to enter . . . with the understanding that he should be permitted to advance from Class to Class with as much rapidity as his exertions would enable him to do." Though "Dr. Witherspoon listened with great attention to so unusual a proposition from so young a person," he turned him down.[16] Hamilton made the same proposal to King's College in New York, which took him on.

Hamilton's formative American years were thus spent in a place that was like and unlike Christiansted: commercial and cosmopolitan, but vastly different in tempo and scale. The population of New York was almost 25,000, slightly more than the whole island of St. Croix; only a fifth of it consisted of slaves. The city was huddled on the southern tip of Manhattan, reaching only a mile up from the fortified Battery. (What is now Foley Square, lined with courthouses, was a deep pond, where people skated in the winter.) New York had already passed Boston in population, and was gaining on Philadelphia, then the second-largest city in the English-speaking world. Unlike the City on the Hill, or the City of Brotherly Love, New York had always been a commercial venture: first, a Dutch post for extracting furs from the interior; then, an English port. Commerce had exploded in mid-century: 700 vessels cleared the port in 1772, compared to 99 in 1746. The British mercantile system was supposed to reserve manufacturing for the mother country, but one visitor noted that New York had "plenty of mechanicks of all kinds," working in rope and snuff factories, breweries, and an ironworks.[17]

"The inhabitants," the same visitor went on, "are in general brisk and lively, kind to strangers [and] dress very gay; the fair sex are . . . said to be very obliging." He claimed that five hundred prostitutes lived by St. Paul's Chapel, near the entrance to King's College. "This is certainly a temptation to the youth." John Adams, passing through on his way to the Continental Congress, thought New Yorkers "talk very loud, very fast, and altogether. If they ask you a question, before you utter three words of your answer, they will break out upon you again and talk away." There were fifteen churches, serving nine denominations and four ethnic groups—English, Dutch, German, and French—plus one synagogue (only Catholicism was forbidden). But religion did not unduly influence behavior. The "readiest way for a stranger to recommend himself," wrote another visitor, was to "drink stoutly" and "talk bawdy."[18]

New York was also a city riven by politics. After the Seven Years' War (called the French and Indian War in North America), Britain tried to pay off its debts by taxing its colonies and tightening up its imperial system. Many in New York were willing to go along; later, they would call themselves Loyalists, and be called Tories. Merchants vacillated between resentment of economic restrictions and fear of disrupted trade. Radicals, like the Sons of Liberty, appealed to the mind—handbills, one resident noted, are "daily and hourly printed, published, pasted up"—and to the mob. "People here live . . . very Comfortable," wrote a British officer, "did they chuse to be contented."[19] But they chose not to be. In the decade before the Revolution, there were twentysome riots or other disturbances, ranging from ideological protests against imperial policy to disorderly British soldiers burning whorehouses. The Stamp Act Congress, the first colonial airing of grievances, met in New York; there was a showdown in New York with British troops before the Boston Massacre, and a tea party in New York harbor after the Boston Tea Party.

Alongside these issues of national and imperial import, old established families jockeyed for position, by any means necessary. In the elections to the provincial assembly in 1769, a member of one family faction, the Livingstons, boasted that "we have by far the best part of the bruisers on our side," while the other faction, the De Lanceys, charged that one of their opponents "dances with, and *kisses (filthy beast!)* those of his own sex." In 1774, Gouverneur Morris, a witty aristocrat in what is now the Bronx, memorably expressed the elites' view: "The mob begin to think, and to reason. Poor reptiles! It is with them a vernal morning; they are struggling to cast off their winter's [skin], they bask in sunshine, and ere noon they will bite."[20] Morris need not have worried about his position: the elites would find ways to manage popular biting for many years to come.

King's College had three teachers, including its president, Dr. Myles Cooper, and about twenty students. Ned Stevens, who was still there, finishing his studies as a doctor, joined Hamilton in a weekly debating club with several other students, including Robert Troup, who became a lifelong friend. Hamilton was already fluent in French, thanks to his mother; we do not know what her thirty-four books were, or what books Hugh Knox had let him read, but King's had a good library, well stocked with legal and political philosophers, and Hamilton worked his way through it. "He used in the evening to sit with my family," Mulligan remembered, and "write dogrel rhymes for their amusement; he was allways amiable and cheerful and extremely attentive to his books."[21]

Politics gave him the chance to write his first journalism in New York. In September and October of 1774, the First Continental Congress met in Philadelphia and proposed an embargo on trade with Britain, to be enforced by a Continental Association with power to proscribe uncooperative merchants. This provoked a spirited attack from Samuel Seabury, an Anglican clergyman in Westchester County. Seabury was an intelligent and principled man; after the Revolution, he would become the first bishop of the Episcopal Church of the United States. Following universal eighteenth-century polemical practice, he wrote under a pseudonym—A. W. Farmer—that was shrewdly chosen: despite the level of frenzy in New York City, most of the farmers in the surrounding counties were content, and suspicious of being forced to trade locally. Seabury stressed England's power and the colonies' weakness, and played on social and regional divisions: the Continental Association was a "venomous brood of scorpions," while Bostonians thought that God "made Boston for Himself, and all the rest of the world for Boston."[22]

Hamilton wrote two responses, "A Full Vindication of the Measures of Congress," and "The Farmer Refuted," which appeared in December 1774 and February 1775 respectively, and together ran to

50,000 words. He was as much a know-it-all as when he approved the measures of the Danish governor, only now he knew more. "Apply yourself, without delay," he told the Farmer, "to the study of the law of nature. I would recommend to your perusal, Grotius, Puffendorff [*sic*], Locke, Montesquieu, and Burlamaqui. I might mention other excellent writers on this subject," he went on, "but if you attend diligently to these, you will not require any." In another place, he told Seabury, "What you say concerning the lumber that is exported from Canada is totally false."

Hamilton turned the tables on Seabury by arguing that the colonies, instead of being weak and divided, were in fact a growing economic threat to the mother country. "The boundless extent of territory we possess, the wholesome temperament of our climate, the luxuriance and fertility of our soil, the variety of our products, the rapidity of the growth of our population, the industry of our countrymen, and the commodiousness of our ports" had caused "a jealousy of our dawning splendor." This passage is striking for its foresight. During the war, George Washington would use the phrase "rising empire." But no other Revolutionary would envisage it so vividly. Hamilton's argument was also striking because he said "our." He signed his pamphlets "A Friend of America," but he wrote them as an American; in two years, the immigrant had become a patriot.

Hamilton appealed to rights as well as power. "The sacred rights of mankind are not to be rummaged for among old parchments or musty records. They are written, as with a sunbeam, in the whole *volume* of human nature, by the hand of the Divinity itself, and can never be erased or obscured by mortal power." In the vein of inspirational rhetoric, this is the finest thing Hamilton ever wrote, and the most Jeffersonian.

He also gave a vivid description of what happens when rights are denied, a state he called "slavery." He meant by this the enslavement of the colonies that would ensue if they continued to be taxed without representation from London, though it is hard not to think that his description gained in vividness from the slavery he had seen firsthand. "I might show that [slavery] is fatal to religion and morality; that it tends to debase the mind, and corrupt its noblest springs of action. I might show that it relaxes the sinews of industry, clips the wings of commerce, and introduces misery and indigence in every shape."

He also made several miscalculations. "There is a certain enthusiasm in liberty," he declared, "that makes human nature rise above itself in acts of bravery and heroism." He would soon discover that this is sometimes true, sometimes not. If Britain chose force, he recommended guerrilla warfare, "harass[ing] and exhaust[ing]" British soldiers "by frequent skirmishes and incursions," rather than "tak[ing] the open field with them." He would also discover the limits of that strategy. Finally, he would come to reassess the "industry" of his new countrymen—not just compared to his own unusual standards, but to the norm of the European world.[23]

Nevertheless, the pamphlets were an impressive performance—so much so that they were attributed to John Jay, a delegate to the First Continental Congress who had graduated from King's College in 1764. Dr. Cooper, a devout Anglican who agreed with Seabury, thought it "absurd to imagine that so young a man" as his own student "could have written" them.[24] Between the publication dates of the two pamphlets, Hamilton turned eighteen.

Late in April, the colonies learned of the battles of Lexington and Concord; argument had become armed defiance. One night in May, a mob came to the college intending to tar and feather Cooper (tarring and feathering was not a prank, but a painful punishment, sometimes fatal). Hamilton and Troup, who were rooming together, heard the commotion and went to Cooper's front steps, where Hamilton "proceeded with great animation and eloquence to harangue the mob on . . . the disgrace it would bring on the cause of liberty."[25] Cooper was able to escape by a back door and take refuge on a British warship.

Another New Yorker who would join Cooper in flight was James Rivington, a printer who had published Seabury's pamphlets, and was accounted a Tory (though he had also published Hamilton's replies). In November, a band of militiamen from Connecticut broke into Rivington's print shop on Hanover Square, smashed his presses, and seized his type. Hamilton lectured this group of patriots too, this time without effect. On their way, for good measure, the raiders scooped up Samuel Seabury.

Historians teach that mobs and other irregular proceedings—popular tribunals, ex post facto laws—are a feature of all revolutions, even ones that are thought of as good and generally orderly. Hamilton never learned this lesson. He opposed mobs and revolutionary justice all his life, sometimes at the risk of his reputation, or his safety. After the Rivington episode, he wrote his first letter to John Jay, who was then serving in the Second Continental Congress: "I am always more or less alarmed at every thing which is done of mere will and pleasure without any proper authority."[26]

Hamilton had been helping the cause in ways more significant than robbing printers and molesting Anglicans. With Troup, he joined a drill company called the Corsicans, who wore green coats and leather caps inscribed LIBERTY OR DEATH, and drilled in a churchyard. The name of the company showed its romantic spirit—Corsica had rebelled against its Italian overlords in mid-century and had been written up by James Boswell. At the end of August 1775, the young soldiers went to the Battery to remove its cannons. Mulligan, who went with them, remembered that "Mr. H . . . gave me his musket to hold" and grabbed one of the cannon ropes. A British battleship in the harbor opened fire on them. "I left his musket in the Battery & retreated." Hamilton retreated with his cannon, and asked Mulligan for his musket. When told that it was back at the fort, "he went for it . . . with as much unconcern as if the vessel had not been there."[27]

This was a fine exploit. But in Boston, war had begun in earnest, and the following summer it came to New York. The British had done badly in Boston. At Lexington and Concord, they had sent a detachment into hostile countryside and it had been mauled. At the battle of Bunker Hill, they had marched, without artillery cover, up a slope, toward an enemy crouched behind a fence. They took the position, but at a cost of 1,500 men. The Americans were elated by their successes, but there was no reason to think the British would continue to perform so ineptly.

After the British evacuated Boston in March, the Continental Army moved south. Thus it was that the Declaration of Independence was first read to the troops in New York on July 9. An equestrian statue of George III at Bowling Green, erected only five years earlier when New Yorkers hoped he would defend them against obnoxious ministers, was pulled down and melted into bullets, and the crown-shaped finials on the iron fence around the green were knocked off. (The green is still there, and so is the fence; the tips of its posts are still rough to the touch.) While the patriots celebrated in town, the British had been massing in the harbor and on Staten Island, where the local farmers welcomed their arrival.

Hamilton, no longer a Corsican, had been made captain of a New York artillery company in March. For the next year, his movements are subsumed in the maneuvers of the rival armies. The fundamental problem facing George Washington, the American commander, was that New York was indefensible. For reasons of politics and prestige, he was expected to hold an island city in a harbor, without a navy. The British, who had the best navy in the world, put it to good use by doing what they had failed to do on the small scale of Bunker Hill: outflank the enemy. In August, they drove Washington out of Long Island, and in September they bisected Manhattan, landing on the east side about three miles north of town. One account claims that Hamilton and his company were in a hilltop fort, below the point of the British landing, and were able to save themselves only because of the timely warning of Major Aaron Burr, son of the late president of Princeton.

Fort Washington, the last American garrison on Manhattan, fell in the middle of November. The city would stay in British hands for seven rough years; three-quarters of it would burn in a fire; the population would plunge to 5,000, then rise to over 30,000, swollen by Tory refugees. Hercules Mulligan stayed on as an American spy, designing British officers' uniforms. Family tradition had it that Hamilton volunteered to lead an assault on Fort Washington; if he did, he was fortunately not asked to do anything so suicidal, for the American army, as 1776 ended, was barely able to hold itself together. Thanks to defeats, desertions, and expiring enlistments, there were at times more American soldiers in British captivity than under Washington's command. As the

Americans retreated across New Jersey, an officer remarked Hamilton. "I noticed a youth, a mere stripling, small, slender, almost delicate in frame, marching beside a piece of artillery with a cocked hat pulled down over his eyes, apparently lost in thought, with his hand resting on the cannon and every now and then patting it as he mused, as if it were a favorite horse or a pet plaything."[28]

Finally, at year's end, the youth got to use his cannon to good effect. Hamilton was in the boats that crossed the Delaware for the dawn assault on Trenton, where he fired at the groggy Hessians. A week later, when the Americans turned the British flank and made their surprise attack on Princeton, he fired on the last holdouts in Nassau Hall. After long delays and frightful costs, liberty had shown some enthusiasm, and Hamilton had gotten into the College of New Jersey.

Chapter Two

*War*

TWO MONTHS AFTER the battle of Princeton, Captain Hamilton was promoted to lieutenant colonel and joined George Washington's "family," or staff of aides. It is not known for certain who recommended him: possibly General Henry Knox, commander of the army's artillery, possibly General Nathanael Greene.

General Washington had been an aide himself, to a British general during the French and Indian War over twenty years ago. His demands on his own aides now were exacting. "[T]hose about me," he wrote, will be "confined from morning to eve, hearing and answering . . . applications and letters." He wanted them for more than paper-shuffling. "They ought . . . to possess the soul of the general; and from a single idea given to them, to convey his meaning in the clearest and fullest manner."[1]

Washington needed such helpers—he had thirty-two over the course of the war—because his duties were so complicated. Most of the commander-in-chief's time was consumed by administration. The American army was a combination of regular troops and militiamen, who signed up for short service. Every new batch of militiamen had to be fashioned into soldiers, so that, periodically, much of the American army was starting from scratch. To pay and equip the troops, money and supplies had to be wrung from Congress and the states. Meanwhile, the war was being fought on a front that stretched from Canada to Georgia. Though there was never simultaneous fighting everywhere, conflict could arise at the most far-flung points. While Washington was besieging Boston and defending New York, the Americans were defeated beneath the walls of Quebec and the British were repulsed from Charleston. When France entered the war as America's ally in 1777, the rebels took on the additional delicate task of dealing with French officers. (Hamilton's French proved useful.) The commander-in-chief of the Continental Army had many of the responsibilities now handled by the president, the secretary of defense, and the secretary of state. Some aides chafed at the routine, and the pressure; some proved to be unsatisfactory: Major Aaron Burr went to Washington's staff early in 1776 but lasted only ten days there. Hamilton stayed at Washington's side for four years.

In March 1777, George Washington had just turned forty-five. The face that Gilbert Stuart made famous was fifteen years in the future. Washington's chestnut hair was beginning to turn grey, and he had put on weight. But he was a vigorous man in his prime, a superb horseman, and at over six feet, a commanding presence. His looks impressed everyone who saw him. His good manners, his reserve, and his evident force of will impressed everyone who dealt with him. By leaving an aristocrat's life to serve without pay, he had impressed the nation with his commitment to republican virtue. The country's need for a hero, and for a patriarchal substitute for Washington's royal namesake, would have caused such traits to be acclaimed in him whether he possessed them or not, at least initially. Happily, he was what he seemed.

Some who came to know him better, especially those whose intelligence was alloyed with envy, discerned other qualities. Years later, Aaron Burr would tell John Adams that he "despised Washington as a man of no talents . . . who could not spell a sentence of common English." Adams replied that Burr was "unreasonable," for to his "certain knowledge, Washington was not so illiterate."[2] Washington was sensitive about his reputation, and apt to be irritable. When truly provoked, his temper could be explosive. He was neither glib nor clever. He enjoyed hearing jokes rather than telling them. He planned everything carefully, including his battles, but if the plans went suddenly awry, he could be slow to react. There were some subjects he knew little about: the arts (except for plays), and finance. Most Americans knew no more about these subjects than he did. Ignorance of the second was potentially fatal for a new nation.

But beneath these limitations, and compensating for them, were virtues that manifested themselves over the arc of his career: judgment (discernment in thinking), prudence (discernment in acting), and the ability to know what he needed and to find it in others. Washington had been introduced to war and glory in his early twenties, when he was impetuous, ambitious, and not above using flattery and backstairs politics to get his way. (His impetuosity, at least, he remembered fondly, if his affection for young officers like Hamilton was any indication.) But the passage of time, his own success in the world, and the seriousness of the issues now at stake, had all refined these traits out of him. He is "no harum-scarum, ranting, swearing fellow," wrote one of the congressmen who had picked him as commander-in-chief, "but sober, steady, and calm."[3]

For the first time in his life—also for the last—Alexander Hamilton was meeting a man who was greater than himself. His father had been a hurtful cipher. Reverend Hugh Knox and Nicholas Cruger were helpful patrons, like good animals in a fairy tale. Myles Cooper and Samuel Seabury, despite being decades older, were easily worsted opponents (Cooper even gave Hamilton the exquisite pleasure of saving an opponent's life). Hamilton's understanding was quicker than Washington's, and his analytical powers were greater. But in every other mental or moral quality, Washington was his equal or superior.

In a few respects, their minds were very similar. Both men had a passion for order. Washington had been trained as a surveyor. Everything from his handwriting to the design of Mount Vernon showed his clean, clear eye. Hamilton could bring order out of masses of information; Washington appreciated it. Both men also had practical temperaments. Washington wanted things done right; Hamilton was confident that he could do them right. His entry into Washington's "family" was the beginning of a twenty-two-year relationship, the most important of his career.

Hamilton had already modified the military ideas he expressed as a patriotic pamphleteer. "Our hopes," he wrote the Reverend Knox in mid-1777, "are not placed in [holding] any city or spot of ground, but in the preserving a good army . . . to take advantage of favorable opportunities, and waste and defeat the enemy by piecemeal."[4] This overview of American strategy superficially resembled the harassing and skirmishing Hamilton had called for in "The Farmer Refuted," but six months of fighting the British in the field had shown him that they could be effectively wasted only by a disciplined and professional force. Washington's task over the next four years, assisted by his staff, was twofold: to take advantage of opportunities and to preserve a good army, under his leadership. Sometimes both tasks involved as much contention with Americans as with the British.

After Princeton, the American army had camped in central New Jersey. In the summer of 1777, the British made two moves. Lord Howe, the commander in New York, put most of his army in his fleet and sailed for points unknown, while General John Burgoyne invaded upstate New York from Canada down the line of Lake Champlain. Hamilton did not fear much from the north. "The geography of the country," he wrote a committee of New York patriots, including Gouverneur Morris, would require the invaders to maintain "a chain of posts," or forts, "and such a number of men at each as would never be practicable. . . . By hanging upon their rear, and seizing every opportunity of skirmishing, their situation might be rendered insupportably uneasy."[5]

By the fall, the situation to the south had become extremely uneasy for the Americans. Howe's fleet appeared in Chesapeake Bay, and Washington, seeing that the enemy's goal was Philadelphia, the nation's capital, hurried to meet them. The British beat him twice, at the battles of Brandywine and Germantown. Hamilton had the job of telling Congress to flee the city; he also had a horse shot in a skirmish.

Howe had marched overland to Philadelphia from northern Maryland, and the Americans still held forts in the Delaware River that could prevent his fleet from sailing up to supply him. Washington also feared that the British might try a last attack before the campaigning season ended. Reinforcements were needed.

But Washington's efforts to get them were complicated by a great American victory. The original American commander in northern New

York, General Philip Schuyler, was the head of an old Dutch landowning family, who had an estate at Saratoga, forty miles north of Albany, in Burgoyne's line of march. He had blocked the invader's path with felled trees and dammed creeks, and fortified the countryside. But Schuyler's unpopularity with the New Englanders under his command had caused him to be replaced by General Horatio Gates, a former major in the British army who had taken America's side in the Revolution. Gates took advantage of Schuyler's preparations, Burgoyne's recklessness, and the abilities of his own second-in-command, General Benedict Arnold. While Washington was losing to the British in the outskirts of Philadelphia, Gates smashed them in the woods near Saratoga, taking Burgoyne and his entire army prisoner.

The battle of Saratoga brought France into the war as America's ally, and Congress, exiled to Reading, Pennsylvania, was so grateful, it struck a gold medal in Gates's honor, and promoted James Wilkinson, the aide who brought them the news, from colonel to brigadier general. Their jubilation had political implications, which did not bode well for Washington. Gates's force had been composed largely of militia, the troops most favored by republican ideology. The "good army" of professional soldiers sought by Washington and Hamilton was a bugbear of American theorists, who saw it as a potential tool of tyrants to overawe the people and the laws. There was also a budgetary angle: since militias were raised by the states, they came cheap, while professional soldiers cost money: "Are we to go on forever in this way, maintaining vast armies in idleness. . . ?"[6] Congressman John Adams had complained earlier in the year. Saratoga looked like a vindication of both antimilitarism and thrift.

The advocates of militias did not take the circumstances into account: Burgoyne, by marching into a wilderness miles from his base, had committed another, larger Bunker Hill, and in such situations militiamen rallied enthusiastically. But for hard battles in succession, or months of tense inaction, only regular troops would serve. Still, victory was victory—Gates had won; Washington had not. Gates at his headquarters in Albany was conscious of his new stature; he sent word of Saratoga directly to Congress, rather than to his commander-in-chief.

Washington gave the job of getting troops from Gates to Hamilton. The twenty-year-old aide had to juggle military and political considerations. Gates had three brigades under his command, and would only release one. Hamilton reluctantly agreed, explaining in a letter to Washington that Gates had "the entire confidence" of the New England states, besides "influence and interest elsewhere" (meaning Congress). But then Hamilton found out (possibly from his classmate Robert Troup, who was serving as an aide to Gates) that the brigade he had been given was seriously understrength. He wrote Gates a sharp letter—"I did not imagine you would pitch upon [such] a brigade"—and demanded another, "without loss of time." Gates thought of complaining to Washington of Hamilton's "dictatorial power," but thought better of it.[7]

Hamilton's efforts turned out to be fruitless (the troops he rounded up reached Philadelphia too late to save the forts on the Delaware, while Howe chose to rest on his laurels). It was not Hamilton's last go-round with Gates. After Germantown, Gates got a letter from Thomas Conway, a vain French officer of Irish descent, who said that "a weak general and bad councillors" (i.e., Washington and his staff) had nearly ruined the country. When the phrase was reported to Washington, he sent Conway a mordant little note, quoting the words, and ending, "I am, sir, your humble obedient servant, George Washington." By not revealing his source, Washington allowed Conway, Gates, and whomever else they had been discussing his weakness with, to suspect each other of tipping him off. Worried, Gates offered two inconsistent defenses of himself: the letter was a forgery, and the offending phrase must have been *"stealingly copied"* by Hamilton when he was on his mission to Albany.[8] Washington then told Gates the truth: that his own aide Wilkinson had blurted the words out in a tavern to another officer, who had passed it along to the commander-in-chief.

"I am wearied to death with the wrangles between military officers," Adams had written early in the war, "scrambling for rank and pay like apes for nuts." Historians still dispute what exactly Gates and Conway were scrambling for, but Washington and his "family" had no doubts: they were convinced that a "cabal" of officers and congressmen wanted to replace him. The Marquis de Lafayette, a nineteen-year-old French nobleman who had arrived in America as a volunteer in August, warned Washington that he was beset by "stupid men. . . . Youth and frienship make perhaps myself too warm, but I feel the greatest concern of all what happens since some time." Hamilton was certain there was a plot: "[I]t unmasked its batteries too soon," wrote the former artillery captain, "but . . . all the true and sensible friends to their country, and of course to a certain great man, ought to be upon the watch. . . ."9

The following summer another difficult general fell by the wayside. The British abandoned Philadelphia and marched back to New York, as the Americans followed indecisively, none of them more indecisive than General Charles Lee. Lee was yet another British veteran who had taken the rebel side, and a capable officer, though not as capable as he thought himself to be. He twice refused command of the advance guard, yielding it to Lafayette, and twice demanded it back. He was in command when the Americans caught the British at Monmouth Courthouse in central New Jersey at the end of June. "The weather was almost too hot to live in," a soldier recalled; the fields felt "like the mouth of a heated oven." Hamilton had given Lee an order from Washington to attack, but when he rode to see how the attack was going, he found Lee's troops in disorder and Lee in a "hurry of spirits." "Do I appear to you to have lost my senses?" Lee asked him. "So singular and unexpected a question," Hamilton wrote later, "was not a little embarrassing." (Lee, for his part, would accuse Hamilton of being in a "frenzy of valor," though any valor might have looked to Lee at that moment as frenzied.) Meanwhile, word came to Washington in another part of the field that Lee had ordered the advance guard to retreat. A soldier overheard Washington say something. "Those that were nearer to him said that his words were 'd———n him.' Whether he did thus express himself or not I do not know. It was certainly very unlike him, but he seemed at the instant to be in a great passion." When Washington finally found Lee, Lee heard him. "I was disconcerted, astonished and confounded," Lee wrote afterward, "by the words and the manner in which His Excellency accosted me."10

Washington retrieved the collapsing situation. "His coolness and firmness were admirable," wrote Hamilton. "He did not hug himself at a distance and leave an Arnold to win laurels for him"—a slap at Gates's generalship at Saratoga—"but by his own presence he brought order out of confusion . . . direct[ing] the whole with the skill of a master workman." One of his tools was Hamilton, who dispatched orders across the field and had another horse shot from under him. Equally important, the American troops showed their mettle. The battle of Monmouth, as it now developed, was not a surprise attack like Trenton, or a clash of advance guards like Princeton, but a face-to-face engagement by the main bodies of two armies in infernal heat, accompanied by a prolonged artillery duel. The years of drilling and leadership paid off. "Our troops," wrote Hamilton, "after the first impulse from mismanagement, behaved with more spirit and moved with greater order than the British troops. You know my way of thinking of our army, and that I am not apt to flatter it. I assure you I never was pleased with them before this day."[11] Though technically the battle was a draw—the British marched off at night before the Americans could reengage—the British had taken note of the new temper of their opponents. Their main army stayed in New York, not risking a major engagement for the rest of the war. Professionals had stood up to professionals.

Lee went to Congress, threatening to resign, *"aye, God damn them, that he would,"* and called Hamilton and the rest of Washington's family "earwigs" and "Toad Eaters."[12] A court-martial suspended him from command.

For the rest of his time on Washington's staff, Hamilton's duties were administrative. The war shifted focus when the British invaded South Carolina in 1780, and Gates was sent to crush them a second time. But without Burgoyne and Arnold to help him, he lost the battle of Camden and retreated with unseemly speed. "One hundred and eighty miles in three days and a half," Hamilton noted. "It does admirable credit to the activity of a man at his time of life."[13] The last important episode in Hamilton's career as an aide offered him no active role, but he gave his friends and historians vivid firsthand accounts of it, which also illuminate his character and his state of mind.

In peace, Benedict Arnold had been a Connecticut merchant, trading in the West Indies, including St. Croix. In war, he had performed feats of generalship even more impressive than Saratoga. But slowness of promotion, investigations of his shady business dealings, and the charms of a young Tory wife had led him into disaffection. In the middle of September 1780, an American soldier stationed along the Hudson River encountered General Arnold on an empty road near Dobbs Ferry. "We met at a [fork] of the roads, and I observed he stopped, and sitting upon his horse, seemed minutely to examine each road. I could not help taking notice of him, and thought it strange to see him quite alone in such a lone place."[14] He was inspecting the approaches to West Point, the riverside fort he planned to deliver to the British. With control of West Point and the lower Hudson, the British might be able to accomplish what Burgoyne had failed to do, striking into the heart of New York State and splitting New England from the rest of the country. As a bonus, Arnold also hoped to capture Washington, who was scheduled to visit the fort with Hamilton, Lafayette, and the rest of his staff.

The plot failed when Major John André, the British officer masterminding it, was captured behind American lines with a plan of West Point in his boot. Arnold fled as soon as he learned of André's fate, leaving behind incriminating papers and his wife. Mrs. Arnold now called Washington to her room, and Hamilton described the scene in a letter.

"It was the most affecting scene I ever was witness to. . . . The General went up to see her, and she upbraided him with being in a plot to murder her child. One moment she raved, another she melted into tears. Sometimes she pressed her infant to her bosom, and lamented its fate, occasioned by the imprudence of its father, in a manner that would have pierced insensibility itself. All the sweetness of beauty, all the loveliness of innocence, all the tenderness of a wife, and all the fondness of a mother showed themselves in her appearance and conduct."

There was more. "This morning she is more composed [although] she is very apprehensive the resentment of her country will fall upon her (who is only unfortunate) for the guilt of her husband. . . . She received us in bed, with every circumstance that would interest our sympathy; and her sufferings were so eloquent that I wished myself her brother, to have a right to become her defender. . . . Could I forgive Arnold for sacrificing his honor, reputation, and duty, I could not forgive him for acting a part that must have forfeited the esteem of so fine a woman."[15]

This was not the first time that Hamilton had sympathized with the wife of a guilty husband—Rachel Faucett had had two, the harsh and grasping John Lavien and Alexander's imprudent father, James—nor would it be the last. Compassion and desire are a potent combination for anyone; for him, given his history, they were almost overpowering. The wish to be Mrs. Arnold's "brother" was a placeholder for both urges. Her maternal fondness awakened the yearnings of a son, while her artfully displayed bosom and bed awakened a different set of yearnings. Hamilton's sympathies, thus aroused, distorted his judgment: Mrs. Arnold had been plotting treason with her husband for a year, and finally joined him in occupied New York. It was also not the only time Hamilton, confronted with guilt, would mistake it for misfortune.

Major André was tried by an American court-martial, which ruled that, since he had been caught in civilian clothes on American-held territory, he must be hanged as a spy. André was twenty-nine years old, handsome, witty (he wrote comic poems in his spare time), and ingenuous. "I am too little accustomed to duplicity to have succeeded," he wrote Washington, the man he had hoped to capture. Wishing to be shot rather than hanged, he felt a shock when he saw that he was to die by the rope. But he quickly overcame it—"It will be but a momentary pang"—and fastened the noose himself.[16]

Hamilton described André's fate and character in a second letter. "To an excellent understanding, well improved by education and travel, he united a peculiar elegance of mind and manners, and the advantage of a pleasing person. . . . His sentiments were elevated, and inspired esteem. . . . His elocution was handsome; his address easy, polite, and insinuating." In their brief acquaintance, André had struck Hamilton as a soul mate and a model: someone he resembled—smart, polite, well spoken—and whom he aspired to resemble more closely. But there are signs in the letter that André was also different, and that Hamilton sensed it. "His knowledge appeared without ostentation, and embellished by a diffidence that rarely accompanies so many talents and accomplishments." Hamilton did not parade his knowledge ostentatiously, but whenever it was relevant, he showed it; "diffidence" was never the word that sprung to anyone's mind concerning him. Moreover, André's military position was only superficially like Hamilton's. When arrested, André was the adjutant-general of Sir Henry Clinton, now the British commander in New York. "By his merit," wrote Hamilton, André "had acquired the unlimited confidence of his general." André's only regret was that Clinton, who had been "too good to me," would blame himself for the operation's end: "[H]e could scarce finish the sentence," Hamilton wrote, "bursting into tears."[17] André was a courtier—talented, romantic, and brave. Hamilton admired the qualities, not the role. He had been twenty when he joined Washington's staff; now he was twenty-three, and beginning to want accomplishments of his own.

. . .

As an aide, Hamilton had demonstrated his skill and his courage to himself, the world, and the man he would be working with for the next two decades. But his years at Washington's side were as important for what he saw as for what he did. Being a staff officer gave him a ringside seat on the country's problems, and a particular perspective on possible solutions. Some key traits of Hamilton's mind—his nationalism, his indifference to the states and their concerns—were in part a function of his foreign birth; one reason he lacked local loyalties was that he came from no American locality. But other immigrants in the founding generation became as fierce partisans of states' rights as native-born politicians. Hamilton's view of his new homeland was also shaped by his experience at army headquarters, and resembled the views of New England Yankees and southern aristocrats who underwent the same experience.

The main problem, from which all others radiated, was money. In "The Farmer Refuted," Hamilton had written as if the "enthusiasm" of liberty would carry all before it. But even the most enthusiastic soldiers required shoes, gunpowder, and food. Paying for them was a perpetual trial. Congress as it was then constituted lacked the power to tax: it could only make requisitions upon the states. Since many of the states were partly occupied by enemy troops, or lacked full-fledged cash economies—Virginia allowed state taxes to be paid in tobacco—the return on requisitions was scant. Congress fell back on two alternatives. It raised $11 million in loans from French and Dutch bankers (since most of the money was spent buying French and Dutch supplies, it was a prudent outlay). Congress also printed money—$200 million worth by the war's end. Like all paper money not backed by gold, silver, or revenue, it quickly became worthless. At one point in 1779, the Continental dollar lost half its value over three weeks.

In March 1778, three months before the battle of Monmouth, Hamilton wrote a letter to New York governor George Clinton, who had been helpful to him when he was on his mission to Gates, assailing "refined politicians" who were too refined to pay the country's bills. "I never can adopt the reasonings of some *American* politicians . . . that no regard is to be paid to national character or the rules of good faith." Such conduct would "bring Government at home in contempt."[18] It certainly brought Congress into contempt of the staff.

Some congressmen made themselves individually contemptible. Samuel Chase of Maryland had signed the Declaration of Independence, and would serve as a justice of the Supreme Court. In the fall of 1778, learning that Congress was about to make secret purchases for provisioning the French fleet, this patriot tried to corner the wheat market. Hamilton published a series of scathing open letters to Chase in a New York newspaper, signed "Publius," a name he had found in Plutarch's *Lives.* You "have the peculiar privilege," he told Chase, "of being universally despised. . . . No man will suspect you of the folly of public spirit—a heart notoriously selfish exempts you from any charge of this nature. . . . You have therefore nothing to fear from the reproaches of your own mind. Your insensibility secures you from remorse."[19] Chase was investigated by the Maryland legislature and cleared on a party-line vote.

Congressmen did not like the criticism, general or personal, and when it came from officers, they feared (not unreasonably) where it might lead. A year after the Chase affair, a rumor made the rounds that Hamilton had declared in a tavern that the people should rise up under Washington's leadership and "turn Congress out of doors." This was unlikely advice from an enemy of mobs, but Hamilton took the rumor seriously and tracked it down to Dr. William Gordon, a gossipy minister who was writing a history of the revolution. Alarmed, Gordon told the young officer he would reveal his source only if Hamilton promised not to challenge him to a duel. "Pleasant terms," Hamilton wrote to a friend. "I am first to be calumniated, and then, if my calumniator takes it into his head, I am to bear a cudgelling from him with Christian patience and forbearance. . . ."[20] Dr. Gordon took his tale to Washington, who told him that if he had any real evidence of mutinous intentions he could present it to a court-martial; if not, he should keep quiet.

The attacks the younger staff officers sustained, and the attacks they made, combined with the pressure of the war to breed in them a spirit of ardent camaraderie. They saw themselves as brothers in honor, risking lives and reputations for an imperiled cause in a desperate time. Their rhetoric, as they contemplated themselves and their duties, could become rapturous. Emotions came to their pens as easily as they came to their hearts. In one letter to Hamilton, Lafayette called himself "a friend who loves you tenderly." James McHenry, an army surgeon attached to the staff, assured Hamilton that he "had not ceased to love you." John Laurens, a colonel from South Carolina, closed a letter to Richard Meade, "Adieu: I embrace you tenderly." Hamilton himself wrote to Laurens: ". . . till you bade us adieu, I hardly knew the value you had taught my heart to set upon you. Indeed, my friend, it was not well done. . . . You should not have taken advantage of my sensibility to steal into my affections without my consent." Since mid-century there had been a vogue for "sentimentality," a term of praise which meant experiencing and expressing the finer emotions—a fashion fed by novelists such as Samuel Richardson and Laurence Sterne. Even George Washington owned an anthology of Sterne. Modern readers unfamiliar with this background, who come upon the effusions of Washington's staff, can misread them as evidence of erotic ties. Hamilton defined their rhetoric truly in another letter to Laurens, when he apologized for having written "several strokes of the true schoolboy sublime."[21] They all felt sublime, and they were little older than schoolboys.

Hamilton and Laurens together came up with a project whose fate sharpened their dismay with politics as usual. The two proposed to raise a regiment of slaves from South Carolina and Georgia, who would be given their freedom in return for their service. Many southern slave-owners in the revolutionary generation deplored slavery, but John Laurens was practically unique in wanting to do something about it; even in the north, Hamilton's opinions on the subject were rare enough (he did get the support of his fellow New Yorker John Jay). The South Carolina legislature rejected the plan. "I was outvoted," Laurens wrote Hamilton, "having only reason on my side." "[T]here is no virtue [in] America," Hamilton wrote Laurens. "That commerce which presided over the birth and education of these states has fitted their inhabitants for the chain . . . the only condition they sincerely desire is that it may be a golden one."[22]

Two points emerge from these controversies. Later in his life, Hamilton's enemies would throw his foreignness at him. His references, sarcastic or despairing, to *"American* politicians" and the absence of virtue in America show that when he was exasperated he could throw his foreignness back at citizens who did not live up to his own standards. Hamilton's bitter ironies about "the folly of public spirit" and his earnest declamation on the chains of commerce—as bad, evidently, as the chains of slavery—were the inverse of his prewar idealism. If the inspiration of liberty was supposed to make "human nature rise above itself," then any sign of unrisen human nature was a betrayal of liberty.

But Hamilton was a practical young man. It went against his grain to brood on his own alienation, or to contemplate abstractions, whether inspiring or distressing. The country, the army, and Congress had a problem. How could it be solved?

Hamilton's first step was to keep educating himself. From the middle of 1777 on, he used the blank pages in the pay book of his former artillery company to jot down interesting items that he had read. Some were from the classics of Greece and Rome—a common source of allusions, ideals, and daydreams for eighteenth-century Americans, though Hamilton was less impressed by the ancient world than many of his contemporaries. A few years later, he would write that for America to imitate "the small ages of Greece and Rome" would be as "ridiculous" as copying Hottentots or Lapps. His favorite classical author, appropriately, was the biographer Plutarch: not a visionary, like Thucydides or Tacitus, spinning out dark theories of history, but a historical journalist purveying observations and anecdotes. Hamilton also copied two revealing extracts from the Athenian orator Demosthenes. Where should Athens attack an enemy? Demosthenes asks, then answers that "war, war itself will discover to you his weak sides, if you seek them." This military advice mirrored Hamilton's style as a controversialist, from "The Farmer Refuted" on: hit the other side with everything, then hit them again. But Hamilton was as interested in governing as in disputing: "[W]ise politicians," said Demosthenes, should "march at the head of affairs," not waiting on "the *event* to know what measures to take; but the measures which they have taken, ought to produce the *event*."23

Economic problems required economic measures, and Hamilton filled his pay book with economic data, much of it from a now unread book, Malachy Postlethwayt's *Universal Dictionary of Trade and Commerce*. Hamilton had skimmed facts from Postlethwayt, and another reference book, Wyndham Beawes's *Lex Mercatoria Rediviva; or, The Merchant's Directory*, in his tangles with Seabury. But now he dug in, covering pages of the pay book with facts: the dimensions of Europe; the recipe for crystal glass; the products of Asia Minor; England's balance of trade with Portugal, Hamburg, and India; rates of exchange; "the quantity of cash necessary to carry on the circulation in a state" (i.e., the money supply); the number of cannons in the French navy, and of horses in Hungary; the trees of Santo Domingo; the size of the British economy (49 million pounds); Aristotle's definition of money. Some of what Hamilton absorbed was tidbits ("Patmos has the best port" in the Aegean, but "nothing else remarkable"); some of it sounded themes that would resonate in his career for years: it takes twenty-five workers to support one hundred people "in all the necessities of life," and three acres to feed one man, at least in England, Hamilton noted, already sizing up the dynamics of a mixed economy.24

Never one to keep his thoughts to himself, he wrote three important letters between late 1779 and early 1781: to Philip Schuyler, who had gone to Congress; to another New York congressman, James

Duane; and to Robert Morris, a rich Philadelphia merchant and investor. All three men were particularly concerned with America's fiscal crisis: in 1776, before the battle of Trenton, Morris had paid for crucial reenlistments out of his own pocket, while Schuyler had complained in a 1779 pamphlet that there was not "one member of Congress adequate to the important business of finance." Hamilton's letters showed that there was one man outside Congress who was trying to become adequate to the related businesses of finance and politics.

"The Confederation itself is defective," Hamilton wrote Duane, "neither fit for war nor peace." He proposed a constitutional convention that would give Congress "perpetual revenues," so that it would not have to beg from the states. Hamilton was willing to take hints from the enemy: America should have a bank like the Bank of England—"had it not been for this, England would never have found sufficient funds to carry on her wars"; with it, "she has done, and is doing, wonders"— though many of his notions of banking were still half baked (he thought changing the denominations of American bills from dollars to pounds would make people trust them).

Hamilton also called for a "proper executive," a suggestion that would naturally occur to a commander-in-chief's aide. "Such a body" as Congress, "numerous as it is, and constantly fluctuating, can never act with sufficient decision. . . . Two thirds of the members, one half the time, cannot know what has gone before." The veteran members "will only give information that promotes the side they espouse . . . and will as often mislead as enlighten."

Hamilton wanted to get the country moving. "There are epochs in human affairs," he told Duane, "when *novelty* even is useful" and "a change is necessary, if it be but for the sake of change." Striking a new note, he wanted to get his countrymen moving as well. The best tax system in the world would not generate revenue if there was insufficient economic activity, and the immigrant's enthusiasm of five years earlier for the energy and enterprise of Americans had abated. "We ought not to suffer our self-love to deceive us," he warned Morris. "We labour less now than any civilized nation of Europe."[25] This was not railing at wicked congressmen but soberly assessing the people they represented.

In later years, Hamilton stayed in touch with all three correspondents: Morris and Duane would help him out professionally, while Schuyler became his father-in-law.

"I give in to no kind of amusement myself," Washington wrote solemnly of the regimen of headquarters, "and consequently those about me can have none." But this was not entirely true, for during even the bleakest winters—and the winter at Valley Forge, 1777–78, was as grim as legend has it—the officers amused themselves with plays and dinner parties. After one dinner, the ladies and gentlemen had a gallant dispute about who should enjoy the company of one Mr. Olney. "Such a scuffle then ensued," wrote Washington, "as any good natured person must suppose. The ladies, as they always ought to be, were victorious." Washington enjoyed flirting. His younger colleagues, Hamilton among them, enjoyed it more seriously. They engaged in cats' cradles of correspondence: young men writing to young women, young women writing back, men writing to each other about women, women writing to each other about men. The letters were just what they should be: conventional revelations, ardent banalities, witticisms complex and stale as old wedding cakes. To his friend Laurens, Hamilton dictated a newspaper ad for a wife: "I lay most stress upon a good shape . . . a little learning will do . . . as to fortune, the larger stock of that the better." If she were a virgin, "I am willing to take the *trouble* of [that] upon myself." This was funny, in its way. To Miss Kitty Livingston, Hamilton solemnly declared: "ALL FOR LOVE is my motto."[26]

The Livingstons were a family of New Jersey gentry that Hamilton had met when he first came to America. (John Jay had married Kitty's sister Sarah.) Another collection of attractive and well-heeled sisters was provided by the Schuyler family. Years later, the youngest of the Schuylers, Catharine, described the impression Hamilton made upon arriving in uniform at their house in the late 1770s. He "exhibited a natural, yet unassuming superiority." A "high expansive forehead, a nose of the Grecian mold, a dark bright eye, and the line of a mouth expressing decision and courage completed the contour of a face never to be forgotten."[27] All of the Schuyler sisters were infatuated with Hamilton, and he was infatuated with all of them. The one he fell in love with was the second-oldest, Elizabeth, also known as Eliza and Betsey: dark-haired, serious, with intense, lovely eyes.

Elizabeth destroyed all the letters she sent Hamilton, an absence that makes her somewhat opaque, and which throws into undue prominence the many surviving letters of her oldest sister, Angelica. Angelica Schuyler had eloped with an Englishman, John Barker Church, who was said to have fled his country in the aftermath of a duel. She too was smitten with Hamilton, and her expressions of regard ring down the years, amplified by her vivid personality. If she appeared in a Jane Austen novel, it would be as one of those minor characters who amuse by their capacity to annoy. Angelica's mode was always to thrust herself into the center of attention. After the birth of a daughter, she wrote Elizabeth: "I intended to have called my little girl Eliza after Mr. Church's mother but she thinks Angelica a much prettier name. Mr. Church is also of that opinion." In other words, I *would* have given my daughter your name, but *everyone* wanted me to give her mine, which is nicer than yours anyway. Some years later, she promised to send Hamilton "every well-written book that I can procure on the subject of finance. I cannot help being diverted at the avidity I express to whatever relates to the subject." Later still, she wrote her "dear Eliza" about "my *Amiable*, by my Amiable you know that I mean your Husband, for I love him very much and if you were as generous as the old Romans, you would lend him to me for a little while [!] but do not be jealous, my dear Eliza [!!], since I am more solicitous to promote his laudable ambition, than any person in the world [more than George Washington? Eliza? Hamilton himself?], and there is no summit of true glory which I do not desire he may attain; provided always that he pleases to give me a little chit-chat, and sometimes to say, I wish our dear Angelica was here."[28]

These, and many, many similar effusions, all returned with interest by Hamilton, led his enemies, and even some of his friends, to assume that Hamilton and Angelica were lovers. (Angelica once told Peggy, a third sister, at a public dinner party that there were no Knights of the Garter in America; "[T]rue sister," Peggy replied, but Hamilton *"would be if you would let him."*)[29] Even apart from the double prohibition of incestuous adultery, it is hard to imagine Hamilton seriously involved with such a woman. But his reaction to Mrs. Arnold showed that his judgment of women could be very erratic.

Not his judgment of Betsey. There were other events and factors in her life, besides the destruction of her letters, which cause her to seem surrounded by silence: the preoccupations of raising a large family; widowhood; the interplay of her temperament and tragedy. But in her twenties, when Hamilton met her, her fundamental nature was more easily discerned. She had "a strong character . . . glowing underneath," wrote James McHenry, "bursting through at times in some emphatic expression." On one outing, "she disdained all assistance" in climbing a hill, wrote another staff officer, "and made herself merry at the distress of the other Ladies." "I have told you, and I told you truly, that I love you too much," Hamilton wrote her in the summer of 1780. "I meet you in every dream, and when I wake I cannot close my eyes for ruminating on your sweetness. . . . To drop figures, my lovely girl, you become dearer to me every moment."[30] They were married at the Schuyler mansion in Saratoga that December; bride and groom were both twenty-three years old. McHenry wrote a wedding poem, in pleasant couplets that mostly steer clear of doggerel, populated with fairies and imps.

In marrying a Schuyler, Hamilton entered the world of upstate New York grandees. He had already encountered some of these people (Gouverneur Morris, for one) in New York City, where they doubled as politicians or merchants. But the source of their wealth and power were huge land grants, sometimes going back to the Dutch (whose rule had ended in 1664). Many of the families—the Van Rensselaers, the Van Cortlandts, the Schuylers—were Dutch. Others, like the Livingstons, had acquired their holdings at the end of the seventeenth century (the New Jersey Livingstons were a lesser sprig of this clan). Unlike planter aristocrats in Charleston or the Virginia tidewater, New York magnates worked their fields primarily with tenant farmers, not slaves. But the New Yorkers enjoyed a status and an opinion of themselves as high as any indigo or tobacco king. Tenant leases in New York ran for ninety-nine years, for one to three lifetimes, or forever, and were encumbered with a variety of feudal restrictions. Some of the estates, or manors, had seats in the state legislature assigned to them, like rotten boroughs in the British parliament. Holders of Dutch grants bore the title *patroon*, or patron. The modern Spanish word *padron*, meaning an employer of indentured labor, captures the economic structure of patroonship; Mr. Collins's simperings about his "patroness," Lady Catherine de Bourgh, in *Pride and Prejudice* capture the social flavor. In the upheavals of the times, most of these landowners had sided with the patriots—"swimming with a Stream which it is impossible to stem," as Robert R. Livingston put it,[31] who swam all the way to the Continental Congress and the committee that drafted the Declaration of Independence—and they had admitted some recruits into their ranks, such as George Clinton, a large landowner west of the Hudson. But their position was secure, and would remain so for decades. Feudal leases were not abolished until the 1840s, and then only after riots; Mr. Henry van der Luyden, the arbiter of New York society in *The Age of Innocence*, set in the 1870s, is still called "Patroon." New York's great families were proud, powerful, and used to having their own way. They were not unprincipled, but their highest principle typically was preserving their own position.

Hamilton was another new man, like Clinton. Philip Schuyler genuinely liked, and even admired him. "You cannot, my dear Sir," he wrote his son-in-law, "be more happy at the connection you have made with my family than I am"—generous words indeed from a patroon to an illegitimate West Indian. More remarkably, Schuyler urged his own son to model himself on Hamilton, in whom he "will see sense, virtue and good manners combined."[32] Besides being sensible, virtuous, and good-mannered, Hamilton would be very useful to Schuyler in navigating the rapids of local politics. New York State at that period, a nineteenth-century historian observed, was divided into three parts: Clintons, Livingstons, and Schuylers. The Clintons had power, the Livingstons had numbers, the Schuylers had Hamilton. But Hamilton never became like his in-laws, or their peers. He never made anywhere near enough money, nor did he ever make the leap into their mind-set. The patroons were possessors; Hamilton was an achiever. Hamilton would have trouble understanding other American gentlemen he encountered.

Shortly after Hamilton was taken into the Schuyler family, he left

Washington's. Hamilton had been discontented for some time. By February 1781, he had been absent from the field for almost four years. Washington, who prized him as an aide, rebuffed all his requests to be reassigned. The break came one day at headquarters. Washington told Hamilton he wanted to see him in his upstairs office, and Hamilton, who was delivering a letter, said he would be back immediately. On his way, however, he was stopped by Lafayette for (he thought) about a minute. When he returned, he found an angry Washington standing at the top of the stairs. "Colonel Hamilton, you have kept me waiting . . . these ten minutes. I must tell you, sir, you treat me with disrespect." Hamilton replied, "without petulancy, but with decision," that he was not conscious of it, but since Washington thought so, "we must part." An hour later, Washington sent another aide to Hamilton offering to patch the quarrel up, but Hamilton answered "that I had taken my resolution in a manner not to be revoked."

These details, from a letter to Philip Schuyler, may have caused the patroon to wonder about his new son-in-law's sense. Hamilton defended his conduct by explaining that Washington was "not remarkable . . . for good temper."[33] This was true enough, though it had not changed over the course of Hamilton's service. The deeper reason was Hamilton's dislike of "personal dependence." In their attacks on the staff, the enemies of the army called Hamilton "the Boy." Washington himself addressed him as "my boy." Hamilton, who had turned twenty-four in January, was old enough, and young enough, to resent the role.

Hamilton did not go public with the details of the rupture. "I shall continue to support [Washington's] popularity," he wrote McHenry, as if that depended on his support. He still wanted a field command. "I am incapable of wishing to obtain any object by importunity," he wrote Washington in May, importuning him for an assignment.[34] Washington gave him an infantry brigade that summer, and Hamilton saw action again at Yorktown.

At the end of a war marked by confusion and crossed signals, the siege of Yorktown was a miracle of coordination. Nathanael Greene, who had replaced the humiliated Horatio Gates in the South, had driven the British under Cornwallis into eastern Virginia. The French navy secured a temporary control of the eastern seaboard. French and American armies moved three hundred miles by land and water from the Hudson River to the York River in five weeks. A wave of hope and valor swept the troops. When the British made their headquarters in the home of Thomas Nelson, governor of Virginia, he told the American artillery to bombard it. Warned by an aide that they were standing too close to the embrasure of a gun emplacement, Washington remarked, "[I]f you think so, you are at liberty to step back." Hamilton had his troops mount the parapet of their trench and perform the order of drill in full view of the enemy. When Hamilton's unit was given the task of making a nighttime assault on a key British redoubt, the soldiers came on so rapidly that they overtook the sappers, the demolition experts who were supposed to prepare the advance. In his report after the redoubt was taken, Hamilton noted simply that "the ardor of the troops was indulged." Washington praised the "intrepidity, coolness and firmness" of the action.[35] The commander-in-chief and the former aide were free to reapproach each other on a more equal footing.

The British surrendered on October 19, though the war, and America's problems, would drag on for years.

Chapter Three

Laws

AS THE FIGHTING drew to a close, Hamilton told his friends that he had put the "public and splendid passions" behind him. His first child, Philip, was born in January 1782, and in November he wrote Lafayette that he was "rocking the cradle." There would be seven more children, five sons and two daughters, and Hamilton was an attentive father. When Philip first went away to school, he wrote the boy a note as wise as it was affectionate. "You remember that I engaged to send for you next Saturday, and I will do it . . . for a promise must never be broken, and I never will make you one which I will not fill as far as I am able; but it has occurred to me that the Christmas holidays are near at hand. . . . Will it not be best, therefore, to put off your journey till the holidays? But determine as you like best, and let me know what will be most pleasing to you. A good night to my darling son." James Hamilton never took such care over his promises, to his sons or to anyone else. "I am already tired" of the "race of ambition," Hamilton wrote Lafayette, "and dare to leave it."[1] He was not leaving just yet, however, for New York had chosen him to be a delegate to Congress, and the domestic situation of the country was as difficult as it had been in the darkest days of the war.

The Congress that Hamilton served in was the sole branch of the national government. It had one house, and state delegations voted as units. This form of Congress, which lasted until 1788, achieved notable things: it resolved conflicting state claims to land beyond the Appalachians and established the procedure for admitting new states; some of its appointments—Washington, Benjamin Franklin as minister of France—were superb, and it presided over a successful war, though from Hamilton's perspective as a staff officer it had caused as many problems as it solved. But the talent level was erratic, as capable men—Patrick Henry, Samuel Adams, Thomas Jefferson—tended to gravitate back to the states. The states drew them because state legislatures held the real power in the country, controlling the national finances and selecting the congressmen themselves. The symbol of Congress's insubstantiality was its lack of a fixed abode: when Hamilton joined, it was sitting in Philadelphia, but it later made a pilgrimage through the towns and cities of the middle states. James McHenry commiserated with Hamilton on Congress's futility: "If you could submit to spend a whole life in dissecting a fly you would be in their opinion one of the greatest men in the world."[2]

One of the best men in Congress when Hamilton arrived was James Madison of Virginia. Six years older than Hamilton, he was the son of a wealthy planter. Brilliant and industrious, he had gone through Princeton in two years, after which he suffered a nervous collapse. Perhaps memories of the episode discouraged Dr. Witherspoon from letting Hamilton study at his own pace. In 1776, Madison missed winning a seat in the Virginia legislature, in part because he refused to follow custom and treat the voters with drinks. But three years later, the state sent the young man to Congress.

A French diplomat later wrote that Madison was "a man whom it is necessary to study for a long time in order to form a just idea of him." Madison moved through life in a thick carapace of reserve. He did not marry until he was forty-three. Dr. Witherspoon, his intellectual mentor, never knew him "to do or to say an improper thing." Among friends he could be relaxed, witty, even (*pace* Dr. Witherspoon) ribald, but with strangers he was cold and silent: "[H]is pride," wrote one, "repels all communication." He disliked public speaking, in part because he had a croaking voice. Another Frenchman, who described Hamilton as "firm" and "decided," with "the determined air of a republican," found in Madison "the meditative air of a politician." Hamilton favored bright waistcoats; Madison dressed in black. Hamilton and Madison were about the same height, though Madison struck one colleague as "little and ordinary."[3]

This sober, silent man shone in small groups and committees, where his knowledge and attention to detail overwhelmed adversaries and allies alike. "He always comes forward the best informed Man of any point in debate," wrote a delegate to the Constitutional Convention, who heard him participate in many.[4] Like Hamilton, he could read a shelf of books and put them to use in arguments or essays. But their minds worked differently—a difference reflected in their educations. Hamilton's, interrupted by war, was continued by reading on the run. Madison, thoroughly tutored and schooled, prepared for later tasks with self-administered courses of study. Hamilton was driven by problems, Madison by theories. Madison's theoretical orientation did not stop him from being an excellent politician—effective for his goals, his side, and himself. His fingertip feel for politics—how points are carried, how deals are made, how people behave and misbehave in pursuit of power, how alliances hang together and disintegrate—informs his theorizing. At his best, he could push a cause with patience, tact, and cunning. If he was beaten, he could keep coming back until he prevailed. His determination would carry him, over the resistance of enemies and the conflicting ambitions of friends, to eight years in the White House.

But in spite of his intellectual power and political skills, his career would be marked by strange shifts. He often got what he wanted, but he wanted drastically different things at different times. Biographers have constructed theories as elaborate as Madison's own in order to reconcile the positions he took during his career. A simpler explanation is that at a deep level of his being James Madison was weak—susceptible to his constituents, and to the influence of stronger personalities. In 1789, Fisher Ames, another congressman who would become, but was not yet, an enemy, laid his finger on this quality of Madison's: "I think him a good man and an able man," but he "seems evidently to want . . . energy of character."[5]

As fellow congressmen, Hamilton and Madison agreed that the government as it was then constituted was in a bad way. Hamilton, in a series of newspaper articles signed "The Continentalist," had described the country as a collection of "petty states . . . jarring, jealous and perverse." The cause of impotence was lack of money. "Power without revenue . . . is a name." In 1782, Congress asked the states for $8 million, and got only $400,000. Robert Morris, then superintendent of finance, said that getting money from the states was "like preaching to the dead."[6]

The minimum program of the reformers was to give Congress the power to collect a 5 percent impost, or tax on imports, without having to go to the states for permission. Since this represented a change in the Articles of Confederation, which were the fundamental laws of the country, it required the unanimous support of all thirteen states. Rhode Island held out, arguing that the power of states to withhold taxes was "the most precious jewel of sovereignty." So it was, which was why Hamilton and Madison wanted to appropriate it. Hamilton did nothing to quiet the fears of Rhode Island when he said, in a January 1783 speech in Congress, that he wanted national revenue collectors "pervading and uniting the States." "Mr. Hamilton," wrote Madison dryly, "had let out the secret."[7] While Congress and Rhode Island wrangled, Virginia withdrew its consent to the impost. The best Congress could agree on was an impost limited to twenty-five years, which would be collected by state revenue agents. Hamilton could not bring himself to vote for such a watered-down measure.

Congress needed money because it still had an army in the field. Though all serious fighting had ended at Yorktown, no peace had yet been signed. Isolated skirmishes continued (Hamilton's friend John Laurens died in one in South Carolina), and the British army still occupied New York City and a dozen frontier posts on nominal American soil. The United States needed to keep the army together, but without revenue, Congress could not pay it directly, nor could it make interest payments on its debts, which would have allowed it to raise a loan abroad. Hamilton, and others in Congress, including Robert Morris, hoped that the army's plight, and perhaps also its pressure, would move Congress to act. George Washington, still at headquarters at Newburgh, New York, was alive to the financial problem. The previous year, he and Morris, drawing from a secret fund, had hired the journalist firebrand Thomas Paine to write articles supporting the cause of fiscal reform. But Washington warned Hamilton that the army "was a dangerous instrument to play with."[8] In March of 1783, a petition, written by an aide to Horatio Gates, circulated through the Newburgh camp calling on the officers to demand redress from Congress. It took all of Washington's prestige to recall the restive officers to their duty.

Three months later, soldiers stationed in Pennsylvania proved more difficult to control. Several hundred of them marched on Congress, and Hamilton, who had warned lawmakers in Philadelphia to flee from the British in 1777, now tried to protect them from the Americans. The Pennsylvania state government, to his chagrin, would not call out the militia. Congress decamped to Princeton, Elias Boudinot, the president of Congress, leaving the announcement of the move sealed on his desk, to be opened only after he was safely gone. Hamilton prepared a resolution calling for a constitutional convention, but he did not bother to offer the motion to such a debilitated body. In July, he quit Congress and rejoined his family in upstate New York. Madison left when his term ended in November.

Hamilton's eight months in Congress had been frustrating. "I often feel a mortification," he had written Washington in March, ". . . that sets my passions at variance with my reason. . . . I have an indifferent opinion of the honesty of this country." (*This* country, not *my* country—a characteristic sign of dismay.) Hamilton was not self-interested—when Congress had debated half-pay for veterans, he had surrendered his own claim to any, so as not to have a stake in the issue—and his efforts to save Congress from the mutinous soldiers showed that he was not a man on horseback (he wanted to use the idea of the suffering army, not the army itself). But he had been impolitic, and impatient. On the other hand, he had made a reputation for himself as a reformer. His friend McHenry put it best: cautious men "think you sometimes intemperate . . . were you to pursue your object with as much cold perseverance as you do with ardor and argument, you would become irresistible."9

Meanwhile, he had to make a living. The career he chose was the law, where he was able to join perseverance, ardor, and argument.

Hamilton began his studies in January 1782, using James Duane's law library. The law of New York was more complicated than that of other states. Based, like all American laws, on the English common law, it had developed many procedural peculiarities, which were often not written down, but committed to the memory of lawyers and judges. ("[W]e had no law of our own," remarked James Kent, a disciple of Hamilton's, many years later, "and no one knew what it was.") Studying for the New York bar examination was thus typically a long task. To accommodate veterans, the legislature delayed the examination of 1782 until July. Hamilton's method of mastering the material was to write himself a small book, which became the basis for study guides in the next century—although the later versions dispensed with some of Hamilton's comments: "[T]here seems to be no Reason for this. . . . this proceeding seems to be without use. . . . There is the usual Confusion in this Doctrine."[10]

Hamilton would practice law off and on until his death. While the war lasted, the New York State Supreme Court sat in Albany; after the British left, it alternated between Albany and New York. Travel between the two places was not quick. The stage took three days, with stops in Peekskill and Rhinebeck; with good winds, a sloop on the Hudson could make the trip in the same amount of time, although with bad winds it might take two weeks. It was easier to move around the Leeward Islands than New York State. The New York bar was a small world; a 1786 directory counted thirty-five lawyers in New York City (one-twelfth the number of prostitutes). Hamilton might argue one case alongside his old King's classmate, Robert Troup, assorted Livingstons, or Aaron Burr, another veteran-turned-lawyer; the next case might find him arguing against them.

Years later, Troup recalled that Hamilton "had only time to read elementary books. Hence he was well grounded in first principles." The explanation is incorrect; Hamilton found the time to read whatever he had to. But Troup accurately describes his method: to establish a principle of the law and build a structure of argument from that, forcing his opponents to fight on his terms. His skill and his successes put him in great demand—one of his clients was his brother-in-law, John Church, whom he helped to set up the Bank of New York—and if he did not become rich from his practice, it was because of the interruptions of public life, and because he charged low fees. In one famous and complex suit, he won a settlement of $120,000 for Lewis Le Guen, a merchant, and billed him for only $1,500. Aaron Burr, who had acted as cocounsel, charged $2,500. At the same time, Hamilton refused a client who said that lawyers liked to make as much as they could—"insinuations," Hamilton informed him coolly, "which cannot be pleasing to any man in the profession."[11] He would defend the honor of the bar against outsiders who wished to hold it to his standards.

The end of the war and the conduct of the victors brought Hamilton a blizzard of cases. The Treaty of Paris was announced in the United States in April 1783, and the British finally evacuated New York at the end of November. Although the treaty forbade reprisals against Loyalists, several states, including New York, passed punitive laws. The population of New York City, which had been swollen by Tory refugees during the war, shrank as boatloads of Tories, refugees once more, sailed for Bermuda or Canada. Distressed by the outflow, which included many merchants and businessmen, Hamilton wrote Robert R. Livingston that "our state will feel for twenty years at least the effects of the popular phrenzy." Livingston agreed that the new laws were often the tools of "the most sordid interest. One [patriot] wishes to possess the house of some wretched Tory, another fears him as a rival in his trade or commerce, and a fourth wishes to get rid of his debts by shaking off his creditor."[12]

Hamilton went, as he had done before, to the newspapers, writing two letters signed "Phocion." Phocion, one of Plutarch's subjects, had been a politician in the declining days of Athens whose bluntness was not appreciated. "When once he gave his opinion to the people," Plutarch wrote, "and was met with the . . . applause of the assembly, turning to some of his friends, he asked them, 'Have I inadvertently said something foolish?'" Hamilton/Phocion appealed to justice, law, interest, and good government. Penalizing former Loyalists as a class violated both "natural justice" and the peace treaty. Driving out prosperous citizens hurt everyone—"carpenters and masons . . . must be content with patching up the houses already built, and building little huts upon the vacant lots, instead of having profitable and durable employment. . . ." Government without law was government by faction: if the state constitution "is slighted, or explained away, upon every frivolous pretext . . . the rights of the subjects will be the sport of every party vicissitude."[13]

Hamilton, who had opened a law office on Wall Street, also argued for former Loyalists in court. "Legislative folly," he wrote Gouverneur Morris, "has afforded so plentiful a harvest to us lawyers that we have scarcely a moment to spare from . . . reaping."[14] The most prominent case he reaped was *Rutgers* v. *Waddington*, a case based on the Trespass Act, which allowed patriots to sue Loyalists who had used their abandoned property during the British occupation. The aggrieved patriot in the case was Elizabeth Rutgers, an elderly widow who had owned a decrepit brewery on what is now Pearl Street before the war began. In 1778, the property was taken over by Joshua Waddington, an agent for two British merchants. The new occupants made 700 pounds' worth of improvements, and from 1780 to 1783 paid rent to a fund for the poor, as directed by the British commander-in-chief. (The Trespass Act, however, forbade defendants from pleading "any military Order or command whatever of the enemy" as justification for their actions.) At war's end, Rutgers's agent asked the merchants for back rent. While they bargained, a fire burned the brewery down, and Mrs. Rutgers sued Waddington for 8,000 pounds. She was represented by the state attorney general, Egbert Benson, who also happened to be her nephew; John Lawrence, who had conducted the court-martial of Major André; and Troup. Waddington retained a Livingston, a Livingston in-law, and Hamilton.

The case went to trial in the Mayor's Court in New York City at the end of June 1784. Standards for conflicts of interest were much laxer then, for one of the judges was a plaintiff in another Trespass Act suit (the defendant in that case was also represented by Hamilton). Some of Hamilton's best thinking went into his courtroom pleading, of which nothing remains except occasional abridged newspaper accounts; Hamilton's notes, marked in the margins with pointing hands, to signify emphasis; or the dim reflections of the praise of listeners. James Kent, who was clerking for Benson at the time of *Rutgers* v. *Waddington*, remembered Livingston as "copious and fluent," and Troup for his "simplicity" and "earnestness," but thought Hamilton's voice, bearing, and reasoning "soared far above all competition. . . . The audience listened with admiration to his impassioned eloquence."[15]

Hamilton presented a learned, three-part challenge to the legality of the Trespass Act. The constitution of New York, he argued, incorporated the common law, which in turn incorporated the law of nations and the laws of war. Under these, Waddington was entitled to do what he had done, whatever the New York legislature subsequently said. In addition, Congress had signed a peace treaty that prohibited punitive suits. If Congress could not speak for the nation in making treaties, "then the Confederation is the shadow of a shade!" If the court found that the Trespass Act violated either the common law or the treaty, then it was obliged to strike it down. "When Statutes contradict the essential policy and maxims of the common law the common law shall be preferred."[16] Before there was a national Supreme Court, Hamilton was advancing an argument for judicial review, and before there was a constitution, he was defining the principles that should guide judges. But if the court would not accept such a grand vision, Hamilton, like any clever lawyer, offered a technicality: Waddington and the merchants he represented were British subjects. Therefore, the Trespass Act, even if legitimate, could not apply to them.

The judgment of the court, delivered in August, by Mayor James Duane, seized the lesser of Hamilton's arguments. Duane accepted the legislature's authority to contravene the law of nations, even to the extent of allowing foreigners to be sued for obeying their own military commanders. But since New York's lawmakers had not explicitly said that this is what they meant to do, then Waddington's British citizenship and the orders of the British commander-in-chief protected him. "[A] subject of the highest national concern" could not "have been *intended* to be struck at in *silence*."[17] Waddington was liable only for the first two years he managed Mrs. Rutgers's property. The jury, adjourning to Simmons' Tavern by City Hall, awarded her less than a tenth what she had asked. Hamilton's fee was 9 pounds, 11 shillings, 3 pence.

The anti-Loyalist party in New York was incensed. The State Assembly resolved that the decision "subver[ted] all law and good order," and an angry open letter in the papers declared that the business of courts was "to declare laws, not to alter them." Hamilton was called many names, including "little, pompous stripling." On the other hand, George Washington, to whom Duane sent a copy of the decision, replied that "reason seems very much in favor of" it.[18] Hamilton went on to argue more than forty other Trespass Act cases. The Assembly finally voted to repeal the law in the spring of 1787, acting on a bill sponsored by Assemblyman Alexander Hamilton.

By then, Hamilton had a larger project in hand, for he was engaged in an effort to rewrite the fundamental laws of the nation.

. . .

The call for a new constitution came, not from the years-long struggle over taxes, but through the side door of commerce. Trade and tariffs were a source of interstate friction, and New York was a major irritant. Its congressional delegation blocked Congress from regulating foreign trade, and it took advantage of the importance of the port of New York to levy tariff duties on imports bound for New Jersey and Connecticut. New Jersey-bound goods that came via Philadelphia were similarly taxed by Pennsylvania, thus causing New Jersey to compare itself to a cask tapped at both ends. Madison persuaded the state of Virginia to call for a commercial conference of the states in Annapolis in September 1786.

Hamilton had been elected to the State Assembly from New York City in April (he polled 332 votes). Thanks to the efforts of Schuyler in the State Senate, and of Troup and William Duer, a fellow West Indian, in the Assembly, Hamilton was picked as one of the delegates to go to Annapolis. There was hardly anything to do there, since only five states sent delegations, and the conference lasted only two weeks. Hamilton used the occasion to offer yet another call for a constitutional convention that would "cement the Union." Madison advised him to phrase it differently, and the report that came out of Annapolis looked forward to an "adjustment . . . of the Federal system" requiring the "united virtue and wisdom" of all the states.[19] The new convention was called to meet in Philadelphia in May 1787.

Two weeks after the Annapolis meeting broke up, the need for adjustments was underlined by an uprising of indebted farmers in western Massachusetts, led by a war veteran, Daniel Shays. Shays and his followers wanted relief from foreclosures and crushing state taxes, which Massachusetts had imposed in a vain effort to cope with its own war debts. Henry Knox sent dire (and exaggerated) reports of a rebel army,

15,000 strong, intent on overturning property throughout New England, and he and others urged George Washington to leave retirement at Mount Vernon and show himself on the scene to influence his former soldiers. Washington replied tartly that "influence is no government."[20] If the government was so feeble, virtue and wisdom would have to come up with a better one.

The call for a Philadelphia convention was resisted in some states by the powers that be, and with special strength in Hamilton's state, where the source of resistance was George Clinton, then serving the tenth of his twenty-one years as governor. Clinton's first election in 1777 had surprised the patroon establishment; Philip Schuyler, who had wanted the job himself, wrote that Clinton's "family and Connections do not Intitle him to so distinguished a predominance." Clinton skillfully cultivated the grandees by giving them important jobs, and he struck Hamilton as a capable wartime governor. After the peace, his political skills inclined him in other directions. Though he had treated Loyalists with moderation during the war, he allied himself with their most frenzied enemies afterward. He balked at giving Congress the power to levy an impost, though he said he favored it in theory. Hamilton explained the gambit in a newspaper article: "He was a friend to an abstract something, which might be any thing or nothing, as he pleased; but he was an enemy to *the thing proposed*."[21] As the state's economy began to prosper in mid-decade—thanks in part to New York City tariffs—Clinton saw himself presiding, if Congress did not interfere, over a booming fiefdom. Hamilton accused him of obstinacy, but it was not the principled obstinacy of Rhode Island. Clinton's politics were passive, protean, and inert. New York sent a delegation of three to Philadelphia: Hamilton, and two Clintonians, John Lansing, the mayor of Albany, and Robert Yates, a New York judge. Since voting at the convention, as in Congress, was by states, Hamilton was outnumbered so long as Lansing and Yates attended. When the two Clinton men left Philadelphia midway through the convention, in disgust at its tendencies, Hamilton did not feel entitled to cast his state's vote by himself, and continued as a nonvoting member. For the duration of the convention, therefore, he was effectively disenfranchised.

The convention opened on May 25 and ran through September 17, meeting in the State House (now Independence Hall), which the Congress had vacated under duress four years earlier. Hamilton did not speak often, and missed all of July, and much of August. William Pierce, who left the most extensive portraits of the delegates, called him "rather a convincing Speaker [than] a blazing Orator. Colo. Hamilton requires time to think,—he enquires into every part of his subject with the searchings of phylosophy. . . . His manners," Pierce added, "are tinctured with stiffness, and sometimes with a degree of vanity that is highly disagreeable." Some who held forth should have spoken less. Pierce wrote of Elbridge Gerry that he "goes extensively into all subjects . . . without respect to elegance or flower of diction," while he judged George Read's "powers of Oratory . . . fatiguing and tiresome to the last degree."[22] But Hamilton was not among the delegates who most regularly supplied guidance or fireworks.

Hamilton's situation with respect to his own state kept him detached. So did his lack of influence on the convention's agenda. The Virginia delegation, which included Madison and Washington, had arrived in Philadelphia early with a plan prepared by Madison, who had been studying foreign and ancient constitutions for the past year, and Virginia's governor Edmund Randolph proposed it on May 29. Delegates alarmed by the sweep of the Virginia plan prepared an alternative, which William Paterson of New Jersey offered on June 15. John Lansing, Hamilton's colleague, was the first delegate to second Paterson's plan, declaring that New York "would never have concurred in sending deputies" if a government according to the Virginia plan were in the offing.[23] Much of the convention's work would involve trading off between the plans and their attendant factions. Hamilton, who had no hand in writing either, and who disagreed with both, felt himself sidelined.

The convention itself, and the exact plan that might emerge, were a way station for him, not a goal. "We have fought side by side to make America free," he had written John Laurens, days before his death, "let us hand in hand struggle to make her happy." He had been calling for a constitutional convention for seven years, not for its own sake, but to make the national government more capable and effective. Changes had not been made, and as a result, he told the convention, the union was now "dissolving or already dissolved."[24] To him, the deliberations in Philadelphia were a frustrating, if necessary, step toward averting evils, and beginning the work of national happiness.

Even so, Hamilton's attendance was not uneventful. In his free time, he had an important talk with Madison that he would remember with puzzlement five years later. "[I]n a long conversation . . . in an afternoon's walk," the two men discussed the problem of state debts, which was no less pressing than the national debt, and which, in Massachusetts, had led to Daniel Shays. The two "were perfectly agreed" that the debts of states that were still outstanding should be assumed by the national government, when (and if) it was reformed; they also agreed that the specifics should be kept out of the Constitution, "from the impolicy of multiplying obstacles to its reception." In Philadelphia, Hamilton and Madison thought the assumption of state debts both necessary and controversial, and they agreed on how to handle it. Their agreement would not last. Hamilton also gave one long speech on June 18, in which he offered a plan of government of his own. The Hamilton plan had no chance of success, which he admitted to his audience; he said he offered it only "to give a more correct view" of his own ideas.[25] These ideas, correctly and incorrectly viewed, would haunt his reputation for the rest of his life, and after his death.

He began by explaining that he had said little, partly out of respect to "the superior abilities, age and experience" of his fellow delegates, partly because of the "delicate situation" of his delegation. But since "we owed it to our Country to do on this emergency whatever we should deem essential to its happiness," he was going to tell the convention that both plans before it were wrong.[26]

Paterson's New Jersey plan was a reformed version of the existing Congress, with additional powers of raising revenue. The Virginia plan called for a bicameral national legislature, which could veto state laws. Congress under both plans would select a national judiciary, and an executive.

Hamilton directed most of his fire at the New Jersey plan, and the continued prominence and distinctness it accorded the states: "It is not in human nature that Virginia and the larger states should consent" to equality of suffrage in Congress. "It shocks . . . the idea of Justice, and every human feeling." Not that he was a partisan of Virginia and the larger states. If all state governments "were extinguished, he was persuaded that great economy might be obtained. . . . He did not mean, however, to shock the public opinion by proposing such a measure." He would only shock the opinion of his fellow delegates. Hamilton also disliked the concentration, in both plans, of whatever power the national government had in Congress. "Giving powers to Congress must eventuate in a bad government or no government." This remark was aimed at the state-dominated Congress of the New Jersey plan, but the former aide-de-camp was suspicious of the institution itself. "Such a body," he had written Duane seven years ago, "can never act with sufficient decision." "What is even the Virginia plan," he asked now, "but pork still, with a little change of the sauce?"[27]

His own plan was based on a blunt analysis of society and its permanent economic interests. "In every community where industry is encouraged there will be a permanent division . . . into the few and the many. Hence separate interests will arise. . . . Give all power to the many, they will oppress the few. Give all power to the few, they will oppress the many. Both therefore ought to have power, that each may defend itself against the other." The power of the few in Hamilton's plan would be wielded by a Senate, elected from special election districts, for good behavior (for life, if the senators behaved well). The many would be represented by an Assembly, elected "by the people," to serve for three years.[28] The balance wheel between them would be a governor, chosen by special electors from the senatorial election districts. Like the senators, the national governor would serve for good behavior; he would also appoint the governors of the states.

The model for Hamilton's plan was seemingly an unusual one to offer a convention that included eight signers of the Declaration of Independence and twenty-one Revolutionary War veterans: Great Britain, with its House of Lords, House of Commons, and king. "The British government," he said, "was the best in the world," and he quoted approvingly the French financier Jacques Necker, who had called it the only government "which united public strength with individual security." He doubted "whether any thing short of it would do in America," though he was "sensible . . . that it would be unwise to propose" anything other than a republican form of government in Philadelphia. His own plan was an attempt to combine Britain's virtues with republicanism, and "he was aware," he admitted, "that it went beyond the ideas of most members." As if to confirm his judgment, three days after he spoke, one delegate (William Samuel Johnson) said he had been "praised by everybody," but "supported by none."[29]

Why such a unanimous vote of no confidence? The Hamilton plan did not much resemble the document that finally emerged, although it was no more different than the Virginia or New Jersey plans. The independent elections of the executive and the legislature provided by Hamilton were closer to the final system than either the Virginia or the New Jersey versions. Nor did the Hamilton plan's singularity arise from the antidemocratic implications of a governor and senators for life. Democracy was not yet a positive totem word in American politics. The delegates in Philadelphia were familiar with all the criticisms that ancient political theory made of democracy, both for its own vices and for its tendency to mutate into tyranny ("the fine and vigorous root from which tyranny grows," as Plato put it). They made the same criticisms themselves. If democracy was the rule of the many, then Shays's Rebellion was democracy, and the Constitutional Convention had been called to thwart it. In some respects Hamilton's ideas had more democratic elements than those of his peers. There is disagreement among the accounts of the half-dozen delegates who took notes on his speeches, but John Lansing recorded him as saying, eight days after his oration, that he would "cheerfully become a martyr" to "the cause of democracy" (Madison wrote, "a martyr . . . for liberty"). Hamilton's Assembly, chosen "by the people" every three years, was as democratic as the final version of the House of Representatives. The delegates believed that just governments must rest on the choice of the people. But they also believed that liberty and justice were better served by passing popular choice through filters of representation. Republican government did not have to be democratic, so long as it was ultimately popular. "Is this a

Republican government?" Hamilton asked of his own plan, and answered that it was—because "all the magistrates are appointed . . . by the people, or a process of election originating with the people."[30]

Hamilton's remoteness from his peers, finally, was not due to his praise of Britain per se. One delegate called the British government an "excellent fabric," another called it "the best constitution in existence," a third pronounced "eulogiums" upon it.[31] The delegates were steeped in British history and precedents, and referred to them constantly.

What was striking about Hamilton was the part of the British Constitution he liked. In his wartime letter to Duane—the same in which he had praised the Bank of England—he had called for a "proper executive." The elected governor-for-life, analogous to the British king, was the "proper executive" of his system. "It will be objected probably," Hamilton said, in the tone of one tarrying while his slower listeners caught up, "that such an Executive will be an *elective Monarch.*" He would not shy at labels: if all executives were kings, then the executive of the Virginia plan was a "monarch for seven years" (the term of office then under discussion). Hamilton proposed giving his executive considerable clout. One of "the great and essential" props of government, he said, was *"influence,"* meaning those "honors and emoluments, which produce an attachment to the government." The king of England dispensed honors and emoluments, and so should America's governor. One of Britain's "ablest politicians," Hamilton added four days later, "had pronounced all that influence on the side of the crown, which went under the name of corruption, an essential part of the weight which maintained the equilibrium of the [British] Constitution. . . . We must take man as we find him, and if we expect him to serve the public must interest his passions in doing so."[32] It was a commonplace of contemporary English thought that the Stuart kings of the seventeenth century had overstepped the limits of their power, and a vocal party believed that the Georges of the eighteenth century, and their ministers, overstepped it still, by the means that Hamilton had described. This reading of history had become gospel in America, where the Revolution was depicted as a crusade against an overweening king and his agents. The able politician cited by Hamilton was the philosopher and historian David Hume, who had recently taken a more benign view of royal influence on the state. Hume, witty and learned, was on every intelligent American's reading list, but his notions of the king's (and by implication the executive's) role in good government went against the American grain. By echoing them, so did Hamilton.

The delegates' reluctance to follow Hamilton's ideas was exacerbated by private monarchical rumblings, inside the convention and out. Gouverneur Morris (serving as a delegate from Pennsylvania, where he had temporarily moved) privately remarked that "we must have a Monarchy sooner or later . . . and the sooner we take [a king], while we are able to make a bargain with him, the better." When Hamilton left the convention for a month, he wrote Washington from New York City that both there and in New Jersey "former habits of thinking are regaining their influence with more rapidity than is generally imagined." In Philadelphia, when the lively society hostess Mrs. Eliza Powell, who concealed a keen intelligence beneath a screen of banter, asked Benjamin Franklin what kind of government the delegates were preparing, Franklin bantered back, "A republic, if you can keep it."[33] Their exchange depended on the knowledge that other notions were being mooted.

Some historians portray Hamilton's speech as either a calculated forensic tack, staking out an extreme position to make the Virginia plan look more moderate, or presenting his "phylosophical searchings" in order to raise the intellectual level of debate. This is overinterpreting. Hamilton presented his ideas because, as usual, he thought they were better than everybody else's. When they failed, he took what he could get. In September, as the convention was completing its work, he said, according to one set of notes, that he would "take any system which promises to save America"; according to another, that the Constitution was "better than nothing."[34] All of the thirty-nine delegates who finally signed the Constitution were in the same position, since none of them had gotten exactly what he wanted.

The Committee of Standing Rules and Orders, on which Hamilton sat, had advised that all deliberations be secret. Years later, Hamilton explained why: so that "experimental propositions might be made . . . merely as suggestions for consideration."[35] The delegates kept their word, as far as publishing went: the first set of notes to be printed (Robert Yates's) did not appear until 1821. But rumors leaked out almost immediately: a report, as precise as it was inaccurate, that the crown of America would be offered to a son of George III, appeared in the newspapers in July and August. Madison would privately show his notes, including the "experimental proposition" on elective monarchs, to his allies in the early 1790s, when he was no longer an ally of Hamilton's.

On the last day of the convention, Hamilton urged all the delegates still present to sign. "No man's ideas," he said, "were more remote from the plan than his were known to be; but is it possible to deliberate between anarchy and Convulsion on one side, and the chance of good . . . on the other?"[36] Hamilton had written Lansing and Yates, asking them to return. They refused, and he was the lone New Yorker to sign.

. . .

The process of bringing the rest of the state along occupied him for the next ten months. The Constitution would go into effect once it was approved by nine states, but approval, to be meaningful, had to include the largest states—Massachusetts, Pennsylvania, and Virginia—as well as New York, which was growing, and centrally located. Governor Clinton knew this as well as anyone. Just as the British had tried to split the United States by invading New York, so Clinton sought to split the Constitution's supporters, or Federalists, by making his state an anti-Federalist bastion.

Hamilton's first recourse was to turn to the press. He planned a series of twenty-five essays defending the document that was so remote from his ideas, to be written with collaborators. At first, he thought of Gouverneur Morris and William Duer, but Morris refused and on second thought Duer was not up to snuff. So Hamilton turned to John Jay and Madison, who happened to be in New York because he had returned to Congress and Congress was sitting there. *The Federalist* appeared, from two to four times a week, in the New York newspapers. Hamilton wrote the first piece in October 1787 on a sloop returning from Albany, where he had been arguing a case before the State Supreme Court. He finished many pieces while the printer waited in a hall for the completed copy. (The story of the waiting printer is so common in accounts of eighteenth-century journalism—compare Samuel Johnson dashing off numbers of the *Rambler*—that it might be dismissed as a narrative convention, except that writers, then as now, have a propensity for running up against deadlines.) When the series was finished in May 1788, it had grown from twenty-five essays to eighty-five, and ran to 175,000 words. Jay fell ill early on, and wrote only a few pieces. Madison wrote over twenty; Hamilton over fifty, or two-thirds of the total.

The collective pen name of Publius was the one he had used in 1778 in his attack on Samuel Chase. Publius Valerius had helped to overthrow Rome's last king and establish the Roman Republic. Plutarch wrote of him that he "resolved to render the government, as well as himself . . . familiar and pleasant to the people. . . . Always, upon his entrance into the assembly [he] lowered" the symbols of his office "to the people, to show, in the strongest way, the republican foundation of the government." So far, Hamilton/Publius would welcome the comparison. But anti-Federalists could have found confirmation of their fears by reading on: "the humility of the man was but a means, not, as [the people] thought, of lessening himself, but merely to abate their envy . . . for whatever he detracted from his authority he added to his real power."[37]

It soon became known who Publius was, though the authors did not take credit for specific essays until years later, and then their accounts disagreed. The articles commonly acknowledged to be Hamilton's are marked with his stylistic and temperamental fingerprints. Jay and Madison can be epigrammatic ("Had every Athenian citizen been a Socrates, every Athenian assembly would still have been a mob") or fussily formal—Madison will number his points, or begin a paragraph with a throat-clearing "Hence." Hamilton is flowing, sometimes overflowing, and agitated. In a few paragraphs at the end of one piece, discussing debt and foreign policy, he throws out the words *avidity, dissension, altercation, complaints, recriminations, quarrels, disgracing, jarring, entangled, pernicious, hates, fears.* He seems always in a hurry, and when he is not moving, he champs at the bit. For all his efforts to be familiar and pleasant, his impatience can show. "It is astonishing that so simple a truth should ever have had an adversary." In No. 24, he described two hypothetical reactions to anti-Federalist polemics: one, from "a man of quick sensibility, or ardent temper," who "pronounc[es] these clamors to be the dishonest artifices of a sinister and unprincipled opposition"; the other, from "a man of calm and dispassionate feelings," who "indulge[s] a sigh for the frailty of human nature."[38] He offered himself to the reader as a composite of both men, though sighing was not his normal mode.

Intellectually, the triple face of Publius blends into one. Hamilton and Madison pass over in silence all they had said in Philadelphia about vetoing state laws or appointing state governors. Hamilton even holds up state legislatures as watchdogs against federal encroachments. Future disagreements between them seem incomprehensible: it is Madison, not Hamilton, who offers the classic formulation of expansive federal power: "wherever the end is required, the means are authorized."[39]

Still, there are different emphases. Madison focused on theoretical and practical politics. His famous discussion of factions in No. 10 is subtle and complex. Though he acknowledged that the unequal distribution of property is the most common cause of faction, he enumerated many others, including sheer frivolity. Next to this, Hamilton's discussion of the few and many in Philadelphia looks bald. In Hamilton's favor, the most serious convulsion in the new republic, Shays's Rebellion, had been a clash of the few and the many. In Madison's favor, the wrangles at the Philadelphia convention had been multiform; perhaps Hamilton would have noticed if he had attended more regularly. Madison's characteristic maneuver is to pit factions and the passions that animate them against each other. "Ambition must be made to counteract ambition."[40] Madison's goal is to block tyranny, and his means is to arrange institutional balance wheels. It was a chestnut of political theory that republics had to be small. But Madison specifically praised the size of the new republic for offering more internal balances—more states, more factions—and more counteracting ambitions.

Hamilton by contrast valued America's size as a potential source of energy. "Under a vigorous national government," he wrote in No. 11, "the natural strength and resources of the country . . . would baffle all the combinations of European jealousy to restrain our growth. . . . The veins of commerce in every part will be replenished and will acquire additional motion and vigor from a free circulation of the commodities of every part." He imagined an America populated by replicas of himself: "the *assiduous* merchant, the *laborious* husbandman, the *active* mechanic, and the *industrious* manufacturer" (emphasis added). This picture recapitulated the student hopefulness of "The Farmer Refuted." But now he understood the role of proper government in making it real. Madison thought it was "vain to say that enlightened statesmen will be able to adjust" all the "clashing interests" in the state. Hamilton was not so gloomy. "[C]onfidence must be placed somewhere . . . the necessity of doing so is implied in the very act of delegating power. . . . it is better to hazard the abuse of that confidence than to embarrass the government and endanger the public safety by impolitic restrictions. . . ."[41]

The subjects Hamilton confidently addressed were war, law, executive power, and administration. The United States had won its revolution four years earlier, but Hamilton foresaw future wars: "A cloud has been for some time hanging over the European world. If it should break forth into a storm, who can insure" that "its fury would not be spent upon us?" He borrowed an argument he had made in *Rutgers v. Waddington* about the common law, and transferred it to the Constitution: "[W]henever a particular statute contravenes the Constitution, it will be the duty of the judicial tribunals to adhere to the latter and disregard the former." "A government ill executed," he noted, "whatever it may be in theory, must be, in practice, a bad government." Finally, he quoted (evidently from memory, since he made a few slips) these lines from Alexander Pope's "Essay on Man":

> *For forms of government let fools contest—*
> *That which is best administered is best.*

He called them "political heresy," then added that "the true test of a good government is its . . . tendency to produce a good administration."[42] Some heresies were less noxious than others.

The complete set of essays was bound and sold to subscribers for six shillings (75 cents). Robert Troup got a plaintive letter from

Archibald McLean, the printer, pointing out that the work had ballooned from one volume of two hundred pages to two volumes of six hundred. "I have several hundred copies remaining on hand, and even allowing they were all sold at the low price I am obliged to sell them at, I would not clear five pounds on the whole [edition]. However I must abide by the consequences, nor could I expect the Gentlemen would make up a loss. . . ."[43] Publishers have changed no more than writers.

Never did a work of world-historical importance have a more slapdash genesis than *The Federalist.* It had its critics. After the Constitution was ratified, William Maclay, a senator from Pennsylvania, made a note to himself to "get if I can the *Federalist,* without buying, it is not worth it." George Washington, who had it reprinted in Richmond, sent Hamilton what would be the majority view: "That Work will merit the Notice of Posterity; because in it are candidly and ably discussed the principles of freedom and the topics of government, which will be always interesting to mankind. . . ."[44] It was quoted in Congress and in court as early as the 1790s. The first justice of the Supreme Court to cite it, ironically, was Samuel Chase.

While Publius was writing, eight states ratified: Delaware, Pennsylvania, and New Jersey by the end of 1787; Georgia and Connecticut in January 1788; Massachusetts (narrowly, and with considerable struggle) in February; Maryland and South Carolina in April and May. But of the remaining five, North Carolina and Rhode Island were hopeless, while New Hampshire, Virginia, and New York, all of whose ratifying conventions would meet in June, were doubtful.

The elections for New York's convention produced nineteen pro-Constitution delegates from New York City, including Robert R. Livingston and two-thirds of Publius (Hamilton and Jay). When they sailed upriver from New York to attend the convention, they were hailed with a thirteen-gun salute from the Battery. So far, *The Federalist* had made its mark. But the "antis" had swept the rest of the state, electing forty-seven delegates, including Lansing, Yates, and Governor Clinton. The convention opened on June 17 in the Hudson River town of Poughkeepsie, halfway between New York and Albany, in the heart of Clinton's rural base.

Hamilton wrote Madison, who was leading the fight in Virginia, to arrange "exact communication" between them, and he also asked a friend and fellow veteran at the New Hampshire state convention to send an express messenger when they ratified. "Let him take the *shortest route . . .* change horses on the road, and use all possible diligence. I shall with pleasure defray all expenses, and give a liberal reward to the person."[45]

The anti-Federalists in Poughkeepsie were sure of their staying power. Hamilton, wrote one, "would probably do much mischief, were the members not as firm as they are." One Federalist was equally sure of anti-Federalist firmness, describing the upstate farmers as "ignorant Dutchmen." Firm or ignorant, there was nothing to be done but address them, which Hamilton proceeded to do. He went through the Constitution point by point, quoting so extensively from *The Federalist* that Governor Clinton asked if he was bringing out a second edition. When he lost his temper—in an exchange with Lansing, who had alluded to the secret debates in Philadelphia—he apologized: "[I am not one of] those indifferent mortals, who either never form opinions, or never make them known." His arguments formed a series of masterly disquisitions on responsibility and trust. "Every one knows that the objects of the general government are numerous, extensive, and important. Every one must acknowledge the necessity of giving powers . . . equal to these objects. . . . Sir, when you have divided and nicely balanced the departments of government, when you have strongly connected the virtue of your rulers with their interest, when, in short, you have rendered your system as perfect as human forms can be, you must place confidence, you must give power."[46]

The psychological situation at Poughkeepsie was quite different from that of Philadelphia. Now there was no possibility of horse-trading, no array of contending goals. Hamilton was at the head of a compact, like-minded, and beleaguered minority, like defense lawyers sitting at the same table. Then he had given one long speech, not to the point. Now he gave many, day after day. The other side might win, but not until he had shown them that they were wrong. Melancthon Smith, the most capable debater on the Clintonite side, publicly admitted that Hamilton's arguing swayed him. A century later, Hamilton's biographer Henry Cabot Lodge (himself a lawmaker) wrote that "anyone familiar with legislative bodies . . . can appreciate the meaning and weight" of such a switch. Hamilton had "changed votes . . . and when party lines are drawn there is nothing so rare."[47] Hamilton was helped by the ratifications of New Hampshire (late June) and Virginia (July), which occurred while the Poughkeepsie convention was sitting.

On July 23, the jubilant Federalists of New York City celebrated the new Constitution, and its advocate, by parading down Broadway behind a twenty-seven-foot ship, the *Hamilton*, manned by thirty seamen and pulled by ten horses. It made "a fine appearance, sailing with flowing sheets and full sails, the canvas waves dashing against her sides." In its wake followed the city's artisans, with regalia and floats of their own. The coopers pulled a barrel of thirteen staves; the tailors carried a banner of Adam and Eve wearing fig leaves, labeled AND THEY SEW'D FIG LEAVES TOGETHER; the brewers hauled Bacchus mounted on a three-hundred-gallon cask. The cartmen, or teamsters, carried standards inscribed with a poem:

> *Behold the federal ship of fame;*
> *The* Hamilton *we call her name;*
> *To every craft she gives employ;*
> *Sure cartmen have their share of joy.*[48]

Hamilton did not see the parade, for the convention in Poughkeepsie was still in session, tying up loose ends, but Nicholas Cruger, the man who first shipped him to New York, did. His apprentice had made good use of his opportunities.

Chapter Four

Treasury Secretary

THE NEW GOVERNMENT met in New York City in the spring of 1789. The city's common council had hired the French architect Pierre L'Enfant to make $65,000 worth of improvements to City Hall, renamed Federal Hall, at the intersection of Wall and Broad Streets. When L'Enfant finished, the building accommodated the House, the Senate, various committee rooms, a library, and a "machinery room," for displaying models of inventions. The Supreme Court met on Broad Street, above a sheep market. Most of the members of the government put up in taverns or boardinghouses. John Adams, who had been elected vice president, rented a farm a mile north of town, in Greenwich Village (Abigail Adams complained that it was "impossible to get a servant . . . that does not drink"). George Washington, who had been unanimously elected president, rented a house near the East River. The president-elect entered the city from New Jersey in a ceremonial barge, rowed by thirteen oarsmen, and took the oath of office from the balcony of Federal Hall on April 30.

Hamilton's first service to the new government was to advise his former chief on etiquette. During his retirement at Mount Vernon, Washington had been deluged with visitors—invited and uninvited, American and foreign, friends, strangers, and idle gawkers—and now that he was president the flow would increase unless it was regulated. Hamilton proposed three kinds of social appearances: a weekly reception, or levee, "the President to remain half an hour," conversing "on indifferent subjects"; small family dinners, with six to eight guests, "the

President never to remain long at table"; and a few formal dinners a year, for the entire Congress, the cabinet, the diplomatic corps, and "distinguished strangers." The number of guests at such functions, Hamilton admitted, would be very large—almost one hundred people. "But there may be separate tables in separate rooms."[1]

The two men's concern for etiquette was symptomatic of a general nervousness, an anxiety to get things right, and a fear that it might not be possible. Americans were haunted by the twin specters of immaturity and decadence. Lexington and Concord had happened only fourteen years ago, yet already one form of government had collapsed and passed away. Another wreck could drag down the country, the republican ideal, and the reputations of everyone involved. When Washington gave his inaugural address, Representative Fisher Ames of Massachusetts noted in a letter "his aspect grave, almost to sadness; his modesty, actually shaking; his voice deep, a little tremulous, and so low as to call for close attention." "This great Man," wrote Senator William Maclay of Pennsylvania in his diary, "was agitated and embarrassed more than he ever was by the levelled Cannon or pointed Musket." The congressmen described similar perturbances in their own bodies. Maclay found the Senate was afflicted with "a rage of speaking," while Ames complained that his colleagues in the House "correct spelling or erase *may* and insert *shall*, and quiddle in a manner which provokes me." Maclay wrote with glee of Vice President Adams's lack of poise: "[W]hen he is at a loss for expressions" he "suffers an unmeaning kind of vacant laugh to escape him." Yet when President Washington called at Maclay's lodgings, he was all aflutter: "This day I ought to note with some extraordinary Mark . . . the greatest Man in the World paid me a Visit."[2]

Of all the principal actors in the new government, James Madison had special cause for distress. Madison and a band of Federalist Young Turks had pushed the Constitution through Virginia's ratifying convention over the opposition of anti-Federalists led by Patrick Henry; in retaliation, Henry and the state legislature, which picked Virginia's senators, had denied him a Senate seat. Consequently, Madison was going to New York only as a member of the House. This rebuke had a profound effect on him. Ames wrote, "[H]e is afraid, even to timidity, of his state," and "sees Patrick Henry's shade at his bedside every night."3

Hamilton was anxious about the new government's powers, and its staying power. In a note to himself after Philadelphia, he had written that the "proposed constitution" might not provide a government of sufficient "consistency . . . for so great a Country," and that the dissolution of the Union seemed "the most likely result." But Washington's election would at least "insure a wise choice of men" at the top, and "perhaps" give the government a chance.4

Hamilton had been making important political choices of his own at the local level, not all wise. New York's ratification of the Constitution had been a victory of the Schuylers and Livingstons over the Clintons, and it seemed right that they should share the spoils. One Senate seat was due to go to Philip Schuyler, the other to New York mayor James Duane, one of the many Livingston in-laws. But Hamilton pushed to give the second seat to Rufus King, a talented lawyer but a newcomer to the state (King had signed the Constitution for Massachusetts). Hamilton got his way, and the enmity of the Livingstons. Governor Clinton, foreseeing this result, covertly backed King.

Washington chose wisely. For chief justice of the Supreme Court, he nominated John Jay. For secretary of war, he picked his artillery commander, Henry Knox. He asked Thomas Jefferson, minister to France, to be secretary of state. Madison and Pennsylvania's other senator, Robert Morris, recommended Hamilton as secretary of the treasury— Morris called him "damned sharp"5— and Washington gave his former aide the nod. Hamilton had been twenty-four when he quit the general's family in frustration and pique. At age thirty-two he was back, at a higher level, and in a more self-sufficient capacity.

The only member of this inner circle that Hamilton did not know was the new secretary of state. Over the next dozen years, he would come to know him, to despise him, and to back him for president. Fourteen years older, Thomas Jefferson had served with distinction in the Virginia legislature and in Congress, and in more trying circumstances as wartime governor of Virginia. (Hamilton touched on the circumstances in his eulogy of Nathanael Greene, when he said that Virginia had been "deficient in order and vigor.") After the war, Hamilton and Jefferson missed serving together in Congress by only four months. In 1784, Congress sent Jefferson to Paris to follow Benjamin Franklin as minister to France. "No one can replace him," he graciously said, "I am only his successor." While in France, he penned some formally flirtatious letters to several women (his wife had died in childbirth), including Angelica Church. "When you come again" to Paris, he wrote, "I will draw a veil over all your good qualities, if I can find one large enough."[6] Angelica Church had the merit of inducing two of the smartest men in America to behave foolishly.

Both as a congressman and a diplomat, Jefferson had chafed at Congress's impotence. "The states must see the rod," he declared at one point. So far, he had agreed with his new colleagues. But other factors in the political crisis of the 1780s appeared differently to him, partly because he viewed them from across the Atlantic. He did not fear Shays's Rebellion. "The tree of liberty must be refreshed from time to time, with the blood of patriots and tyrants. It is its natural manure." He did fear the new Constitution when he first learned of it. It "mend[s] a small hole," he complained to his friend James Madison, "by covering the whole garment." At least it should have a bill of rights (Jefferson would later advise Lafayette and other French reformers on a French Declaration of the Rights of Man). Hamilton, in *The Federalist*, No. 84, had made a lawyerly argument against putting a bill of rights in the Constitution, since it "would contain various exceptions to powers which are not granted; and, on this very account, would afford a colorable pretext to claim" them. But several states made their ratification conditional on a bill of rights, and that, along with Madison's explanations of the document as a whole, brought Jefferson around. When he received a copy of *The Federalist*, he wrote Madison that he had "read it with care, pleasure, and improvement."[7]

In a 1791 portrait of the secretary of state by Charles Willson Peale, Jefferson's high forehead, bright button eyes, and swept-back red hair make him look like some strange but alert bird. A description by Senator Maclay conveys the same combination of detachment and awareness. "His cloaths seem too small for him [Jefferson was tall—six feet two]. He sits in a lounging manner on one hip commonly, and with one of his shoulders elevated much above the other. . . . His whole figure has a loose shackling [or ramshackle] air. He had a rambling vacant look & nothing of that firm deportment which I expected would dignify the presence of a Secretary. . . . Yet he scattered information wherever he went, and some even brilliant sentiments sparkled from him."[8]

Jefferson had such a long life—he did his greatest deed, drafting the Declaration of Independence, when Hamilton was still a teenager, and reached his highest office, the presidency, after Hamilton's career was over—that there was much in his character that Hamilton never encountered. But two not-so-obvious facets of the Virginian would have a great impact on him.

Jefferson was a squire. He was obviously a Virginia planter, but to call him a squire fixes the type of which Virginia planters were a provincial offshoot. Even as upstate New York had been defined by the Dutch patroons of the mid seventeenth century, so Virginia had been defined by the English country gentlemen who settled it at the same time. Like many provincial copies, the Virginia version was gaudier than the home model, having more land, more dash, more obvious pride. The sources of a Virginia gentleman's wealth were also more evident. The slaves of Sir Thomas Bertram of Mansfield Park lived in remote Antigua; the slaves of Thomas Jefferson lived at Monticello. Certain forms, finally, were different: Sir Thomas was a baronet; Thomas was proud to live in a land without titles. But both were squires.

Squires had their own politics. English country gentlemen feared lords greater than themselves, powerful ministers, businessmen, and London. All these fears were transferred to the colonies, where they helped breed the Revolution; after independence, they were replaced by local analogues. The politics of squires enabled Jefferson (and Madison, Washington, and other Virginians) to speak without hypocrisy of "the people." They were more powerful than any other people in Virginia, but they were of the people nevertheless. The enemies of the people were in London, or even (as some of them came to fear) closer to home.

Jefferson's station as a squire also explained his paeans to agrarian life. In his only book, *Notes on the State of Virginia*, published shortly after he arrived in Paris, he proclaimed that "those who labor in the earth are the chosen people of God." None of the laboring in the earth of Monticello was done by Jefferson, yet he was not being consciously insincere. He embodied a type, expressed in a tradition of pastoral polemic running back through English literature, and beyond, to Horace and Virgil. In France he saw the decadence of the type—Marie Antoinette dressing as a milkmaid. Unlike her, Jefferson lived on a real farm, where he kept track of crops and seeds and bills. He knew other ways of life existed, but he could not imagine any that were better. Between him and a man raised on islands where many of the plantations were owned by absentees and only the counting houses offered opportunity, a gulf was fixed.

Jefferson was also a politician. This was a calling that his enemies sometimes discerned only after it was too late, and which Jefferson concealed as he grew older. Jefferson's greatness as a politician came partly from the plainness of his ideas, which reflected the force of his character. Madison's thoughts at their best are brilliant constructs. Jefferson's are visions. Jefferson's elaborations of his aperçus are unconvincing, sometimes even ludicrous, but at the first moment of perception, they shine like searchlights. Which is more compelling, Madison's *hence*'s, or Jefferson's trees of liberty? As important as Jefferson's ideas and words were his silences. Jefferson had the patience to wait problems out; he could even leave them altogether. Madison or some other earnest junior partner could mind the store. After the Constitution had been ratified, a correspondent asked Jefferson if he were a Federalist or an anti-Federalist. "If I could not go to heaven but with a party," Jefferson answered, "I would not go there at all. . . . I am of neither party, nor yet a trimmer between parties."[9] Because he meant it, he was the most skillful partisan of his generation. Only Washington had equivalent cunning and tact, and Washington had only ten years to live.

Hamilton had the least experience of any of his colleagues. Knox had been a general and Jefferson an ambassador; Hamilton had written a few letters on finance and helped some New York bankers. But he could also expect the least interference from Washington, who was qualified to be his own secretary of war and of state, but not of the treasury. Congress confirmed his appointment on September 11, 1789, a

Friday. On Sunday, Hamilton went to the Treasury Department, on Broadway below Trinity Church, and went to work.

. . .

Hamilton had some models for a modern finance minister to guide him. Jacques Necker, whose high opinion of the British government he had quoted at the Constitutional Convention, was a Swiss banker who had been called upon, from 1776 to 1781 and again in 1788, to reform the chaotic finances of France. He had a very high opinion of his role— "If men are made in the image of God," he wrote, "then the minister of finance, next to the king, must be the man who most closely approximates to that image"[10]—and during his years out of power, he wrote three volumes of self-justifying memoirs that impressed Hamilton. Necker sought to bolster France's credit by cutting wasteful royal spending and by simplifying and strengthening its tax system. He also issued the first public budget in French history, which was one of the reasons he had been fired in 1781. As important as his policies was his rhetoric: he wrote about finance in an inspiring, even heroic way.

But Necker had not been a successful hero. For models of effective finance ministers and financing, Hamilton looked—as he had in his wartime letter to James Duane—to Britain's lords of the treasury and the Bank of England.

During the preceding century, Britain's financial institutions had performed prodigies. Over that time, tax revenues sextupled, and the national debt rose by fifteenfold. Thirty to forty percent of government spending had to be covered by loans, and military spending alone consumed 9 to 14 percent of the national income. Yet during this period of exploding expense and debt, Britain rose from being a marginal European state, which had with difficulty beaten Holland in a series of naval wars, to an empire with outposts on three continents and the wherewithal to subsidize entire European armies.

Britain's debt represented strength, rather than bankruptcy, because of the care and skill with which it was financed. At the end of the seventeenth century, Britain was awash with schemes for raising money: lotteries, taxes on leather, short-term loans. The scheme that took root was the Bank of England, founded (with fifty-four clerks) in 1694. The bank raised money for the government by issuing long-term bonds, which could be traded in the open market. The market in bonds acted both as a check on the government's behavior, and as an advertisement to investors of its good behavior. As a result, the British government was able to raise money, at relatively low rates of interest, whenever it needed it.

"Credit," a contemporary economist wrote, "is only begot by certain and punctual payments."[11] Britain was able to make such payments to its bondholders because of an efficient (by eighteenth-century standards) tax system, which Necker sought in vain to emulate. Among the many cogs of the British revenue system, before he moved to America, was Thomas Paine, who had been a collector of excise taxes.

Presiding over the structure were successive first lords of the treasury, who often doubled as prime minister, the most famous being Robert Walpole, a hard-living squire's son, who dominated British politics for much of the early eighteenth century. His tool of political control was what Hamilton, following Hume, had called "influence." Walpole used influence quite baldly—he paid off members of Parliament with lucrative government offices. Several rich plums went to his own family, and Walpole himself accumulated a collection of paintings that was later snapped up by Catherine the Great.

This century-long development had not unfolded without setbacks. An early rival of the Bank of England, the South Sea Company, overhyped itself and burst in a bubble in 1720. Britain's attempt to extend its tax system to its colonies provoked the American Revolution. As a young revolutionary, Hamilton expected Britain's debts to bring it down: "Great Britain, already tottering under her burthens, will be obliged to increase them, 'till they become altogether insupportable." Paine, the former exciseman, agreed. "As a nation, she is the poorest in Europe; for if the whole kingdom [were] put up to sale like the estate of a bankrupt, it would not fetch as much as she owes."[12] But Britain always managed to go again to the market for loans, and to move on. Her latest expedient had been a "sinking fund"—revenues earmarked to retire the debt—proposed by the current prime minister and first lord of the treasury, William Pitt, in 1786. The fund would never have worked even if Britain had not taken on huge new military expenses as the century ended, but as a sign of the government's seriousness, it restored investor confidence. William Bingham, a Philadelphia merchant who had been in London at the time, wrote Hamilton in November 1789 that "this stroke of finance operated like a charm."

Britain's financial revolution—for it amounted to nothing less—was greeted by many Englishmen, and most English writers, with incomprehension, suspicion, and dismay. Troops of pundits, from geniuses like Daniel Defoe, Jonathan Swift, and Alexander Pope, to dispossessed politicians and nameless Grub Street scribblers, covered acres of paper with abuse of the Bank, the government, and its ministers, especially Walpole; none of it is now readable, except for *Gulliver's Travels.* "I had the honour," wrote Gulliver solemnly of Lilliput, "to be a *Nardac,* which the Treasurer himself is not; for, as all the world knows, he is only a *Clumglum,* a title inferior by one degree. . . ."[13] So, in fantasy, Walpole's enemies mocked his "influence." Bank phobia was, however, the particular property of English squires—and many of their transatlantic cousins.

Hamilton was guided in his conduct of day-to-day business by neither Necker nor Walpole but by his own administrative style. Years later, John Marshall wrote that he had "a patient industry, not always the companion of genius." The Treasury was the largest government department. He worked harder than his colleagues and he had more work to do. Jefferson and Knox had fewer than twenty clerks between them. Congress, in part to guard against the possibility of theft, had given the secretary of the treasury a staff of five assistants and auditors. William Duer, Hamilton's acquaintance from New York, was briefly his assistant; Oliver Wolcott, a young man from Connecticut who prided himself on his "orderly and proper manner," served as auditor, then comptroller. Hamilton also oversaw five hundred customs collectors, spread along the coast from Maine to Georgia. He immediately sent off a barrage of letters to them, and to knowledgeable outsiders, concerning counterfeiting, smuggling, lighthouses, the French debt, and duties on brandy and tea. He asked Bingham for "any thoughts"; "send me your thoughts," he wrote Madison. Hamilton's activity was not busy work, nor was it micromanaging. He needed to establish the procedures of a large, new organization, much as Washington had had to impose a routine on the army. He also needed information to gauge the economic problem, and what resources were available for meeting it. "Absolute precision is not expected," he assured his customs collectors when he asked them for an account of the duties they received, but he did want their answers "as speedily as possible."[14]

His first problem was establishing America's credit. This could only be done by resolving the problem of its outstanding debt. The debt had two potentially controversial aspects. The United States had issued a great number of securities, or IOUs, during the war, which now traded at 20 to 25 percent of their face value. The largest class of security-holders were veterans; it was a hard thing to have given men who had risked their lives only a piece of paper in return, though it was better than giving them worthless American paper money. But many of the securities—anywhere from 60 to 75 percent of them—had been sold, at a discount, by their original possessors: some in return for goods or services, some for cash. Many of these were now in the hands of speculators. Should the government discriminate between speculators and soldiers? One of Hamilton's correspondents who thought not was Madison's mentor, John Witherspoon. Suppose, he wrote Hamilton, a clerk in the Bank of England were to tell a person redeeming securities, "'Where did you get these? You are a Speculator . . . we will not pay you the full Value of them.' Such a Thing reported and believed on the Exchange of London would bring the whole National Debt to the Ground in two Hours." Madison himself wrote him from Virginia only that he had not yet formed "any precise ideas" on the question of debt.[15]

The second tangle of the American debt was the debts owed by states. Some states had paid off their wartime obligations, but others had not. If the federal government took on, or assumed, the unpaid debts, the states that had no debts to assume would balk. Complicating the picture was the fact that some of the debt-free states had achieved this condition by shady means: North Carolina had paid off its debts by knocking their value down to 20 percent; Rhode Island had balanced its books by inflation, causing Washington to refer to its politicians as a "paper-money junto."[16]

Hamilton's "Report on Credit" was presented to the House on January 14, 1790. It began with a strong statement on national obligations. "States, like individuals, who observe their engagements are respected and trusted, while the reverse is the fate of those who pursue an opposite conduct." This was the argument from expediency, sharpened by the comparison to private life. But Hamilton cited "still greater authority . . . the immutable principles of moral obligation." Happily, doing right would mean doing well: the prospect that the new Constitution might lead to payment of America's debts had already caused the price of securities to rise.

He came down firmly against discrimination, attacking the notion of credulous sellers and conniving buyers. "How shall it be ascertained, in any [particular] case, that the money which the original holder obtained for his security was not more beneficial to him, than if he had held it to the present time?" Conversely, "how shall it be known whether, if the purchaser had employed his money in some other way, he would not be in a better situation . . . though he should now receive the . . . full amount? . . . Questions of this sort, on a close inspection, multiply themselves without end, and demonstrate the injustice of a discrimination, even on the most subtile calculations of equity, abstracted from the obligations of contract." He supported assuming the state debts equally strongly: if fourteen separate governments were trying simultaneously to settle their obligations, "collision," "confusion," and "interfering regulations" would be the result. He suggested a schedule for paying off security-holders, a "sinking fund" not so much to extinguish the debt as to stabilize its value, and a list of import duties to raise revenue, singling out tea, coffee, and spirits as luxury items that could be taxed—perhaps, in the case of "pernicious" luxuries, taxed out of existence. "The consumption of ardent spirits," he observed, "is carried to an extreme which is truly to be regretted, as well in regard to the health and morals as to the economy of the community."

Along the way, he made a far-reaching forecast. "It is a well-known fact that, in countries in which the national debt is properly funded, and an object of established confidence, it answers most of the purposes of money." Government paper, "in the principal transactions of business, passes current as specie" (meaning, it is as good as gold). "The same thing would, in all probability, happen here under the like circumstances."[17] Hamilton did not fear money; he proposed to turn the United States into a cash economy. He would lift it into capitalism (a word that did not yet exist) by creating capital.

The "Report on Credit" was 20,000 words long, not counting appendices. When it had been read, the overwhelmed House sat silent.

The silence did not last long. The House and Senate, and all New York, began to hum with speculation, in both senses of the word. People either discussed how to make money out of the secretary's proposals, or deplored other people for doing so. "I call not at a single house," wrote Senator Maclay in his diary, observing the first behavior while practicing the second, without encountering "traces of Speculation." One of the most active speculators, unbeknownst to Hamilton, was his assistant William Duer, who formed a syndicate with William Bingham, among others, to buy up veterans' securities in the southern backcountry. Maclay filled his diary with gossip: a senator from North Carolina, on his way to New York, had passed "two expresses with very large sums of money" headed south, while a congressman from Connecticut had "sent off two small vessels" on the same errand. Hamilton's proposals, Maclay concluded, would "damn [his] Character . . . forever." In the House, James Jackson, a vehement congressman from the Georgia frontier, assailed the "spirit of havoc, speculation, and ruin. . . . My soul rises indignant at the avaricious and immoral turpitude which so vile a conduct displays." When Jackson got going, his voice rose along with his soul so that the Senate, meeting upstairs, had to shut its windows "to keep out the din."[18]

Meanwhile, Madison, the de facto leader of the House—"our first man," Ames had called him back in May 1789—had finally developed his ideas. In February, he committed himself publicly for discrimination, and against assumption. Throughout the eighties, he had taken the opposite positions on both issues. (As late as the Constitutional Convention, he had agreed with Hamilton, in their afternoon walk, that

86

state debts ought to be assumed.) Fisher Ames attributed Madison's shifts to his home-state political problems. Modern historians have argued that, as far as discrimination was concerned, he was genuinely appalled by the upsurge in speculative activity. If true, this reason reflects better on his sensibility than on his understanding: where freedom of exchange is allowed, speculation will always heat up as the day of reckoning approaches. With respect to assumption, Madison proposed that all state war debts, both those that had been paid, and those that had not, be taken up by the federal government. States like Virginia, which had paid their debts, would go into the black. This proposal would involve doubling the nation's debt—in effect, killing the goose by asking it to lay golden eggs. While seeming to be zealously—even overzealously—for assumption, Madison's proposal would in fact sink it.

Madison framed his new arguments, Ames thought, "with great care," but his reasoning "will not bear a strict examination." Everyone, meanwhile, was sure of his own reasoning. "I have written very dogmatically," Ames ended one letter, but "why should I affect doubts when I entertain none?" "When is it that I do not think well of my own arguments?" Maclay asked himself in his diary.[19] Hamilton listened to the speeches of the clashing congressmen from the galleries.

Discrimination was rejected at the end of February, but the debate on assumption dragged on through the spring. Paradoxically, delay gave more leeway to the speculators the delayers decried. Moreover, men like Maclay and Jackson were not simply virtuous enemies of unseemly profit-seekers. They, and many other Americans, speculated in unsettled public land, west of the Alleghenies. Duer (who, fortunately for the honor of the Treasury Department, resigned in April) was involved in a huge Ohio Valley land syndicate as well as his venture in securities. It might be argued that land was a more honorable object of speculation than the pay of soldiers, but western land, much of it occupied by Indians, would require the exertions of new soldiers before it was open to white settlement. Many investors in securities hedged their positions with land, and vice versa. There were also bulls and bears in both markets. Any simple morality play based on the response to the "Report on Credit" breaks down under examination.

The issue of assumption became entangled with another: the permanent location of the capital. New York had spent considerable sums on its public buildings, and was willing to spend still more, but powerful forces in Congress wished to pull the capital to a more central location, either in Pennsylvania or along the Potomac. The president, who lived on the Potomac, and who fancied the river as a channel for inland commerce, was a strong, though silent, advocate. Assumption was not making any progress in Congress. (Maclay maliciously observed during one Senate debate that Hamilton's father-in-law's "Hair stood on end, as if the Indians had fired at him.")[20] It was time for Hamilton to make some deals.

At the beginning of June, he arranged to meet Pennsylvania senator Robert Morris, as if by accident, during a morning stroll on the Battery (the same spot from which he had hauled his cannon fourteen years earlier). Morris agreed to try to round up votes in return for a Pennsylvania site. Later in the month, Hamilton had a meeting that is more famous, because it was recorded by Thomas Jefferson.

The secretary of state ran into Hamilton one day outside the president's door. (Washington had moved to a house on Broadway.) "His look," wrote Jefferson, "was sombre, haggard, and dejected beyond description. Even his dress [was] uncouth and neglected." Jefferson's accounts of meetings with Hamilton, all written up years later, must be treated with care; it is surprising that an elegant dresser like Hamilton would be perceived by such a careless one as Jefferson as looking "uncouth," though Jefferson does present this detail as surprising. Hamilton said he was worried about the fate of assumption. Jefferson suggested a "friendly discussion" over dinner at his lodgings the following night, between Hamilton and Madison. When the former associates arrived, Jefferson professed not to understand the subject, but "encouraged them to consider the thing together."[21] The result of their considerations was an agreement to pass assumption, in return for a move to the Potomac. Pennsylvania would be soothed by making Philadelphia the interim site. Some interim site was needed since the Potomac location was unpeopled swamp. What Jefferson left out of his account was that Virginia was angling for a more favorable settlement of its wartime accounts, as well as a Potomac site, and Hamilton obliged them. Hamilton's adroitness in juggling capitals and ledgers shows his politicking at its best.

So Hamilton betrayed his city for his vision. When the deal was broached in Congress, Hamilton's friend Rufus King, loyal to his adopted state, burst into tears. The story of grandiose plans for the District of Columbia—President Washington envisioned a national university there, and Jefferson proposed bringing the faculty of the University of Geneva over en masse—coupled with pitiful fulfillment, has lasted for two centuries. Hamilton was willing that the capital be a wilderness monstrosity, so long as the country flourished. The price he had paid, he admitted, was "bad . . . but it will preserve the funding system."[22]

The national government returned to Philadelphia in the fall of 1790. Abigail Adams, who was hard to please, thought that "etiquette was not to be found" in its richest homes. This was a minority opinion. New York was the country's coming city, but Philadelphia, which with its suburbs had a population of over 35,000, was still its most impressive—"a London in wealth," as Representative Ames wrote, "and more than a London already in arrogance." Its sober Quaker elite had been replaced with a showier lapsed Quaker and Episcopalian upper class. One guest at President Washington's table noted "an elegant variety of roast beef, veal, turkey, ducks, fowl, ham, puddings, jellies, oranges, apples, nuts, almonds, figs, raisins and a variety of wines and punch."[23] The streets (thanks to Benjamin Franklin) were cleaned and swept; in New York, garbage had been removed by rainwater and wild pigs. The only serious inconvenience of Philadelphia life was yellow fever, a disease that no one then understood, and which emptied town in summers when it struck. For all of the new capital's size and sophistication, the government remained a simple affair. One visitor to the Treasury Department reported that the files sat on planks, supported by trestles, and that the secretary worked at a plain pine desk, covered with green cloth. The furnishings in the room did not seem to be worth more than $10.

The first important project Hamilton worked on in Philadelphia was his next great report to Congress, calling for a national bank, the

Bank of the United States. The report, delivered in December of 1790, called for a bank with a capital of $10 million (the capital of the existing banks in the country added up to only $2 million). Hamilton recited for Congress the advantages of a national bank: by making loans, it in effect multiplied its hard currency reserves ("credit keeps circulating, performing in every stage the office of money"); in emergencies, it could serve as a source of loans to the government. He rebutted common fears, e.g., that interest paid to foreign depositors would suck money out of the country (that interest "arises from the employment of the[ir] capital by our own citizens"), or that banks only benefit financial wheeler-dealers ("they more frequently enable honest and industrious men, of small, or, perhaps, of no capital, to undertake and prosecute business"). All this was true of the Bank of England; but Hamilton also proposed innovations on that model. His bank would be run by private individuals. Public control would "corrode the vitals" of a bank's credit. "The keen, steady and . . . magnetic" self-interest of private proprietors was "the only security that can always be relied upon for a careful and prudent administration." The bank, and not the government, would have the power to issue paper money. "[T]he wisdom of the government will be shown in never trusting itself with the use of so seducing and dangerous an expedient."[24] The national government would supply one-fifth of the capital, in payments funded by customs duties and excise taxes; the rest would be raised by private subscriptions. The bank's charter would run for twenty years.

Even more important than the report on the bank was Hamilton's defense of it against an attack from an unexpected quarter. Compared with the months-long wrangle over assumption, the bill to charter a bank went through Congress fairly quickly. But in the House, James Madison raised a damaging question: was a national bank constitutional? Chartering a bank, or any other corporation, was not a power of government enumerated in the Constitution. Then it must fall under the clause of the Constitution that allows Congress "to make all laws which shall be necessary and proper" to carry out enumerated powers—a clause Madison had defended in *The Federalist* ("wherever the end is required, the means are authorized"). Madison, reversing himself once more, now argued that too wide a definition of necessity could encompass "every object of legislation."[25] Behind the scenes, he argued to Marylanders and Virginians (including George Washington) that a national bank located in Philadelphia with a twenty-year charter would anchor the capital there, and prevent it from moving to the Potomac as promised. Robert Morris was indeed scheming for just such a result. The attorney general, former Virginia governor Edmund Randolph, and the secretary of state sent opinions to Washington supporting Madison's constitutional objections.

Washington asked Hamilton for a rebuttal. Like a lawyer preparing for his day in court, Hamilton paced in a friend's garden for an afternoon, rehearsing his arguments aloud. Then, over the night of February 22–23, he wrote his opinion on the constitutionality of the bank.

Hamilton began by considering the nature of government itself. It was "*inherent* in the very *definition* of government . . . that every power vested in a government is in its nature *sovereign*, and includes, by the *force* of [that] *term*, a right to employ all the *means* requisite. . . ." It was characteristic of Hamilton's legal reasoning that, though he could shuffle precedents and chop logic with the best of them, his attention gravitated to essences, located in the nature of things. In this case the essential proposition was that ends encapsulate means, though Hamilton admitted that certain means were forbidden: those that were "precluded by restrictions and exceptions specified in the Constitution," those that were "immoral," and those that were "contrary to the *essential ends* of political society." The first category of forbidden means stood Madison's argument on its head: instead of enumerated powers, Hamilton focused on enumerated prohibitions. But by citing morality and political society, he looked once more behind the tapestry of law to nature.

He then became specific. "The only question" is "whether the means to be employed, or, in this instance, the corporation to be erected, has a natural relation to any of the acknowledged objects or lawful ends of the government." Congress, he went on, could not form a corporation to supervise the Philadelphia police, "because they are not authorized to regulate the police of that city." But a corporation related to tax collection or trade could be erected "because it is the province of the Federal Government to regulate those objects," and because regulating a thing means "employ[ing] all the means" that are "to the best and greatest advantage."

He next proceeded to demonstrate that a bank was the most advantageous means of fulfilling the government's powers. Among his many examples were war loans. "A nation is threatened with war [and] large sums are wanted on a sudden to make the requisite preparations. Taxes are laid for the purpose, but it requires time to obtain the benefit of them. . . . If there be a bank the supply can at once be had. If there be none, loans from individuals must be sought [but] the progress of these is often too slow."

He sharpened the point. "The essentiality" of a bank "is exemplified at this very moment. An Indian expedition is to be prosecuted"— to the Miami River in the old Northwest Territory, in what would become the state of Indiana. An army sent to the Northwest the previous year had been repelled by the Indians, with heavy losses, and Congress and the president had decided to send another. "The only fund out of which the money can arise . . . is a tax, which only begins to be collected in July next. The preparations, however, are instantly to be made. The money must, therefore, be borrowed—and of whom could it be borrowed if there were no public banks? It happens," he added, "that there are institutions of this kind, but if there were none, it would be indispensable to create one."[26] For future loans, perhaps during greater wars, and for many other purposes of government, it was indispensable to create a national bank.

There was a sweep and relentlessness to Hamilton's legal reasoning that overwhelmed opposition. Chief Justice John Marshall would echo Hamilton's letter to Washington when the constitutionality of the second Bank of the United States came before the Supreme Court in *McCullough v. Maryland* twenty-eight years later. Washington, satisfied with his former aide's defense, and assured that the capital would move to the Potomac—the president had already been laying out lots on a site a few miles from Mount Vernon—signed the bank bill into law.

Washington took a tour of the southern states, where he found the ladies "handsome" and the roads "indifferent," and the rest of the government fled the Philadelphia summer. All but Hamilton, who stayed in town to work on his third great report, which he presented to Congress at the end of the year. Formally, he was responding to a request made by the House in January 1790 that he prepare a plan to make the United States "independent of other nations . . . for military supplies."[27] What he gave them, in his "Report on Manufactures," delivered in December 1791, was another window on his vision for America.

Hamilton's research into the subject went back to his days as a colonel, jotting down facts from Malachy Postlethwayt in his old pay book. More recently, he drew on his correspondence with customs collectors, and with businessmen as far afield as Liverpool, Glasgow, and Canton. He also relied on the arguments of the man who had replaced William Duer as assistant treasury secretary, the Philadelphia merchant Tench Coxe. Coxe had been a Tory during the early years of the war: after Hamilton had warned Congress to flee Philadelphia in 1777, Coxe had reentered his hometown with the British army. But he had converted to patriotism, and even smuggled a model of Arkwright's spinning jenny out of Britain after the war. Cotton was the keystone of British manufacturing, and securing a model of British machinery was an important act of industrial espionage. In 1787, Coxe wrote *An Enquiry into the Principles on Which a Commercial System for the United States of America Should Be Founded,* in which he argued that manufactures might be "the means of our POLITICAL SALVATION."[28]

At his inauguration, George Washington had worn a suit of Connecticut broadcloth in symbolic support for American manufacturing, but there was as yet little to support. The great majority of Americans were farmers. In the cities, where there was a class of people engaged in business, merchants and their employees outnumbered manufacturers and artisans. Hamilton and Coxe were arguing a minority case.

The "Report on Manufactures" was in two parts—visionary and programmatic. The more important visionary part was offered as an answer to the question whether manufacturing added to "the produce and revenue" of society or whether it merely diverted useful effort from agriculture. Hamilton listed seven proofs for the productivity of manufacturing. The division of labor—among artisans, and between artisans and farmers—led to greater concentration and skill. Machines were "an artificial force brought in aid of the natural force of man" ("unencumbered," he noted, "by the expense of maintaining the laborer"). Manufacturing encouraged the immigration of skilled workmen and businessmen—an important point in a still-barren country.

Two of Hamilton's proofs strike a modern ear as unsayably blunt. Manufacturing increased "the surplus produce of the soil. . . . The bowels as well as the surface of the earth are ransacked for articles which were before neglected. Animals, plants, and minerals acquire a utility" previously "unexplored." Manufacturing also pried the idle out of the home. "Women and children are rendered more useful, and the latter more early useful, by manufacturing establishments, than they would otherwise be. Of the number of persons employed" in British cotton mills, he went on enthusiastically, "it is computed that four sevenths, nearly, are women and children, of whom the greatest proportion are children, and many of them of a tender age." Later, he called the labor of women and children "a very pregnant and instructive fact."[29]

Opinions on both nature and the factory system were about to change, or were already changing, in ways that would make these sentiments seem wicked, or bizarre. Only seven years after Hamilton wrote, William Wordsworth would find in nature

The anchor of my purest thoughts, the nurse,
The guide, the guardian of my heart, and soul
Of all my moral being.

But Hamilton thought "ransack[ing]" it for items of "utility" was a good thing. Similarly, the charge that nineteenth-century socialists and reactionaries alike would hurl against the factory system like a battering ram—that it employed women and children—awakened no premonitory echo in him. So impervious was he to it that he used *pregnant* in a discussion of woman and child labor with no sense of rhetorical dissonance. Hamilton was writing from his own experience: he grew up in one of the garden spots of the earth, but its beauty had meant nothing for most of the people who lived there, because of the poverty and degradation of their condition. Hamilton, though not degraded to slavery, was poor enough to have gone to work at nine: why shouldn't American children, and their mothers, do the same?

The two remaining proofs also reflect Hamilton's experience, and his character. A diverse economy, he argued, develops society. "The spirit of enterprise . . . must be less in a nation of mere cultivators, than in a nation of cultivators and merchants; less in a nation of cultivators and merchants, than in a nation of cultivators, artificers, and merchants. . . . Every new scene which is opened to the busy nature of man to rouse and exert itself, is the addition of a new energy to the general stock of effort." Equally important, a diverse economy develops individuals. "Minds of the strongest and most active powers . . . fall below mediocrity, and labor without effect, if confined to uncongenial pursuits. [But] when all the different kinds of industry obtain in a community, each individual can find his proper element, and can call into activity the whole vigor of his nature." *Busy, rouse, exert, energy, effort, enterprise, strongest, active, activity, vigor*—these are all Hamiltonian touchstones, field markings as distinctive as DNA or the folds of the ear. But they became so for him only because of luck and work: if Nicholas Cruger and the Reverend Hugh Knox had been different men, if Hamilton himself had been marginally less remarkable, he, with all his intelligence and talents, might have been buried in St. Croix. Hamilton wanted to improve the odds for future Hamiltons.

The balance of the report sketched how this might be done. He expected the necessary capital to come from domestic banks and foreign investors. Government would help by encouraging domestic manufacturers with bounties, or subsidies. Bounties were, "generally speaking, essential to the overcoming of the obstacles which arise from the competitions of superior skill and maturity" of foreign producers—especially when foreign governments awarded bounties of their own.[30] (Hamilton proposed to use protective tariffs more sparingly—so sparingly that some modern protectionists disown him as a false forerunner.) He acknowledged that such regulations raised prices in the short run, but argued that competition among domestic manufacturers would lower them permanently over time.

A private venture in large-scale manufacturing, planned by Hamilton and Coxe, was already under way before Hamilton delivered his report: the Society for Establishing Useful Manufactures. The society planned to develop seven hundred acres beside the falls of the Passaic River in northeastern New Jersey. Hamilton and Washington had picnicked at the spot in July 1778, after the battle of Monmouth Courthouse: there the river drops seventy feet from the ridges of the interior to the coastal plain, fifty feet in one steep swoop. Using the power of the falls, the society proposed to produce a range of items, from straw hats to iron wire. The charter granted by the State of New Jersey (drawn up by Hamilton) gave the society a ten-year exemption from property taxes, and perpetual freedom from taxes on its capital investments. In gratitude, the society named its site Paterson, after New Jersey's governor (the same William Paterson who had proposed the New Jersey plan at the Constitutional Convention). William Duer was chosen to preside over the board of directors, a collection of New York and Philadelphia money men. Pierre L'Enfant, who had remodeled Federal Hall, and who was already at work on plans for the new federal city along the Potomac, was hired to lay out Paterson. As a soldier, Hamilton had seen the nation's capital flit from Philadelphia to Princeton, and as treasury secretary, he had bargained it away from New York, to Philadelphia, to the swamps of Maryland. One can imagine that he was more invested in the location of its future economic center.

The report and the society together were the most ambitious of Hamilton's projects. There were some problems with them, especially on the practical side. Hamilton asked, without answering, the question of when bounties should end. Continuing them "on manufactures long established must almost always be . . . questionable," he admitted. On the other hand, "in new undertakings, they are as justifiable as they are oftentimes necessary."[31] The implied resolution, as it often was with him, was, Leave it to me. Some modern historians have questioned whether American capitalists were ready, in the 1790s, to sustain a project like Paterson (the industrial cities of New England were still a generation away). The question would not get a fair trial, because of more immediate problems that the society encountered.

Hamilton's passionate analysis of economic diversity refutes charge that he was a tool of the rich—as well as the nobler estimate, that he was a pragmatist, using the economy to cement the union. "[Y]ou wanted to organize the country," wrote William Carlos Williams, author of *Paterson*, the modernist epic poem about the city Hamilton created, "so that we should all / stick together and make a little money."[32]

Hamilton certainly was pragmatic. "Ideas of contrariety of interests" between the North and the South, he wrote hopefully in his report, are "as unfounded as they are mischievous. The diversity of circumstances" between the regions in fact leads to a "contrary conclusion," because "mutual wants constitute one of the strongest links of political connection."[33] If the South wanted to be a region of farms, let the North supply her hats and wire.

But he was also, and primarily, an idealist. Having risen from island poverty, he never forgot that economies are about the people who work in them. Like revolutions, they must compensate for whatever evils they produced by "bring[ing] to light talents and virtues which might otherwise have languished in obscurity." The "Report on Manufactures" was Hamilton's program for universalizing the trajectory he had outlined in his eulogy of Nathanael Greene in St. Paul's Chapel two and a half years earlier. •

. . .

Hamilton was busy with one other activity in the second half of 1791, which also reflected his experience and his character. He began an affair with a married woman.

Sometime in July, when Betsey had left the hot, unhealthy city to stay with her family in upstate New York, a Mrs. Maria Reynolds called at the Hamilton residence. She was twenty-three years old—eleven years younger than Hamilton—and came from a respectable New York family (her brother-in-law was a minor Livingston). Two extended descriptions of Mrs. Reynolds survive, both written years later—one by Hamilton himself; one by Richard Folwell, a Philadelphia publisher who was briefly her landlord. Hamilton mentions her "simplicity and earnestness," Folwell her "innocent countenance." She told Hamilton that her husband, "who had for a long time treated her very cruelly," had recently abandoned her in Philadelphia without means; therefore she applied to his "humanity" for help in getting back to New York. Hamilton thought the story was "odd," but he also thought she was a "pretty woman in distress."[34] He told her he had no money on hand, but he would call at her lodgings that night and give her a bank bill. When he came, he gave her more than the bank bill.

Over the following months, as he worked on the "Report on Manufactures," he had assignations with Mrs. Reynolds, who seemed to have forgotten about returning home. He wrote clumsily deceitful letters to Betsey, telling her how much he missed her, but that she should stay where she was. "I am so anxious for . . . your health that I am willing to make a great sacrifice. . . ." Meanwhile, James Reynolds, the cruel husband, appeared on the scene. During the war, he had worked in the Commissary Department, supplying the army. In 1790, when the question of discrimination was being agitated, he hired himself out to a New York merchant to scour the backwoods of Virginia and North Carolina, buying up veterans' back-pay certificates. Now he reconciled with his wife, and told Hamilton that he could point out speculators in the Treasury Department. He also told him he might like a job as a clerk. Hamilton listened to his information and turned down his job application. "The intercourse with Mrs. Reynolds, in the mean time, continued." Hamilton suspected "some concert" between the Reynoldses, "yet her conduct made it extremely difficult to disentangle myself."[35]

Mrs. Reynolds was a temperamental, as well as compelling, woman. "The variety of shapes," Hamilton wrote in bafflement, that she "could assume was endless." Folwell, who was a better judge of her, described her as "far from being tranquil or consistent. . . . almost at the same Minute that she would declare her Respect for her Husband, cry, and feel distressed," these emotions "would vanish, and Levity would succeed, with bitter Execrations on her Husband." One reason for her bitterness, she told Folwell, was that her husband insisted she meet "certain high and influential Characters . . . and actually prostitute herself to gull Money from them."[36]

Ten days after presenting the "Report on Manufactures," Hamilton felt the trap close. He got a letter each from the husband and wife. The wife was sad: "Oh my God I feel more for you than myself and wish I had never been born to give you so mutch unhappiness. . . ." The husband was angry and threatening. "You have acted the part of the most Cruelist man in existence. . . . it shant be onely one family thats miserable."[37] After two interviews with Hamilton, Mr. Reynolds stated that he would forget Hamilton's cruelty for $1,000. Hamilton had to pay the money in two installments, and borrow from Robert Troup to make up the sum.

A month later, in January 1792, the Reynoldses wrote him again. James wrote that Maria wanted to see him: "I have not the Least Objections to your Calling, as a friend. . . ." "Do something to Ease My heart," wrote Maria, "Or Els I no not what I shall do for so I cannot live."[38] Hamilton resumed the affair.

A plain statement of the facts is that Mrs. Reynolds was a whore, her husband was a pimp, and both were blackmailers; Hamilton was a john and a gull. While true, this ignores the emotional currents. Maria Reynolds was probably fond of everyone she slept with, including her husband and Hamilton. She used sex and helplessness to manipulate men; she felt aggrieved by them, but her behavior brought grief upon her. James Reynolds was a small-time all-purpose operator, willing to deal in supplies, securities, and his wife. But he did not always like his work. Sometimes, wrote Hamilton, he would "relapse into discontent," abusing his wife and her lover, and threatening to reveal all to Betsey Hamilton. "The same man might be corrupt enough to compound for his wife's chastity, and yet have sensibility enough to be restless in the situation. . . ."[39]

What of Hamilton himself? In the only flash of self-knowledge in his long backward look at the affair, he admitted that "perhaps . . . vanity" drew him on.[40] But it was vanity of a particular kind. Sheer pride in his power and prestige could have lured him into beginning the affair. But elementary self-interest should have made him cautious when Mr. Reynolds reappeared, and driven him away altogether after he was actually blackmailed. But Hamilton was being driven, not by the pride of a man, but by the pride of a boy. The "pretty woman in distress," who had already reappeared as Mrs. Arnold at West Point, was originally Rachel Faucett in the West Indies. He could be his father, saving her from John Lavien. He could be himself, consoling her after his ne'er-do-well father had vanished—only this time, his consolations could be effectual, because he was no longer a helpless boy, but secretary of the treasury, calling into activity the whole vigor of a nation.

This makes the Reynolds affair an interesting, as well as a sordid, episode. The nation would learn of it soon enough.

Chapter Five

Fighting

HAMILTON'S REPORTS were not discrete projects. They formed a coherent design. Settling America's debts would fortify its credit; credit would allow manufactures to develop; a diverse and flourishing economy would generate the revenue that would ensure the debt's proper funding. "All his measures. . . ," wrote one observer to James Madison in 1792, are "like the links of a chain . . . acquir[ing] additional strength by their union & concert."[1]

Similarly, the criticisms of his enemies—and the "links of a chain" letter was written by an enemy—were not scattershot. Madison's switches, and Senator Maclay's asperities, reflected, or responded to, definite ideas about money, finance, and power. The conflict between these ideas and Hamilton's were the main domestic factor in the rise of political parties—Hamilton's allies calling themselves the Federalists, carrying the name over from the dispute on ratifying the Constitution; the opposition calling themselves the Republicans.

A coherent opposition was something Hamilton had not encountered since his collegiate quarrels with Samuel Seabury. George Clinton in 1788 had not been a principled opponent of the Constitution; he would go on to serve ten of his twenty-one years as governor under the document he had fought. Hamilton's new opponents, like Hamilton himself, were men of ideas. Hamilton would spend the rest of the Washington administration, and the rest of his life, contending with them.

Representative Fisher Ames thought he understood Republicanism. In one of his letters to Boston friends that was not merely acidulous, he

described it as a southern affliction, which could be explained by ana-
lyzing the sociology of the South. "At the southward, a few gentlemen
govern; the law is their coat of mail; it keeps off . . . their creditors and
at the same time it governs the multitude. . . . A debt-compelling government," such as Hamilton had put in place, "is no [use] to men who
have lands and negroes, and debts and luxury, but neither trade nor
credit, nor cash, nor the habits of industry, or of submission to a rigid
execution of the law. . . . The pride of the strong is not soothed by yielding to a stronger." Ames acknowledged that "as men," southerners "are
mostly enlightened, clever fellows. I speak of the tendency of things,
upon their politics, not their morals."[2]

This was true enough of most southern gentlemen (with some exceptions: the merchants of Charleston, and scattered individuals—
among them, George Washington). But Hamilton's opponents were not
all southerners. Senator Maclay was too prickly to be an effective opponent, or supporter, of anything, and indeed lost his Senate seat in 1791.
But he was a Pennsylvanian, and he was not the only northerner who
came to dislike the new financial order.

In a rich and resonant coincidence, Adam Smith's *Wealth of Nations*
was published in the same year as the Declaration of Independence, as if
to signal that the United States was the twin of the free market. But
many Americans harbored a powerful distrust of markets and finance,
especially of any profit arising from money. In their view, financiers
turned the medium of exchange into a prop in a magician's trick. This
ancient insight—or denial of insight, depending on whether one shared
it—flourished in the world's newest nation. "Every dollar of a bank bill
that is issued beyond the quantity of gold and silver in the vaults repre-
sents nothing, and is therefore a cheat upon somebody," declared John
Adams. John Taylor of Caroline, a learned Virginia planter, agreed that
banking was theft, "whereby labour suffers the imposition of paying an
interest on the circulating medium." "I have ever been the enemy of
banks," wrote Thomas Jefferson in his old age, and of "the tribe of
bank-mongers, who were seeking to filch from the public their swin-
dling, and barren gains." "The Stock holder," wrote Maclay, meaning
holders of government bonds, "is an unproductive character. . . . It is

enough that we have seen one generation of them. Let us not perpetuate the breed."[3]

The only solid asset, such founders believed, apart from labor, was land. A contemporary school of French economists, the Physiocrats, had fitted this insight up in modern dress, but it too was an old one, especially popular among landowning aristocracies. In America, attachment to land was a more democratic sentiment, since the continent seemed infinite, and land was cheap, once it had been wrested away from Indians or foreign powers. Hamilton's opponents asked why the superstructure of banks and taxes and a funded debt could not simply be replaced by land sales. "The western lands are the natural fund for the redemption of our national debt," wrote Maclay. "I would be happy to see" all government stock made nonnegotiable, except by "commutation into lands. And let it die with the obstinate speculator who refuses such commutation."[4]

But Hamilton's enemies knew why he refused such an obvious expedient. He desired the superstructure for its own sake, as a lever of power, and a source of patronage, or influence. This they had learned from the squires' politics of England. All the apparatus of ministries and corruption and debts and taxes—the entire imperial carapace that the Revolution had thrown off—was being reimposed across the Atlantic. As early as December 1790, the Virginia legislature passed a remonstrance, attacking Hamilton's system for its "striking resemblance" to Britain's. "Is this then the precipice to which we would reduce the rising nation of North America?" asked Maclay.[5]

This is not to deny that Hamilton had acquired some opponents through the usual accidents of politics. The Livingstons of New York, whom he had offended by depriving their in-law of a Senate seat in 1789, retaliated in the spring of 1791. Senators served for six years, but in order to stagger elections, two-thirds of the Senators in the First Congress were given short terms. In New York the senator up for early reelection was Philip Schuyler. Governor Clinton, and his new Livingston allies, awarded the seat to the New York attorney general, Aaron Burr. Burr, a successful lawyer, had joined Hamilton and other Federalists in an unsuccessful effort to defeat Clinton in the previous gubernatorial election; in the next, he would let it be known that he was willing to run against Clinton himself. But in the meantime, he was willing to accept Clinton's backing to get into the Senate. Hamilton thereafter regarded him with a baleful eye. "As a public man," he wrote, Burr "is one of the worst sort—a friend to nothing but as it suits his interest and ambition."[6]

Principle and accident had combined to give Hamilton his most formidable opponent—his colleague, the secretary of state. Hamilton's relations with Jefferson had been, for over a year, civil. While the capital was in New York, President Washington had taken the two men sailing off Sandy Hook to catch bluefish. At a time when Madison was combating Hamilton's measures in the House, Jefferson had brokered the deal between them that secured the funding of the debt. In January of 1791, Hamilton was elected to the American Philosophical Society in Philadelphia—a group of gentlemen savants of which Jefferson was the guiding spirit. A month later, the philosophers were disagreeing over the constitutionality of the national bank—an issue as divisive as funding, but not necessarily more sundering.

The rupture, in Jefferson's mind at least, came in April. The president, preparing to go on his tour of the South, asked his cabinet to meet together in his absence. One evening, Jefferson had Hamilton, Knox, and Adams over for dinner. Talk turned to the British constitution. According to Jefferson's recollection, "Mr. Adams observed, 'purge that constitution of its corruption . . . and it would be the most perfect constitution ever devised by the wit of man.' Hamilton paused and said, 'purge it of its corruption . . . and it would become an *impracticable* government: as it stands at present, with all its supposed defects, it is the most perfect government which ever existed.'"[7]

This after-dinner chat was the kind of comparative politics that any intelligent American might indulge in (and politics was the subject on which Americans most effectively exercised their intelligence). But to Jefferson, or any American similarly disposed, the man who had just secured a Bank of the United States was now praising the very ends to which unscrupulous ministers put the Bank of England. A national bank required taxes to make payments on the government bonds it held, and in return it provided the government with a source of loans. Taxation and loans allowed the government to multiply its offices. Giving offices to legislators, or their friends and relatives, was corruption. After finishing his building, the architect had revealed its purpose.

Hamilton's foreign birth, one of the sources of his nationalism, was also a factor in his indiscretion. A man raised among Americans might have anticipated the alarms that praise of "corruption" would set off. Or perhaps his temperament made him incapable of anticipation. Why say something in a veiled manner, or leave it unsaid, if it was interesting and right?

Jefferson said nothing that night. But he took two actions soon thereafter. The first was directed against his old friend, John Adams, the lesser offender, who had praised Britain, though not corruption. Thomas Paine's *Rights of Man* had recently arrived in America in manuscript. At the end of April, Jefferson wrote a note to a relative of the printer, hailing the work as an antidote to "political heresies which have sprung up among us."[8] The evident reference was to John Adams's *Discourses on Davila*, a long work of political theory that had been running as a serial in a Philadelphia newspaper, but Jefferson may also have had after-dinner discourse on his mind; what Adams had written in the papers echoed what he had said at Jefferson's. When the *Rights of Man* was published, Jefferson's note was published with it. Adams complained; Jefferson tried—unpersuasively—to soothe him.

In May and June, Jefferson moved against the more important heretic. He and James Madison made a tour of New England and New York, to collect natural specimens. They admired Lake George, shot squirrels, and studied the Hessian fly, a grain pest, for the American Philosophical Society. Hamilton's old friend Robert Troup thought that nature was not the only purpose of their tour. When the Virginians stopped in New York City, Troup wrote Hamilton, "there was every appearance of a passionate courtship" between them, Livingston, and Senator Burr. "*Delenda est Carthago* is the maxim adopted with respect to you. . . ."[9] The phrase, a slogan of the Roman politician Cato the Elder, meant "Carthage must be destroyed"—which, in the Third

Punic War, Rome did. No reader of Plutarch would need to have the reference explained.

Did Hamilton believe it? In the summer of 1791, trying to patch up the feud between the vice president and the secretary of state, Hamilton told Jefferson that he himself believed "the present government" did not "answer the ends of society," though, unlike Adams, he did not publish his opinions. "However," he went on, "since we have undertaken the experiment, I am for giving it a fair course. . . . The success indeed so far, is greater than I had expected."[10] Such hopes, coming from him, were as bad as doubts. Jefferson made a note of Hamilton's latest indiscretion.

Jefferson could also consult Madison's notes on Hamilton's indiscretions in Philadelphia four years earlier. At the Constitutional Convention, he had quoted Necker praising the British government as "the best in the world," and Hume praising "that influence . . . which went under the name of corruption." Madison's notes also quoted him as saying he would willingly be a "martyr . . . for liberty," but men often read what they want, or what they fear.

If Hamilton had held his tongue at dinner, or later, his split with Jefferson might have been delayed, not avoided. Two men so ambitious, so intelligent, and so different could not have worked together indefinitely. But their opposition—or at least Jefferson's to him—had become open half a year before the "Report on Manufactures" was presented.

. . .

The year 1792 brought problems that Hamilton could not fail to acknowledge. In March, William Duer went bust, bringing down the Society for the Establishment of Useful Manufactures with him.

Duer, like Hamilton, had Caribbean connections, albeit grand ones: his father owned plantations in Antigua and Dominica. Duer had moved to New York in 1768, and tried to make money as a contractor for the Royal Navy. When the Revolution came, he joined the American army, then became a contractor for it. In the postwar years, he served as secretary of the Treasury Board, the committee that handled the budget and finances, where he left behind an unexplained debit in the accounts of almost a quarter of a million dollars. For nine months, he had assisted Hamilton at the Treasury Department. In every phase, he looked to make killings in land, in securities, in whatever was going. "You are sanguine, my friend," Hamilton admonished him, at the time Duer was stepping in as director of the Manufacturing Society. "You ought to be aware of it yourself, and to be on your guard against the propensity."[11]

Vain words. In the new year, Duer had two schemes afoot—to take over the Bank of New York, and to corner the market in one kind of government bond. But Duer was trying to make his move in a bull market and lacked the resources. In his frantic efforts to buy, he took out loans wherever he could, including loaning himself the surplus funds of the Manufacturing Society. The bubble was pricked by Oliver Wolcott, who on March 12 initiated a suit against Duer for his unsettled Treasury Board accounts. Duer wrote frantically to Hamilton that if he did not stop the suit "my ruin is complete." Hamilton let justice, and ruin, take their course. Duer fled his creditors—"shopkeepers, widows, orphans . . . even the noted Bawd Mrs. Macarty"—in a debtors' prison.[12] Hamilton had acted honestly and, by adroit maneuvers, prevented the panic from sweeping away the entire market. But Duer gave the nation a symbol of extravagance and corruption in high places. The Society for the Establishment of Useful Manufactures never recovered, and the "Report on Manufactures" was a dead letter.

As Duer was going down, Hamilton was attacked in the press. Since 1789, the principal political newspaper, first in New York, then in Philadelphia, where it moved along with the government, had been John Fenno's *Gazette of the United States,* a journal that would in a modern third-world country be called "semiofficial." It carried governmental reports, essays by administration figures (such as the *Discourses on Davila*), and Treasury Department ads. In October 1791, it had been joined by another political newspaper, the *National Gazette,* edited by Philip Freneau. Freneau had gone to Princeton with James Madison, and was as talented a poet as the country possessed ("The Indian Burying Ground" is still included in large anthologies, as a sop to literary nationalism: "By midnight moons, o'er moistening dews; / In habit for the chase arrayed, / The hunter still the deer pursues, / The hunter and the deer, a shade!"). In the summer of 1791, Jefferson hired Freneau as a translator at the State Department. His real purpose was to advance Madison's and Jefferson's views through the *National Gazette*, which began publishing in October. By March 1792, Freneau went hunting for Hamilton.

The debt, the *National Gazette* declared, was "hereditary monarchy in another shape"; Hamilton's taxes were "copied from British statute books." Were not "some amongst us . . . advocates for monarchy and aristocracy?" Would they not make the Constitution, by "stretching its powers," a "stalking horse [for] hereditary government?"[13] Freneau wrote many of his squibs himself; others were contributed, pseudonymously, by Madison, Attorney General Edmund Randolph, and Senator James Monroe of Virginia.

When an attack appeared in the press, Hamilton finally recognized it, and he responded in his characteristic mode, writing under a series of pseudonyms: "An American," "Anti-Defamer," "A Plain Honest Man," and many others. He asked why a government clerk like Freneau should be campaigning against the government, and he ridiculed Jefferson's judgment by arraigning a number of his pre-1789 views, such as his hesitations about supporting the Constitution. One of Hamilton's congressional allies, William Loughton Smith of South Carolina, went further, mocking Jefferson's military record, his idiosyncratic inventions, and his theorizing, in the *Notes on Virginia*, that blacks smell because they secrete more through their skin than their kidneys. Hamilton also wrote a long, private letter to Edward Carrington, a fellow veteran and a friendly Virginian, lamenting his break with Madison, and affirming his republicanism: "I [am] affectionately attached to the republican theory. This is the real language of my heart." Even now, however, he could not leave well enough alone: "[I]n candor, I ought also to add that . . . I consider its success as yet a problem."[14]

The journalistic din was bound to come to the attention of President Washington, who was a careful reader of newspapers all his life; in any case, he was also receiving personal appeals from his secretary of state to recognize the bad effects of the secretary of the treasury's system. In July, he sent Hamilton a letter, arranging Jefferson's critique in twenty-one questions, ostensibly from Washington's neighbor, George Mason. Hamilton sent back a 14,000-word reply, rebutting each point, and portraying his attackers as the true enemies of republican government. The only way to "throw affairs into confusion . . . is by flattering the prejudices of the people, and exciting their jealousies and apprehensions. . . ."[15]

Missing from his letters to Carrington, Washington, and the newspapers, was any recognition that his enemies had a worldview. Hamilton correctly identified their ignorance and their ambition. (Senator Aaron Burr was testing the waters for a possible run for the vice presidency, which filled Hamilton with alarm.) He could not see that they had their reasons. He knew he was not a monarchist; he had fought to throw monarchy off. But he could not understand how his proposals, and his manner, might excite fears, however unjustified.

Washington had fuller knowledge than anyone of Hamilton's patriotism in action, and he had sided with him on every major contested point of his presidency. But he also did not want members of his administration, and their friends, abusing each other in the press. In August, he wrote Hamilton and Jefferson asking them to cease their attacks. By chance, each wrote a characteristic reply on the same day, in the second week of September. Hamilton admitted writing his essays, offered to resign if Jefferson would, but also offered to stay, without further journalistic guerrilla warfare, if his assailants would abide by the same rules of conduct.

Jefferson answered with a long *cri de coeur*, which made no more effort to understand his rival than Hamilton had made to understand him, and which was a good deal less candid. He blamed Hamilton for tricking him on the funding question, and assailed the tendency of his measures. He disclaimed any role in urging Freneau to set up his newspaper. This was not a simple lie. Jefferson disliked controversy, especially being the subject of it, and could deny to himself his own role in it. He made no effort to deny his opinion of Hamilton, whom he called "a man whose history, from the moment *at which history can stoop to notice him*, is a tissue of machinations against the liberty of the country" (emphasis added).[16]

In a lifetime of memorable phrases, that phrase about stooping history stands out as one of Jefferson's iciest, and ugliest. John Adams's wild assault—"the bastard brat of a Scotch pedlar"—only attacked Hamilton's birth; Jefferson's maligned his career. History never stooped to Hamilton; he rose to meet it. Jefferson's only excuse is that he was expressing the pride of a patriot, as well as the pride of a snob. Where had Hamilton been, when Jefferson, and the other demigods, had pledged their lives, their fortunes, and their sacred honor in Philadelphia in 1776? He, of course, had been pledging his life as an artillery captain in New York. But he had not been at the epicenter. What right did he have now to instruct the founding fathers, to ignore their fears, and to redesign their institutions?

Hamilton and Jefferson stayed at their posts, and the salvos in the press continued.

In December 1792, Hamilton received an unexpected hit: three congressmen visited him, asking about James Reynolds. Hamilton had returned to his lover earlier in the year, even though he knew her to be a blackmailer, and the affair had continued through the spring, before he finally summoned the will to disentangle himself. Meanwhile, he had made Betsey pregnant with their fifth child, who was born in August. Some of Hamilton's wrath at Jefferson and his other enemies may well have been displaced anger at his own betrayal and folly. Then, in November, James Reynolds got into serious trouble: he and a partner, one Jacob Clingman, had been trying to collect the back pay of a dead war veteran, acting as executors of his estate. But, as Maria brightly put it, the soldier inconveniently "came to life,"[17] whereupon Reynolds and Clingman went to jail. The two crooks tried to save themselves in different ways: Reynolds repeated the tale he had once told Hamilton, that he knew of corruption in the Treasury Department. Clingman told a former employer that he and his partner had information implicating the secretary of the treasury himself, including letters from Hamilton to Reynolds. As it happened, Clingman's former employer was Frederick Muhlenberg, Speaker of the House.

On December 15, Muhlenburg, Senator Monroe, and Representative Abraham Venable of Virginia appeared at Hamilton's office. They had thought of taking their story to the president, they said, but they wanted to present it to him first. Hamilton asked them to come to his house that night, and asked Oliver Wolcott to be there as well.

When the three lawmakers arrived, Hamilton admitted that he knew Reynolds, admitted that he had given him money, but explained that the source of the connection was no corrupt scheme, but his affair with Reynolds's wife. He produced a cache of letters from his lover, and his procurer, to prove his words. "Before I had gotten through the communication," Hamilton wrote later, Muhlenberg and Venable "delicately urged me to discontinue it as unnecessary. I insisted upon going through the whole and did so." The congressmen apologized for the "trouble and embarrassment" they had caused, and took their leave.[18] Monroe retained the letters that Clingman had originally given them.

The visit had a postscript that Hamilton would not learn of until years later. Clingman called on Monroe after the new year to say that Maria Reynolds denied Hamilton's story: she had "appeared much shocked at it & wept immoderately."[19] The Reynoldses were not strangers to guilt or shame, after their fashion: just as James did not always like knowing what he did, so Maria did not like others to know what she did.

Hamilton had had a narrow escape, if it was an escape. He could hardly imagine that a secret known to three politicians would rest with them, though he might reasonably expect that they accepted his public probity, if not his private morality.

At the end of January 1793, Hamilton's public probity was challenged in the House of Representatives. Concerned by seeming irregularities in Hamilton's juggling of various foreign loans and debts, another Virginia congressman, William Branch Giles, offered a series of resolutions asking for information. Most historians have not taken Giles too seriously, thanks in part to one of Maclay's catty pen portraits, which made him out to be a heavy-drinking blowhard. But Giles was not acting alone: Jefferson helped him draw up his resolutions, and Madison gave him his solid support. Giles asked, in effect, for a full account of the Treasury Department's transactions for three and a half years. Since Congress was set to adjourn at the beginning of March, it was assumed that Giles's questions would hang, unanswered, over the length of the recess. Hamilton managed to produce an answer—60,000 words, plus appendices—in four weeks, showing that the "irregularities" arose from Giles's failure to understand the principles of accounting. Undeterred, Giles offered a new set of resolutions condemning Hamilton's conduct, which were defeated by overwhelming margins— not surprisingly, wrote Jefferson, since a third of the House consisted of "bank directors and stock jobbers."[20] Hamilton's enemies had only been beaten, not convinced, and Congress would continue to investigate him (without result) throughout his tenure.

. . .

The journalistic fighting of 1792, which brought Washington's first term to such a rancorous close, was known as the Newspaper War. Beginning in 1793, Washington's second term would be consumed by actual fighting, at home and abroad. We have edited this out of our memory of the founders, to whom we attribute dispositions as smooth and magisterial as the statuary that commemorates them. When they disagree, we imagine them doing it in intellectual forums, at the Philadelphia convention, or in *Federalist*-style essays in the newspapers. It is an old error. In his first memorable speech, the young Abraham Lincoln looked back to a time when "jealousy, envy, and avarice" were "smothered," while "the deep-rooted principles of *hate* and . . . *revenge*" were reserved for foreign enemies.[21] In fact, the last years of the eighteenth century in America were marked by warfare, insurrection, and riot, actual or threatened; Americans directed jealousy, envy, hatred, and revenge at each other. Politics became so bad that the contending parties imagined it was even worse—that their enemies were more despicable, and that they themselves might be driven to more desperate measures, than they commonly were.

The foreign cause of America's discontents was the French Revolution. Hamilton's hero, Necker, had summoned the Estates General (moribund for 175 years) to support his reforms, but events went faster than Necker, or anyone, had foreseen. The Bastille fell three months after Washington's inauguration; Lafayette sent the key to the president;

1. The street where Hamilton clerked in Christiansted, St. Croix.

2. General Washington at Monmouth, with Colonel Hamilton and General Lafayette following.

3. Elizabeth Hamilton, seven years after her marriage.

4. Philip Schuyler.

5. Fanciful images of Maria Reynolds and her lover.

6. Rivals as forty-somethings: an old Alexander Hamilton (left), and a young Thomas Jefferson (above).

7. The State and Treasury Department offices (left) in Philadelphia.

8. Alexander Hamilton by James Sharples—
the family's favorite portrait.

9. A young James Madison.

10. Celebrating the ratification of the Constitution.

11. The Grange, as
a country house.

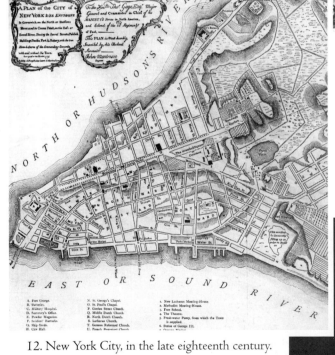

12. New York City, in the late eighteenth century.

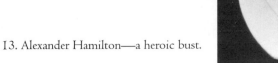

13. Alexander Hamilton—a heroic bust.

14. Aaron Burr.

15. John Church's pistols.

16. The site of Paterson, New Jersey.

17. Hamilton's grave at Trinity Church, Wall Street, New York City.

18. The Grange as it appears today, on Convent Avenue in Harlem, New York City.

19. Betsey Hamilton in her eighties.

20. Alexander Hamilton by John Trumbull.

the messenger who conveyed it was Thomas Paine, who had been in France on business ("A share in two revolutions," Paine wrote Washington excitedly, "is living to some purpose"). The three veterans of the American Revolution believed the French would be a replica of theirs. Washington hung the Bastille key in his official residence, next to a portrait of Louis XVI, with no sense of incongruity; it was imagined that the monarch who had helped the United States win its freedom would soon preside over a reformed and free nation of his own. Hamilton, almost alone in America, expressed some unease over France's prospects. As early as October 1789, he wrote Lafayette that he was following events "with a mixture of pleasure and apprehension." Why the latter? Hamilton listed four features of the French scene that worried him: "disagreements" among reformers, "the vehement character of your people," "the interested refractoriness of your nobles," and "the reveries of your philosophic politicians." It took the French a while to become aware of Hamilton's reservations; in October 1792, he was named, along with Washington and Madison, a friend of "humanity and society," and a French citizen. The letter of notification was addressed to "M. Jean Hamilton, dans les États-Unis de l'Amérique." "Curious example of French finesse," noted Hamilton when he filed it.[22]

But France was not a mirror of America, as America's heroes discovered—Lafayette had to flee the country, and Paine was jailed and slated for execution. As the French Revolution developed into a combination of a crusade and a traditional European great-power war, American opinion on it divided. Jefferson, Madison, and the Republicans looked to France to rebuke the power of Britain. Jefferson, at one point, hoped to have tea in London with conquering French generals. Hamilton and the Federalists viewed both French friendship and French bellicosity with alarm, and felt a common interest with Britain. "We *think in English*," Hamilton assured a British diplomat in a private talk.[23] This was a commercial, as much as a cultural, sentiment: since nine-tenths of federal revenue came from customs duties, and three-quarters of that was generated by commerce with Britain, Hamilton's financial calculations depended in a very direct way on continued Anglo-American trade. It was one of the chief links in the chain of his measures.

How should American inclinations be embodied in action? Republicans advocated a policy of ardent frugality. Their expressions of sympathy with France could be rapturous. Rather than see the Revolution fail, wrote Jefferson, "I would have seen half the earth desolated. Were there but an Adam and an Eve left in every country, and left free, it would be better than as it now is." (This, in a letter from the secretary of state to the American chargé d'affaires in Paris.) But since Republicans feared military establishments as much as financial ones, a government fashioned by them would have been in no position to give French Adams and Eves much assistance. By contrast, Hamilton had been for a strong army since his days in the army. "A nation, despicable by its weakness," he had written in *The Federalist*, No. 11, "forfeits even the privilege of being neutral."[24]

Foreign policy was also an issue in domestic politics, as Americans used French or British sympathies as tests for assigning virtue or blame to each other. "The successes of republicanism in France," wrote Jefferson, "have given the coup de grace to [Federalist] prospects, and I hope to their projects." "The spirit of jacobinism" in America, wrote Hamilton, may produce "calamities of which the dreadful incidents of the French revolution afford a very faint image."[25] Federalists and Republicans made each other out to be guillotiners, or fit victims of the guillotine. No working guillotines were ever built on American soil, but Republicans toasted the machine and displayed models of it at their festivities, while Federalists invoked it in their polemics.

The Eurotropism of American rhetoric exacerbated controversy over Hamilton's economic measures. If his system was copied from "British statute books," as the *National Gazette* claimed, then it was no longer simply a bogey of abstract political theory, but an imitation of a belligerent in a world war. Local resentment of specific fiscal policies could be cast, by both the locals and the federal government, in the language of revolution and treason. Foreign ideologies became placeholders for actual ideologies that Americans did not trouble themselves to understand in each other. It was much easier to talk about monarchy and Jacobinism than about what Hamilton and Jefferson were really thinking.

In March 1793, just after the Giles resolutions had been beaten,

America learned of the decapitation of Louis XVI. The king had been deposed the year before, but his death was still a shock. His portrait had hung in the Senate, as well as in Washington's residence; his birthday had been an American holiday. Thomas Paine, not yet in jail, quixotically argued to the last that the former king should be sent to America for republican reeducation. "Revolutions," Paine was told by an angry Frenchman, "are not made with rosewater."[26]

Early the following month, a new French ambassador arrived in America. Edmond Charles Genet, known as Citizen Genet to his brothers in revolution, is sometimes misidentified as a Jacobin; his faction was actually the Girondins, a group that was every bit as bloodthirsty as the Jacobins, and more bumptious in their foreign policy. Genet's mission was to attack France's enemies (chiefly Britain and Spain) from American soil, to ask for an early payment of the American debt, and to promote fraternal solidarity between the two peoples. In pursuit of the last goal, he landed not in Philadelphia but in Charleston, and made a twenty-eight-day progress to the capital, which was, as he put it, a string of "perpetual fêtes." Genet was encouraged in his hopes by these celebrations, and by the reactions of prominent Americans, including Jefferson, who was at first taken with him. The secretary of state gave one of Genet's agents, a French botanist, a letter of introduction to the governor of Kentucky; the "botanist's" real purpose—botany was a useful Jeffersonian cover story—was to plan a private invasion of frontiersmen into Spanish Louisiana. Hamilton, meanwhile, warned in the *Gazette of the United States* (from fresh personal experience) that the true patriot "will regard his country as a wife, to whom he is bound to be exclusively faithful"; foreign countries were "mistress[es] that may pervert his fidelity, and mar his happiness."[27]

The president held continuous meetings of his cabinet (Hamilton, Jefferson, Knox, and Attorney General Randolph) to discuss the French situation. The foreign policy of the Washington administration, unlike its economics, was Washington's own. He had been involved in diplomacy and warfare for forty years. At different times in his life, he had worked with Frenchmen and with Englishmen; he had also killed them. His guiding principle was to keep the United States out of their conflicts. He consulted with his colleagues to decide how this should be done, and to engineer consensus among them (one of his greatest feats of engineering had been to keep an increasingly unhappy Jefferson on the team).

America's special problem with France was that there existed a treaty of alliance going back to the Revolutionary War. No one in the cabinet, including Jefferson, wanted the United States to give France active military assistance. Hamilton argued baldly that the treaty had been made with Louis XVI and his heirs; since Louis had been executed and France was now a republic, the treaty was no longer in force. Washington did not want to be so blunt; he directed the attorney general to draw up a proclamation which, though it did not use the word "neutrality," was universally known as the Neutrality Proclamation.

As he had with the Constitution, Hamilton defended the document he had not entirely agreed with in a series of newspaper articles, signed "Pacificus"—a sharp and sober explication of national interest as the principle of national action. Gratitude, Pacificus wrote, was a proper emotion "between individuals." But "among nations . . . the predominant motive of good offices . . . is the interest or advantage of the nation which performs them." It had been thus with the French during the American Revolution. Why had they helped the United States? Because it was in their interest to hurt Britain. America now should be guided by the same motive, not by phantoms of affection. Foreign friendships are "hollow," foreign attachments make us "dupes. . . . Foreign influence is truly the Grecian horse to a republic. We cannot be too careful to exclude its influence."[28]

Jefferson read the articles with dismay. "For God's sake," he wrote Madison, "take up your pen, and . . . cut him to pieces."[29] But Hamilton did all the cutting, with help from none other than Genet: in a fresh series of articles, entitled "No Jacobin," he revealed that Genet had been sending increasingly strident messages to the government, including offensive references to George Washington. Popular reaction was swift: public meetings, from New England to Richmond, denounced Genet and supported the Neutrality Proclamation. Jefferson instructed Madison and other Republicans to abandon Genet to his fate. The United

States asked France to recall him (Hamilton wanted a public request, but Washington once again held back from a definitive confrontation). The Girondins having fallen from power in France, Genet decided that he would be safer settling in upstate New York, where he married a daughter of Governor Clinton.

The next public crisis was caused by taxes. One source of revenue that Hamilton had proposed to tap in his "Report on Credit" was "ardent spirits," which he had classed with other luxuries. But to the inhabitants of the frontier, which ran beyond the Appalachians, whiskey was a necessity. Their spokesmen claimed that distilling grain into whiskey was the most convenient way of transporting a crop to market, a claim repeated by historians ever since. But the main reason the frontiersmen, mostly recent immigrants from Ulster and the Scotch-English border, made whiskey was because they liked to drink it. They deeply disliked paying any taxes on it, an attitude reflected in the twentieth-century moonshiner's song "Copper Kettle."

> My daddy, he made whiskey,
> My grandaddy made it too.
> We ain't paid no whiskey tax
> Since 1792.

Hamilton acknowledged that the whiskey tax was being passed on to consumers. His solutions to the problem were that frontiersmen should drink less, and that the government should crack down on scofflaw distillers. "It depends on" the frontiersmen "themselves" to "diminish . . . consumption," he told Congress in 1792, while urging the president in the same year to "exert the full force of the law. . . . Moderation enough has been shown; it is time to assume a different tone."[30]

Both sides took a different tone in 1794. Ironically, the year began with an amelioration of the excise laws, proposed by Hamilton, whereby distillers accused of breaking them could answer the charges in state courts if federal courts were inconvenient. This meant that cases arising in western Pennsylvania, a center of discontent, could be tried in Pittsburgh, instead of across the state in Philadelphia. Pending cases, however, were still subject to the old procedures, and Hamilton meant to enforce the law, wherever the cases were tried. In July, western Pennsylvania erupted. The federal excise inspector fought a two-day gun battle, besieged in his house, with the local militia, in which at least two people were killed, the mail was robbed, and 7,000 angry men met in a field outside Pittsburgh, which they threatened to burn. Maybe they would do more. "Should an attempt be made to suppress these people," wrote Hugh Henry Brackenridge, a local politician, they might march on Philadelphia. "There can be no equality of contest between the rage of a forest, and the abundance, indolence, and opulence of a city."[31]

This was rant; Philadelphia was not about to be invaded by an army of backwoodsmen. Local politicians were caught in the bind that awaits inflammatory moderates, fulminating against the excise law, then trying to restrain their wilder fellows from violence. Brackenridge was one such. Another was Albert Gallatin, a Swiss (like Hamilton's idol, Jacques Necker), who had immigrated to the United States in 1780, and who had already been elected to Congress, where he had succeeded the hapless Giles as Hamilton's chief Republican gadfly. But the politicians among the Whiskey Rebels did not define the situation, nor did they control it. There had been unrest in Maryland, Virginia, North Carolina, Kentucky, and what would become Ohio. Unhappy westerners had sent out feelers to Britain, looking for relief from the former colonial power (the British embassy in Philadelphia reported treasonous approaches to Hamilton).

Early in August, Washington collected the opinions of his cabinet. Jefferson had retired at the end of 1793, disheartened by Hamilton's role in the administration, and intuiting, in his own unstated way, that he could best attend to his political fortunes as an outsider. His replacement as secretary of state, former Attorney General Edmund Randolph, suggested sending a commission to western Pennsylvania to try to arrange a compromise. Hamilton, backed by Henry Knox, wanted to send out the militias of the neighboring states. "The very existence of Government demands this course. . . . The force ought, if attainable, to be an imposing one," to "deter . . . opposition" and "save the effusion of

. . . blood." William Bradford, the new attorney general, suggested what Washington actually did: prepare to summon the state militias, while sending out commissioners to judge the temper of the countryside, and to demonstrate that the government was not acting rashly: "the public mind [must] be satisfied that all other means in the power of the Executive have failed" before the government turned to force.[32]

While the commissioners went to the scene, Hamilton took once more to the newspapers. His pen name this time was "Tully," another name for Cicero, one of the last and most eloquent defenders of the Roman Republic. Evoking Cicero was a predictable rhetorical maneuver; anyone in America, not just members of the Republican party, would want to depict himself, by historical analogy, as a champion of republican government. But Hamilton's pose was also sincere. He wrote, not just as the administrator defending his handiwork, or the tax collector defending his taxes, but as the college student who had shamed New York mobs, and the lawyer who had upheld the natural justice of the law. The "question . . . is plainly this—Shall the majority govern or be governed? shall the nation rule or be ruled? shall the general will prevail, or the will of a faction? shall there be government or no government. . . . The instruments by which [government] must act are either the AUTHORITY of the laws or FORCE. If the first be destroyed, the last must be substituted; and where this becomes the ordinary instrument of government, there is an end to liberty!"[33] The Whiskey Rebels assumed the forms of civil society: the mob that attacked the excise inspector's house was constituted as the local militia. But it acted as a mob nonetheless. The rebels had other recourse open to them—Gallatin, after all, was a congressman. Hamilton recommended a show of force to overawe the force of the lawless, and to restore republican authority.

The commissioners reported in early September that, although the moderates had won a close vote in one meeting, the hotheads still talked of erecting guillotines, and over 12,000 militiamen from Pennsylvania and three other states were ordered out. Hamilton asked Washington if he could accompany the army: "[T]he person who is understood to be the adviser or proposer of a measure, which involves danger to his fellow-citizens" should "partake in that danger." The president reviewed the troops east of the Alleghenies, then returned to Philadelphia. Hamilton went over the mountains—a decision presented, then and since, as thrusting and officious. But the nominal commander of the army, Governor Henry Lee of Virginia, was a reckless, if energetic, man, which Hamilton knew from the war (Lee had proposed at one point that deserters be beheaded), so perhaps it was just as well for western Pennsylvania that Hamilton accompanied him. "The duties of the army," Hamilton instructed Lee, on Washington's authority, "are confined to the attacking and subduing of armed opponents of the laws." None appeared. The most zealous rebels fled down the Ohio. Hamilton decided that there was nothing to link Brackenridge or the "Swiss-born incendiary" to any criminal action.[34] The army brought 150 prisoners back to Philadelphia, of whom only two were convicted of treason, the president pardoning them both. Still-born crises are the hardest to judge. After the initial violence, the Whiskey Rebellion petered out. But that was arguably because of the massive and deliberate effort the government had made to stifle it.

After Hamilton returned to Philadelphia, he notified Washington that he would be returning to New York City and private life at the beginning of 1795, after his thirty-eighth birthday. The state of public affairs allowed him to retire. American finances were in good order: by this time, the United States had the highest credit rating in Europe of any nation, some of its bonds selling at 10 percent over par (in other words, investors were paying premiums to hold them). His successes had paradoxically the same effect on him as they had on Jefferson two years earlier: Jefferson thought he could accomplish nothing by staying, Hamilton believed he had accomplished enough. If more were needed, Hamilton could send advice to Washington, or to his replacement as treasury secretary, Oliver Wolcott.

On a personal level, Hamilton's health was suffering from a combination of overwork, and summers in Philadelphia. He would have died during one yellow fever outbreak had he not been treated by his childhood friend Edward Stevens, who understood the causes of the disease no better than any other doctor, but who at least did not prescribe treatments that were positively harmful. While Hamilton had been off to western Pennsylvania, his wife had miscarried. His family's finances demanded that he return to private law practice. One man who saw him at work was Talleyrand, the French politician and diplomat, temporarily out of favor at home, who had been given an introduction to the Hamiltons by Angelica Church ("he is extremely agreeable," Angelica wrote Betsey, "and very much improves on acquaintance"). Passing Hamilton's office in New York one night, the Frenchman was astonished to see the American at his desk, writing by candlelight. "I have just come from viewing a man who had made the fortune of his country," Talleyrand wrote, "but now is working all night in order to support his family."[35]

New York had not forgotten him. In 1791, five merchants had commissioned John Trumbull to paint a full-length portrait. The merchants wanted something suitable for display in City Hall, the former Federal Hall; Hamilton wanted the painting to be "unconnected" with political life.[36] Trumbull compromised, introducing standard props of the grand manner: an arch, a column, a cloak draped over a chair. Hamilton stands in front of these items, in a simple and elegant suit, one hand resting on a desk. What draws the eye, apart from his bright face and ruffled shirt front, are the quiet highlights on his watch fob, his inkstand, and a row of upholstery tacks on the edge of the desktop. This man's most important work, the picture says, is done at his desk, not in neoclassical forums. In February 1795, the New York Chamber of Commerce gave him a valedictory banquet, with toasts to Commerce, Integrity and Knowledge, Liberty and Law, and nine cheers for Hamilton.

But the end of the Washington administration would not be a peaceful time for him, for New York, or for anyone. The cause of the final uproar would be foreign affairs. No sooner had Citizen Genet been cashiered and French diplomacy entered a more restrained phase, than Britain passed a series of maritime Orders in Council, resulting in the seizures of hundreds of American ships, on the grounds that they carried French contraband. British naval officers profited from the seizures, and hence had an incentive to make them. "Ah, those were pleasant days when I had the *Laconia*," says Captain Wentworth in *Persuasion.* "How fast I made money in her!" Hamilton might have assured the British minister that Americans thought *"in English,"* but Englishmen did not know that. Sometimes literally: a friend of Fisher Ames wrote from London that "a very sensible man" had asked him "what language we talked in America."[37] Preoccupied with Europe, Britain did not think of America in any consistent fashion. The French Revolution, which sucked America into European patterns of thought, caused distracted Europeans to give America short shrift.

The two countries had a variety of other grievances, some of them unresolved since the end of the Revolutionary War. Britain was trying to restrict American trade with the West Indies; British troops still occupied ten forts on American soil, two of them in upstate New York, and hence monopolized the fur trade; Britain had not compensated American slave-owners for slaves they had liberated during the war; and the British navy seized sailors from American ships in British ports and on the high seas, and impressed them into British crews. America, for its part, had not compensated Loyalists for confiscated property (Hamilton had warned, in his arguments on Trespass Act cases, that failure to do so would encourage the British to stay in their forts); many of the seamen impressed by the British navy were British nationals or even deserters; and British merchants had yet to collect 3 million pounds in prewar American debts, most of it owed by tobacco planters.

Northern Federalist senators, anxious to forestall a Republican embargo on trade with Britain, urged Washington to send Hamilton to London as a special envoy to address these issues. Washington told them that he lacked "the confidence of the country" and decided to send Chief Justice Jay instead.[38] The president had confidence enough in Hamilton, however, to ask him to draw up Jay's instructions. Jay set off in the spring of 1794, two months before the Whiskey Rebellion began.

The finished treaty arrived in the United States in March 1795. Not even the Federalists liked all of it. Jay had gotten American ships access to the West Indies only under onerous restrictions. Seized ships, Loyalist claims, and American debts would be adjudicated by commissions. Slaves and impressment had been omitted altogether. Britain agreed to vacate the frontier forts.

Washington submitted the treaty to the Senate, which passed it except for the article on West Indies trade, without publishing its contents. The air of mystery stoked Republican fears. They burst into flame when the *Aurora*, successor to the defunct *National Gazette*, published the text. A Republican senator had sold his copy to the French ambassador, who had given it to the newspaper, just in time for the Fourth of July.

Six years of aping British policies seemed, to Republicans, to have culminated in a servile treaty with Britain's monarch. Jay's name was the subject of punning toasts—"clipped wings, lame legs . . . and an empty crop to all Jays"[39]—and Jay's effigy was burned up and down the coast. Copies of his treaty were burned along with him, and rioters in Philadelphia broke windows in the houses of the British ambassador and a Federalist senator—and why not, since in the rioters' eyes the two were ideologically indistinguishable?

In this crisis, Washington turned to his former aide for advice, which Hamilton gave freely and judiciously. Hamilton wrote at the beginning of July that the "greatest interest" of the country was peace. "With peace, the force of circumstances will enable us to make our way sufficiently fast in trade," whatever particular treaties America signed. War, on the other hand, would "wound . . . our growth and prosperity. Can we escape it for ten or twelve years more," he prophesied, "we may then meet it without much inquietude."[40] In seventeen years, the United States would find itself at war once again with Britain, and thanks to its own incompetence would suffer numerous disasters. But the nation by then was strong enough not to be crushed by them.

At the end of July, Hamilton went to his desk to prepare a series of newspaper articles entitled "The Defence." His pen name this time was Camillus, a Roman general of the fourth century B.C. who saved the Republic from an invasion of the proto-French tribe, the Gauls. Hamilton may have felt a personal affinity for this identity, for, as Plutarch explained, before the Gauls attacked, Camillus had "taken to a private life," because the people had been "exasperated against him." In "The Defence," Hamilton went through the virtues of the treaty, and the objections to it, in exhaustive detail, covering everything from impressment and the fur trade to the morality of just contracts and the nature of international law. His two underlying themes were realism and honor. "It is not for young and weak nations to attempt to enforce novelties or pretensions of equivocal validity. . . . [We should] exert all our prudence and address to keep out of war as long as it shall be possible; to defer, to a state of manhood, a struggle to which infancy is ill adapted." "True honor is a rational thing. It is as distinguishable from Quixotism as true courage from the spirit of a bravo. . . . Honor cannot be wounded by consulting moderation."[41]

After seeing the first number of "The Defence," Washington complimented Hamilton on his "clear, distinct and satisfactory manner," adding that the enemies of "good government" (i.e., the Republicans) "are always working like bees to distil their poison," while its friends, relying "*too much* and *too long* upon the sense" of the people, "neglect the means" of appealing to it. He need not have worried. Altogether, Hamilton, with some help from Rufus King, wrote thirty-eight essays, which appeared over the course of half a year. The treaty's journalistic assailants, led by Robert R. Livingston, were overwhelmed. Hamilton's energy wrung a tribute from Jefferson, who was advising Madison from Monticello: "Hamilton is really a colossus to the anti-republican party. Without numbers, he is an host within himself." By the end of this performance, he had worn down even his friends. "Jove's eagle," complained Fisher Ames, hurls his bolts "not at the Titans, but at sparrows and mice."[42] In the end, Washington signed the treaty, and House Republicans, led by Madison and Gallatin, failed in an effort to sabotage it by withholding the necessary appropriations.

But the debate over Jay's Treaty was not conducted only at Hamilton's desk, or in arguments for the president or the people. On Saturday, July 18, New York Republicans called for a public meeting in front of City Hall to express New York's disapproval of the treaty. Five to seven thousand people showed up, stretching a block down Broad Street, and west up Wall Street toward Trinity Church. The church and the old City Hall building have been replaced by early nineteenth-century substitutes, and every other building is a twentieth-century temple of finance, casting dark slabs of shade, but the streets are the same—narrow, winding paths, except for Broad Street, a wide marketlike plaza. Hamilton, Senator King, and a group of treaty supporters gathered on the steps of an old Dutch house on Broad Street to make sure that the meeting would not be unanimous. The meeting instead was chaotic, impeded by boos, hisses, simultaneous speeches, and vain calls for order. Various Livingstons (one of them John Jay's brother-in-law) denounced the treaty. At one point, a party of Republicans marched away to the Battery to burn it. Hamilton moved that the meeting express "full confidence in the wisdom and virtue of the President," and no opinion on the treaty. *We'll hear no more of it, tear it up,* shouted the crowd, which began throwing stones at the Federalists. "We have the better part of the bruisers on our side," a member of the Livingston faction had boasted in 1769. An old empire had passed away, and a new one arisen, but the families were still the same, and so were the bruisers. One stone hit Hamilton in the head, drawing blood. He left, making a joke (different accounts have him speaking of "knock down" or "striking arguments").[43]

On Wall Street, Hamilton's party encountered one James Nicholson, and fell into a smaller but equally nasty scene. Nicholson had been the commander of the *Hamilton* in the parade celebrating the Constitution seven years earlier. Since then, his politics had changed (he had also become Albert Gallatin's father-in-law). Nicholson had been spreading a rumor that Hamilton had skimmed 100,000 pounds of government money while he was treasury secretary and stuck it in a British bank. Nicholson and one of Hamilton's companions fell to quarreling. Hamilton tried to calm them, whereupon Nicholson turned on him, calling him an "abettor of Tories" and accusing him of backing out of a duel.

"No man can affirm that with truth," Hamilton exclaimed. Later that afternoon, Hamilton's party found another quarrel, in front of one of the Livingstons' houses. Senator King tried to break it up, Hamilton volunteered "to fight the whole *'Detestable faction'* one by one." "Judge how much he must be mortified at his loss of influence," Edward Livingston wrote, to "descend to language that would have become a street bully."[44] True—but who do stones and slanders become?

Neither argument resulted in a duel, though Hamilton made up a will, naming Troup as executor. He left mostly debts. His largest creditor was John Church, Angelica's husband, whose American business affairs Hamilton handled. He wrote Troup regretting that Church's affairs "will not have been as profitable to him as they ought to have been & as they would have been if I could have paid more attention."[45]

Mass meetings called for symbolic purposes, pointless and turbulent; angry knots of friends and families, patrolling the tight streets, offering insults and violence to each other; all in the heat of New York in July—it was a page from Thucydides, Machiavelli, or some other historian of city-states. Everyone had lowered himself. Hamilton went beyond the moment, leaving the streets to write "The Defence." But the day could not have aroused comfortable associations in the man who had defended Myles Cooper and tried to defend James Rivington. In *The Federalist*, No. 9, Hamilton had written of the "tempestuous waves of sedition and party anarchy" that had marked the ancient world. "It is impossible to read the history of the petty republics of Greece and Italy without feeling sensations of horror and disgust at the distractions with which they were continually agitated." From such disorders, he went on, "the advocates of despotism have drawn arguments . . . against the very principles of civil liberty." But "happily for mankind, stupendous fabrics reared on the basis of liberty . . . have, in a few glorious instances, refuted their gloomy sophisms. And I trust America will be the broad and solid foundation of other edifices, not less magnificent."[46] The mid-1790s had tested this trust.

Chapter Six

Losing

THE LAST MAJOR SERVICE Hamilton performed for President Washington was drafting his Farewell Address. Washington had asked Madison to prepare a farewell as early as 1792, when he considered stepping down after one term, which Madison had done, though he, and all of Washington's feuding advisors, had asked him to stay on for another four years (they were afraid of being left alone with each other). In May 1796, the president sent Madison's old text to Hamilton, with additions of his own, and with permission to cut it if he thought it "too verbose." Hamilton instead expanded the text, making it Washington's longest public paper. The president preferred Hamilton's version "greatly," and it appeared in the *American Daily Advertiser,* a Philadelphia newspaper, on September 19.[1]

Structurally, the style of the Farewell Address was Hamilton's, in its length and its lawyerly elaboration of its points. Here and there are phrases that are pure Hamilton, such as "the point in your political fortress against which the batteries of internal and external enemies will be directed . . . "[2]—which is not only a military metaphor (Washington rarely used them), but an artillery metaphor. Yet sentence by sentence, Hamilton strove to shape his style to Washington's, making it graver and more apothegmatic. Most of the dozens of small changes that Washington made in Hamilton's draft made it more terse and solid still. For the opening paragraphs, Hamilton retained Madison's 1792 address. It was their last collaboration.

The theme of the address was the blessings of Union, and the dangers that threatened it. "The continuance of the UNION" was "a primary object of Patriotic desire. . . . The name of AMERICAN . . . must always exalt the just pride of Patriotism, more than any appellation derived from local discriminations." Twenty years after Hamilton's first polemics as an American, flickers of tension still played around his identity. Washington's first draft had used the phrase "We may all be considered as the Children of one common Country." Hamilton changed this to "Children for the most part of a common country," which Washington amended to "Citizens by birth or choice, of a common country."[3] Taking the metaphor literally, Hamilton excluded himself; Washington returned him to the fold.

The Union rested on the Constitution, public opinion, and self-interest: "[A]ll the parts combined cannot fail to find" the "united mass of [their] means and efforts" yielding "greater strength, greater resource," and "greater security." These blessings could be undermined by excessive attachment to regional feeling, domestic factions, or foreign allies. "There can be no greater error," the address declared, echoing Pacificus, "than to expect, or calculate upon real favours from Nation to Nation."[4] The Farewell Address covered Hamilton's, and Washington's, major goals and worries, from the Constitutional Convention to Jay's Treaty. The worries especially would preoccupy the nation for the next four years.

Hamilton never discussed his role in the Farewell Address, and the documents that established it were not published until 1859, though his close friends and family knew. Walking down Broadway with Betsey one day, Hamilton was offered a copy by a veteran who was hawking them. "That man," he said to her, "does not know he has asked me to purchase my own work."[5]

Some readers saw Hamilton's hand. "You will have noticed the lies it contains," wrote Pierre Adet, the new French minister, "the insolent tone that governs it, the immorality which characterizes it. . . . You will have recognized immediately the doctrine of the former Secretary of the Treasury, Hamilton. . . ."[6]

Washington's announcement set off a scramble to replace him—a subdued scramble to our eyes, since the candidates did not publicly campaign, nor even so much as announce their availability. Strenuous politicking nevertheless went on, much of it (since most presidential electors were chosen by state legislatures) behind the scenes. The result was that John Adams became president by a three-vote margin in the Electoral College. At his inaugural in March 1797, Adams thought his departing predecessor looked at him as if to say, "I'm fairly out, and you fairly in. See which of us will be happiest!"[7]

The transition from the first to the second president posed a new set of problems. One arose from the voting rules of the Electoral College prescribed by the Constitution. Before the Twelfth Amendment was adopted, electors did not cast one vote for a two-man ticket, but two votes for two men. The candidate with the most votes became president; the runner-up became vice president. In a close contest, it took a fine touch to ensure that a party's first and second choices finished in that order. The Federalists, though they were riding the popularity of Washington and the success of Jay's Treaty, failed in electoral finesse, with the result that the man most of them considered their second candidate, South Carolina grandee Thomas Pinckney, finished third behind the Republican favorite, Thomas Jefferson. (The Republican second choice, Senator Aaron Burr, came in a distant fourth.)

Adams also faced, for the first time, the question of how to handle a predecessor's cabinet. There was no tradition requiring it to depart with the outgoing president. What should be done with it? The problem was exacerbated by the fact that Washington's last cabinet was as mediocre as his first had been distinguished (the rancor of national politics was driving first-rate figures from public life). The best man in it was probably Hamilton's successor at Treasury, Oliver Wolcott—a man of no genius, but hardworking and able. The secretary of war was Hamilton's old army comrade James McHenry. While not positively incompetent, McHenry's real talents were for the arts of peace. "I have planted gardens," he wrote Hamilton in 1795, "I have planted trees, I have written little essays, I have made poetry once a year to please my wife, at times got children and at all times thought myself happy." Unable to find anyone else to take on the War Department, Washington had lured him from these enjoyments. The most vivid, and least satisfactory, of the holdovers was Secretary of State Timothy Pickering. Like Hamilton and McHenry, Pickering had served on Washington's staff during the war, though he had no respect for the commander-in-chief, and had dabbled in the Conway Cabal. Pickering could deal skillfully and humanely with people so long as they were remote from him: early in the decade, he negotiated a treaty with the Seneca Indians, and later in his life, he sympathized with Haiti, the hemisphere's second republic. But with his fellow Americans, particularly his colleagues, he was prickly and self-righteous. "While all sorts of people are greased with pomatum and whitened with powder," Pickering once wrote, "my bald head and lank locks remain in *status quo.*" This perfectly captures his special tone of virtue regarding itself in a mirror. His temper was "sour," wrote Abigail Adams, and his resentments "implacable." There was "something warm and angular in his temper," Hamilton agreed, which required "a vigilant moderating eye."[8] Washington had tapped Pickering to be secretary of state only after six other men had turned the job down. Adams decided to keep the three problematic secretaries at their posts.

Adams's cabinet posed a special problem for Hamilton—a problem disguised as an opportunity. All these men were closer to him than they were to their chief. Wolcott had worked under him; McHenry was an old friend; one of the few people Pickering admired was Hamilton, though he did not always listen to him. Hamilton had advised Washington on a variety of matters after he had returned to New York and his legal career. The holdover cabinet continued to turn to him for advice.

But the greatest domestic problem facing the new president was John Adams. It is impossible not to love John Adams. Our affection is engendered by his openness. In an age composed of distant, not easily penetrable figures—whether reserved, like Washington, or changeable and multifaceted, like Jefferson—Adams strikes us like a blast of fresh air. His journals, letters, and conversations present every mood and thought new-picked. Frequently, his first thoughts were harsh and unjust, but then he was likely to be harsh on himself for thinking so. He had another rare quality: humor. Some of the founders had a bright and somewhat arid form of wit, but Adams was one of the few who could be funny—most often when he was unhinged by hatred, but funny nonetheless. The similar qualities of his wife Abigail endear him to us even as they endear her. A man with such a mate and correspondent, we think, must have been worthy of her.

At times, Adams was more than an intriguing character. His eloquence and tenacity in the Second Continental Congress, culminating in his great speech of July 2, 1776, would be a high point in anyone's career. At that moment, one delegate wrote, he was "the Atlas of American independence"; his "power of thought and expression," wrote Jefferson, "moved us from our seats."[9] The sentiments that inspired him then guided him all his life. The most attractive portrait of him, painted about 1793 by John Trumbull, which shows a surprisingly mild face and a bald forehead bathed in light, is interpreted by one critic as an allegory of his intelligence. But the light is not self-generated; it falls on him from above, as on a saint, suggesting rather his devotion to his guiding principle, the cause of his country.

None of these traits prepared him to be a good president. Adams had no executive experience. He had been successively a lawyer, a congressman, a diplomat, and the first vice president to complain about the inconsequence of the job. As president, Adams made some excellent appointments, Chief Justice John Marshall among them. But the ability to harmonize a team, to project and oversee an operation, was simply not there. He was a hands-off administrator, spending inordinate amounts of time at his home in Braintree, doing business by mail. When he acted, he acted impulsively and without consultation. Years later, he complained that "I was as president a mere cipher," meaning that Hamilton pulled the strings in his cabinet.[10] Hamilton's role was not quite what Adams thought, and to the degree that he was a cipher, it was because he made himself one.

There were finally the shadows cast over his character by his virtues—his pride in the role he had played in Philadelphia, and his insecurity about his place in history. No forts had been named after him, he complained when he was president, "except perhaps a diminutive work at Rhode Island." Washington and Franklin, he fretted, would overshadow him. He could not deny their achievements. But younger men who challenged, or seemed to challenge him, provoked his ire. He "holds cheap any reputation," wrote Ames, "that was not . . . founded and top't off" in 1776.[11]

Hamilton had worked well enough with Adams during the Washington administration, and had defended him during the newspaper wars of 1792 for his "early intrepid, faithful, persevering, and comprehensively useful services to his country."[12] But Hamilton's efforts during the election of 1796 to keep Jefferson out of office by ensuring that Federalist electors in New England cast ballots for Pinckney as well as Adams were widely interpreted as an attempt to slip Pinckney in ahead of Adams. Among those who so interpreted them was Adams himself.

Hamilton's first crisis of the new administration, however, was an eruption from the past. In June and July, there appeared in Philadelphia a series of pamphlets entitled *The History of the United States for 1796*, by James T. Callender. Callender was a Scottish journalist who had left Britain after attacking George III. In America, he enlisted with the Republicans; his *History* unctuously ranked Jefferson's prose with that of Xenophon and Polybius. Jefferson, for his part, considered Callender "a man of science fled from persecution," and gave him small amounts of money.[13] Callender came to general notice when Nos. 5 and 6 of his *History* revealed the Reynolds affair.

Callender, who had clearly been briefed by an insider, did not dwell on the affair. That, he wrote, was a cover story. Hamilton's real partner in the Reynolds household was James, with whom he was engaged in corrupt speculation, as the three congressmen who had confronted him in 1792 had at first believed. And if Reynolds "was *one* agent . . . it may well be conceived, though it cannot yet be proved, that our secretary had twenty others."[14]

Hamilton learned of the pamphlet when he was sent a copy by Wolcott, who urged him to respond cautiously, though Hamilton was soon driven to anything but a cautious state of mind. Frederick Muhlenberg and Abraham Venable quickly wrote that they had had nothing to do with Callender, and would state that they accepted Hamilton's version of events. James Monroe also denied leaking the story; he had deposited his copies of the Reynolds correspondence with "a respectable character in Virginia" (almost certainly, Thomas Jefferson). But he would not now tell the public what he had told Hamilton privately five years earlier. Whether Callender's charges "are well or ill founded," he wrote, "depends upon the facts . . . & upon your defense."[15] Monroe may have been swayed by Jacob Clingman's report that Maria Reynolds denied Hamilton's denial; or perhaps the intervening years of political warfare had hardened him.

Hamilton turned to the medium that had so often served and assailed him, bringing out in August his own pamphlet, *Observations on Certain Documents . . . In Which the Charge of Speculation Against Alexander Hamilton, Late Secretary of the Treasury, is Fully Refuted. Written by Himself.* "The charge against me," he declared, after some preliminary drubbing of "jacobinism" and "calumny," "is a connection with one James Reynolds for purposes of improper pecuniary speculation. My real crime is an amorous connection with his wife."[16]

The performance was by turns convincing, embarrassing, and astonishing. He demolished the foundation of Callender's story by showing how implausible it was. "It is very extraordinary, if the head of the money department of a country" would play for such puny stakes, and with such a small-time partner. He toted up the sums Reynolds had asked for: $50 here, $300 there. "[I] must have been a clumsy knave . . . to risk [my] character in such bad hands and in so huckstering way." His account of the affair was appallingly thorough. Just as on the December night five years ago, when Muhlenberg and Venable had begged him to desist, he insisted upon going through the whole. His thoroughness may have been self-punishment, and indeed he had much to punish himself for: his wife gave birth to their sixth child as he was preparing his defense. "I can never cease to condemn myself for the pang," he wrote, which his confession "may [!] inflict in a bosom eminently intitled to all my gratitude. . . . But that bosom will approve that even at so great an expense, I should effectually wipe away a more serious stain from a name, which it cherishes. . . ." Hamilton's discomfort radiated from his synecdoches—the verbal mufflers that turned Betsey into a *bosom* and himself into a *name*. At the end, he recovered his poise. "I have paid pretty severely for the folly and can never recollect it without disgust and self-condemnation. It might seem affectation to say more."[17]

The Reynolds pamphlet produced a full gamut of reactions. "A curious specimen of the ingenious folly of its author," wrote Madison to Jefferson. "Humiliating in the extreme," agreed Henry Knox. Knox's correspondent took a longer view: "[I]f he fornicates with every female in the cities of New York and Philadelphia, he will rise again, for purity of character . . . is not necessary for public patronage." Betsey Hamilton stood by her husband; to her, his accusers were "scoundrels."[18] No doubt it was easier to blame others. Betsey had made her choice two decades ago, and she stuck with it.

Hamilton got one note which mentioned nothing, but said much. "Not for any intrinsic value the thing possesses, but as a token of my sincere regard and friendship for you, and as a remembrancer of me; I pray you to accept a Wine cooler for four bottles. . . . I pray you to present my best wishes, in which Mrs. Washington joins me, to Mrs. Hamilton & the family; and that you would be persuaded, that with every sentiment of the highest regard, I remain your sincere friend, and affectionate Hble. Servant. Go: Washington."[19]

Mere journalists did not merit a rebuttal as self-exposing as the Reynolds pamphlet, or indeed any rebuttal at all. But Hamilton believed Monroe's silence had forced his hand. The two men carried on an increasingly acrid correspondence, which might well have ended in a duel had not Monroe been soothed by former Senator Aaron Burr. Hamilton felt the need for some defense, from others or from himself, because his reputation as a public servant was at stake. He would not have agreed that purity of character was irrelevant to public service. The Farewell Address, which he had ghosted, praised religion and morality as the "firmest props" of "political prosperity." But character manifested itself in public as well as private life, and of the two the public record was more important. Hamilton considered corruption a "more heinous charge" against a public servant than adultery. Only the need to defend himself against it could have "extorted" from him "so painful an indecorum" as the Reynolds pamphlet.[20]

. . .

The political class had other things to think about besides Alexander Hamilton's adultery. America's problems with Britain—smoothed for a time by Jay's Treaty—had been immediately replaced by problems with France.

Internal French politics made France more bellicose. Though the Jacobins, who had replaced the Girondins in 1793, instituted a Reign of Terror at home, they followed a policy of not picking unnecessary quarrels abroad; hence their dismissal of Citizen Genet. Succeeding revolutionary regimes, culminating in a five-man committee called the Directory, allowed Frenchmen to breathe easier, but returned France to adventurism abroad, spearheaded by the exploits of a rising young general, Napoleon Bonaparte. France's new rulers interpreted America's treaty with Britain as a threat to them, and during the election of 1796, their ambassador, Pierre Adet, published a series of menacing essays, trying to swing the contest to Jefferson. (Hamilton, who had called foreign influence the "Grecian horse" of republics, feared that this would be another "melancholy example" of it.)[21] The French also announced that they would seize American ships carrying goods bound for Britain.

In the waning days of the Washington administration, Hamilton had suggested sending a three-man commission, including his enemy James Madison, to try to negotiate a Jay's Treaty with France. President Adams, shortly after his inauguration, asked Vice President Jefferson if he could persuade Madison to go, or perhaps even go himself. A unity commission including Madison or Jefferson would have bound the Republicans to the administration's diplomacy; precisely for that reason, Jefferson and Madison had no intention of taking part. But Adams and Hamilton were at that point both determined that all reasonable efforts to head off a war should be made, and that they should be made reasonably. "We ought to do every thing to avoid rupture," Hamilton told Wolcott in a letter; and in another, "Real *firmness* is good for every thing.

Strut is good for nothing." A three-man commission was dispatched by June 1797: Elbridge Gerry of Massachusetts; Thomas Pinckney's brother Charles; and a Federalist lawyer and veteran from Virginia, John Marshall. Pickering's instructions to the commissioners, which may have had Hamilton's input, were moderate in tone: they were to seek "mutual satisfaction . . . without referring to the merits of our respective complaints."[22]

The new minister of exterior relations who would deal with them was Hamilton's acquaintance, Talleyrand, restored to office thanks to the lobbying of a former mistress. Over a forty-five-year career, Talleyrand would serve a republic, an emperor, and three kings, though the only king to whom he was loyal was Brie, the king of cheeses. For him, ideology was secondary to maintaining France's position within a balance of power. One of the reasons Talleyrand was impressed with Hamilton (apart from being amazed that he worked for a living) was the fact that the American's perspective on foreign policy was similar to his own. "Standing, as it were, in the midst of falling empires," Hamilton wrote during this period, "it should be our aim to assume a station . . . which will preserve us from being overwhelmed in their ruins." This was a thought that Talleyrand could understand. Hamilton, he wrote, "divined" European affairs, even though he had never been there.[23]

There were certain things that Talleyrand had not divined about the United States, even though he had lived there, as his dealings with the American commissioners would show. Talleyrand's other great principle in public life, besides patriotism and the balance of power, was getting rich. This he did by taking percentages and selling access, a practice followed in many regimes, *ancien* and revolutionary.

When the commissioners arrived in Paris in early October, they had a fifteen-minute audience with the minister of exterior relations. But they did not then get down to work. Instead, a series of unofficial visitors, all describing themselves as friends of Talleyrand's, appeared to feel them out privately. France, which was considering invading England, wanted a "considerable loan." Talleyrand and the members of the Directory also required "something for the pocket"—quite a bit, it turned out: 50,000 pounds sterling. "No! No! Not a sixpence!" Pinckney cried in unfeigned surprise and indignation.[24] When the shakedown produced no results, the intermediaries added threats.

Disturbed by the long silence from Paris, Adams in January asked his secretaries for advice. Hamilton's, relayed via McHenry, was firm but prudent. He wanted to raise what was for the time a very large peacetime army of 20,000 men, expandable to 50,000, to defend against possible attack, or to seize Florida and Louisiana, territories of France's new ally Spain. He wanted warships built, or bought from Britain, to protect American shipping. He advised, however, against declaring war, or against a formal alliance with France's enemy, Britain. "'Twill be best not to be entangled."[25] Some Federalists, notably Pickering, wanted to be openly pro-British. But the Republicans dismissed all talk of standing up to France as warmongering.

Then the political world somersaulted. In March, President Adams finally received an account from Marshall of French diplomacy, identifying the extortionate intermediaries as X, Y and Z, and early in April he gave it to Congress. France stood revealed as a compound of revolutionary hubris and old-world vice. Pinckney's exclamation, transformed into "Millions for defense, not one cent for tribute," became a toast and a rallying cry. Republican die-hards tried to fix blame for French rascality on Talleyrand personally, but their strength in Congress, until then a majority, shrank away. "The wretches looked round," wrote Fisher Ames gleefully, "like Milton's devils when first recovering from the stunning force of their fall from Heaven. . . ." Popular opinion rallied around the President, who was kept so busy answering messages of support that Abigail Adams feared for his health. He also gave rein to his talents as a speechmaker. "The finger of destiny," he told one audience, "writes on the wall the word: war!"[26]

Hamilton's diplomatic and military advice hardly changed. In a letter to Pickering, written after the XYZ letters were received, he repeated the suggestions he had made to McHenry a month earlier, hoping that Adams would be "*temperate*, but *grave, solemn*, and *firm*." Talleyrand's greed was a small item on the world stage. Napoleon's armies had conquered Italy; two mutinies had struck the British fleet; the Bank of England had suspended payments in specie. "Wise men," wrote Hamilton, "look for prodigies, and prepare for them with foresight and energy." But not with theatrics. "The attitude of *calm defiance* suits us."[27]

But foreign policy was also a theme of domestic politics, and there Hamilton, like Adams and the rest of the Federalists, sought to take advantage of the situation. In March, he began a series of essays, entitled "The Stand," and signed "Titus Manlius," this time a hero from Livy, a Roman David who had killed a Gaulish Goliath in single combat and wrested a golden collar from his neck. As the scourge of Gauls, Hamilton reiterated his advice to McHenry and Pickering, and his call for "calm defiance." But he also assailed the French Revolution as an engine of atheism and immorality, and accused Republicans, whom he called the "foreign faction," of colluding with it.[28]

Congress went further. Ames gave the watchword: "Zeal is now better than logic." The Federalist majority passed an Alien Act that allowed the President to expel any noncitizen foreigner he found "dangerous to the peace and safety of the United States." The Federalist journalist William Cobbett, who wrote under the name Peter Porcupine (not drawn from Plutarch or Livy), and who was himself a foreigner, gave the rationale: thousands of "factious villains, which Great Britain and Ireland have vomitted from their shores" had settled in the United States. "Nothing short of a state of rebellion can content these wretches. All governments are to them alike hateful. Like Lucifer, they carry a hell about with them in their own minds; and thus they prowl from country to country." A Sedition Act made it a federal crime to publish "false, scandalous and malicious" writings against the Congress or the president.[29] States had their own laws against seditious libel, and the Sedition Act was more liberal than current common law, which did not accept truth as a defense. Nevertheless, a federal sedition law (nine years after Congress had written the First Amendment) was an innovation.

The Alien and Sedition Acts were justified, in the eyes of Federalists, by the memory of Citizen Genet and the Whiskey Rebellion. Within the last five years, France had meddled in American affairs, and the country had put down an armed uprising. Weren't strong measures required to prevent a conjunction of the two? Hamilton objected to earlier, even more stringent, versions of both acts. "Let us not be cruel or violent," he wrote Pickering of the draft of the alien law, while he told Wolcott the draft of the sedition law, which made treason (i.e., support for France) a peacetime crime, was "highly exceptionable. . . . if we push things to an extreme, we shall then give to faction *body* and solidity." But he supported both acts in their final forms. Although the Alien Act was never invoked, the Sedition Act struck a dozen victims, including James Callender, for calling John Adams "a hideous, hermaphroditical character," among other things.[30]

During all the upheavals of the last two and a half years, Hamilton had been pouring out his advice and his journalism while trying to earn a living. His law office migrated from Wall Street to Pine Street to Broadway. His letter to Wolcott on the sedition bill contains the hurried sentence: "I have not time to point out my objections by this post, but I will do it tomorrow."

Hamilton would soon be returning to public life. The sixty-six-year-old George Washington had been called out of retirement to command the expanded army, with a commission dated July 4, 1798. Since he did not propose to leave Mount Vernon unless the French attacked, organizing the army would depend on his seconds-in-command. The three major generals under him were to be Henry Knox, Charles Pinckney (once he returned from France), and Hamilton. But in what order? The cabinet wanted Hamilton first. Washington wondered whether Pinckney should not rank first, as a gesture to the South. Knox was convinced that he deserved the highest rank, by virtue of his seniority during the Revolution.

President Adams wanted Hamilton to be third, if not lower. In one letter, he suggested ranking him below Horatio Gates, who was pushing seventy; in another (unsent), he complained that Hamilton was a foreigner, who had scarcely been in the country longer than Albert Gallatin. One source of Adams's dislike was his aversion to standing armies, and Hamilton's evident fondness for them. He put his main reason for balking in a letter to McHenry: "There has been too much intrigue in this business." Years later, Adams called Hamilton "the most restless, impatient, artful, indefatigable and unprincipled in-

triguer in the United States, if not in the world." In his view, Hamilton
had intrigued to keep him out of the presidency, and now he was intriguing to become de facto commander-in-chief. Interestingly, he did
not mention the Reynolds affair as a disqualification, though he had
deplored it: Hamilton, he complained, was "as debauched . . . as old
Franklin."[31] The logjam was broken by Washington, who came down
for his sometime aide, and Adams confirmed the appointments, in the
order Hamilton, Pinckney, and Knox, in October—a victory Hamilton might better not have won.

Hamilton held his post for a year and nine months, and the army
never fired a shot in anger. But he was continually occupied, throwing
himself into matters great and small: fretting over the lack of engineers
and artillerists; considering a draft in case of invasion; regulating the
length of the infantry's step ("[I]n the theories of military writers, and
in the establishments of military nations, there is great diversity in this
important article. For example: while our step is two feet English, that
of France [and it is believed of Russia] is two feet French, or about
twenty six inches English; that of Great Britain, two feet six inches English. . . ."); proposing taxes to pay for it all (a stamp duty on hats; salt—
25 cents a bushel; male servants, $1 each; saddle horses, the same). He
worried about cavalry: "The service of the cavalry in this country has
never been but imperfectly understood." He worried about uniforms:
"Nothing is more necessary than to stimulate the vanity of soldiers. To
this end, a smart dress is essential." He offered opinions on New Yorkers who applied to be officers: "Unknown. . . . Unworthy. . . . Drunken.
. . . Democratic, but upon the whole eligible as Second Lieutenant."[32]

He also cast an eye on foreign policy. Spain, originally an enemy of
revolutionary France, had become, out of fear and weakness, an ally;
Hamilton had mentioned the desirability of attacking and acquiring
Spanish Louisiana and Florida in his first letters on the crisis in the
spring of 1798. A grander plan presented itself, in the person of Fran-
cisco de Miranda, a Venezuelan patriot and soldier of fortune Hamilton had met after the Revolutionary War. Miranda's hopes for his own
country's independence being discovered by the Spanish, he roamed
through Europe looking vainly for sponsors. The Girondins made him

a brigadier general; Catherine the Great made him a lover; the Jacobins put him in prison. He returned to the United States, where Hamilton was taken with him. An American army and a British fleet assisting Miranda, Hamilton thought, could liberate the continent. "The command in this case," he wrote Rufus King, then ambassador to London, "would very naturally fall upon me, and I hope I shall disappoint no favorable anticipation."[33] His goal was an independent South American government, granting equal commercial privileges to its two Anglo-Saxon sponsors.

Nothing ever came of the idea, and Miranda, after various false starts, was betrayed to the Spanish by his fellow patriots and died in prison. It is hard to judge a scheme that bore no fruit. It certainly had all the marks of fantasy and disaster: Hamilton, though fluent in French, knew no Spanish, and his only experience of Latin America was hoping that Nicholas Cruger's captains could avoid the Spanish coast guard. When something like Hamilton's plan was effectuated twenty-five years later by the Monroe Doctrine, the work of liberation had been accomplished by the Latin Americans themselves, and no North American armies had to be involved.

His interest in seizing Louisiana and Florida was more practical. Those territories had little pre-existing European culture, and whoever controlled the Mississippi and New Orleans controlled the economic life of the frontier. To advance this project, he chose a collaborator even odder than Miranda: James Wilkinson, Gates's deputy during the Conway Cabal. McHenry and Robert Troup warned Hamilton that Wilkinson was not to be trusted. His character, Hamilton admitted to Washington, "gives room for doubt."[34] But he recommended him for a promotion anyway. Hamilton may have thought a shady figure appropriate to a grey international situation. A decade later, America would learn that Wilkinson had been a Spanish agent since the 1780s.

The Federalists' projects soon ran into trouble. At the end of 1798, Kentucky and Virginia passed resolutions, secretly written by Jefferson and Madison, denouncing the Alien and Sedition Acts as unconstitutional and calling on the states to "interpose for arresting . . . the evil." Madison had imagined a similar situation in *The Federalist*, No. 46, when he wrote that "ambitious encroachments of the federal government" on the states "would be signals of general alarm." No general alarm sounded now. Four states made no comment on the Virginia and Kentucky Resolutions and ten rejected them, arguing that it was up to the judiciary to pass on the constitutionality of laws. Republican tempers in Virginia and Kentucky were not appeased. John Randolph, in his maiden race for Congress from Virginia, called for resistance "by force."[35]

In March 1799, force was used in Pennsylvania, where 140 armed farmers, stirred up by Republican propaganda—President Adams, it was said, was planning to marry his son to a daughter of George III—drove off a United States marshal who was trying to enforce a land tax. This rebellion was not in the state's wild west, but in the town of Bethlehem in the east; the farmers, led by a man named John Fries, were normally placid Germans who returned to their homes after chasing the marshal away.

Hamilton took the intellectual arguments of the Virginia and Kentucky Resolutions seriously. The notion that states could judge or thwart federal laws struck him as "gangrene," and an effort "to change the government." In a letter to a Federalist senator, he jotted down some proposed changes of his own: an amendment allowing the government to build interstate canals, which would knit the country together (interestingly, he did not rely on the "necessary and proper" clause, but assumed that an amendment was needed); and another, to break up the larger states: "Great states will always feel a rivalship with the common head. . . ." Writing to a Federalist congressman, he proposed to "put Virginia to the test" by marching an army through it.[36] He never made that suggestion to the commander-in-chief, and nothing came of it.

His advice to McHenry about how to handle Fries's rebellion was adopted, however. "Beware, my dear sir, of magnifying a riot into an insurrection, by employing in the first instance an inadequate force. . . . Whenever the government appears in arms, it ought to appear like a *Hercules*. . . ."[37] This was the principle the government had followed to good effect in the Whiskey Rebellion, once it moved. What Hamilton was forgetting was that Washington had moved only after prudently weighing his options, and—equally important—conveying the impression of prudence. A force commanded by a brigadier general swept through the "rebellious" countryside, arresting sixty men; three, including Fries, were convicted of treason by Hamilton's old target Samuel Chase, now a justice of the Supreme Court and a bigoted Federalist. President Adams ultimately pardoned them, to Hamilton's distress.

But the most important obstacles to administration policy were both farther away and closer to home. The global balance of power changed almost as soon as the United States became alarmed by it. In August of 1798, in the battle of the Nile, Britain had destroyed a French fleet supporting Napoleon in an invasion of Egypt. France would not be able to challenge Britain's hegemony in the East, or to invade the United States. Louisiana would continue to be both an opportunity and a threat, as Hamilton recognized, but the immediate danger had passed. President Adams meanwhile began hearing from American diplomats that Talleyrand was sending out feelers for new negotiations on Franco-American relations.

Also changing was the balance of power in John Adams's mind, particularly as he considered the two clashing parties. Political parties were an anomaly in American political thought. Hamilton, it is true, thought there were permanent social divisions based on wealth, and Madison had written subtly in *The Federalist* of factions. But permanently organized parties expressing coalitions of interest seemed strange and unwholesome, and while two parties had in fact emerged, they still had trouble thinking of themselves, or their enemies, in partisan terms. The Federalists were the friends of government, and dismissed their rivals as "the faction"; the Republicans were the defenders of the country's principles, and dismissed their enemies as secret monarchists. Even so, by 1798, all the founders and their junior partners were partisans, including even George Washington.

All except John Adams. The president was probably the last enemy of parties left in America. He was associated with the Federalists, because he had been vice president in the Washington administration; because he had unwisely praised monarchy, in conversation and in print; and because he despised French philosophy and the French Revolution. But he was also neutral, or hostile to, several Federalist policies, especially those developed by Hamilton (a national bank, a stronger army). Practically, he was an Anglophobe, hating the British government "in everything but its theory," as Ames observed. Fundamentally, he was a man of '76, when all (except Tories) had pulled together. If he could not impose unity on the country's contending factions, he could achieve equilibrium. "Jefferson had a party, Hamilton had a party, but the commonwealth had none,"[38] Adams would say in later years. He would fill the gap. When Jefferson said such things, though he meant them, he behaved otherwise. Adams was determined to live his rhetoric.

For both sets of reasons, foreign and domestic, Adams announced in February 1799 that he was appointing a special envoy to France. The Federalists reacted, in Abigail's words, "like a flock of frightened pigeons." Well they might, since Adams had consulted with no one in his cabinet, or "his" party, but simply dropped the news from on high. "The step," Hamilton wrote a Massachusetts Federalist, "would astonish, if any thing from that quarter [i.e., from Adams] could astonish. But as it has happened . . . the measure should go into effect."[39]

It took eight months for the American mission to be off. During that time, France lost battles, Talleyrand fell from power, and the president sent out conflicting signals. In October, he left Braintree for Trenton, where the government was sitting to avoid Philadelphia's yellow fever, to have a last meeting with his sullen cabinet. Also there to meet him was Hamilton, who had come from army headquarters in Newark, ostensibly to settle some military appointments. Years later, Adams wrote that "the little man" was "wrought up . . . to a degree of heat and effervescence." The object of Hamilton's heat was the proposed mission, which he tried to dissuade the president from sending. Hamilton, Adams added smugly, displayed a "total ignorance of everything in Europe."[40] This was an overstatement. Hamilton wrongly argued that the French Republic was finished, and that a royal restoration was around the corner, whereas Napoleon (escaped from Egypt) would manage to beat France's enemies back. But Hamilton also told the president that the Directory was tottering, and that it would be foolish to negotiate with lame ducks. This turned out to be true. But Adams was unmoved. The mission left for France, and Hamilton left for Newark.

The mission doomed the army. The only reason to have continued trying to organize it would have been to use it as a geopolitical counter to Spanish or French designs in the South and West. But no political groundwork had been laid for such exertions. The United States had blazed up in response to French high-handedness. Now that France seemed more reasonable, most Americans wanted calm. In any case the commander-in-chief died in December 1799. "[H]e was an *Aegis very essential to me*," Hamilton wrote Washington's secretary—under the circumstances, somewhat egotistically (the greatest man of the age had died; was the most important loss the loss to Hamilton?) unless one appreciates the context. Hamilton had had no effective paternal aegis, or shield, for the first twenty years of his life. They had quarreled, and misunderstood each other, but in every important controversy, Washington had given Hamilton his head. "If virtue can secure happiness in another world," Hamilton went on, "he is happy. In this the seal is now put upon *his* glory."[41] The emphasis suggests that Hamilton felt his own was still unsealed. Congress ordered the army disbanded, which Hamilton accomplished by June 1800. By then, the American mission was in Paris negotiating with Bonaparte, who had supplanted the Directory. The day after they signed their treaty, Bonaparte compelled Spain to give him Louisiana, which would be a source of disquiet to America for three years.

. . .

There was political groundwork to be laid for the next presidential election. John Adams might not believe in parties, but that did not make the parties go away—and the Republicans had been doing very well. They campaigned against the Alien and Sedition Acts, and watched as the rapprochement with France removed the curse of Francophilia from them. The Federalists meanwhile were split in two. Until the day he died, Adams would portray his peace feeler as a bold and lonely stroke for the good of the country, an interpretation that popular history has accepted. Whatever the good of it, the manner in which he executed it, both secretive and fitful, divided his base even more than necessary. One part, grateful for peace, clung to him. Another, caught up in the war fever that he had done as much as any man to inflame, reacted with wrath. "This extravagant opinion of himself," Ames raged about Adams in a letter to Wolcott, "this ignorance of parties and characters . . . this caprice . . . that forbid him ever to have a sober, reflected system . . ." Adams returned anger with anger, demanding McHenry's resignation in a tantrum, firing Pickering, and branding his enemies a "British faction," with Hamilton at its head. For good measure, he called Hamilton a "Bastard" and a "foreigner."[42]

Hamilton, for his part, concluded that Adams was "mad," and wrote him two notes demanding an explanation of the "British faction" charge. Receiving no answer, he decided to write a letter of his own. The work swelled into a pamphlet, *Letter from Alexander Hamilton, Concerning the Public Conduct and Character of John Adams, Esq., President of the United States,* which appeared at the end of October 1800. Adams, Hamilton admitted, had "patriotism and integrity, and even talents of a certain kind." But there were also "defects of character": an "eccentric" imagination; no "sound judgment" or "steady perseverance"; "extreme egotism"; "unfitness for the station contemplated." On and on it went, until the surprise ending: as in 1796, the most important goal was to keep Thomas Jefferson out, in pursuit of which the author "resolved not to advise . . . withholding from [Adams] a single vote." Adams's running mate this time was to be Charles Pinckney, and Hamilton urged Federalists to support them equally. He concluded with a call to "cultivat[e] harmony."[43]

As wonderful as the development of his argument, like yanking a bridle in full gallop, was his plan for disseminating it: he had the letter printed for private circulation among two hundred Federalist leaders. What happened instead was that Aaron Burr got a copy almost immediately, and published it far and wide.

The *Letter* delighted Republicans even more than the Reynolds pamphlet. "I rejoice with you," Madison wrote Jefferson. One Republican editor wondered whether such attacks on the president were not liable for prosecution under the Sedition Act. Ames gently chided his hero: "Though I think it one of your best performances," he wrote

Hamilton, the *Letter* was "more unlucky [for] federal men than any thing you ever wrote."[44]

Hamilton soon had more on his mind than John Adams, or even Thomas Jefferson. The first bellwether of the presidential election had already occurred: the election for the New York State Assembly in the spring of 1800. New York was one of ten states whose electoral votes were cast by the state legislatures, and the elections for the Assembly were a crucial test. Hamilton and his friends campaigned hard for the Federalist slate. "Every day he is seen in the streets," wrote a Republican newspaper, "hurrying this way, and darting that." "I have not eaten dinner for three days," sighed Troup, "and have been constantly upon my legs from 7 in the morning till 7 in the afternoon."[45] To put himself even more in the public eye, Hamilton took on the defense of Levi Weeks, a laborer accused of stuffing his girlfriend down a well.

But the Republicans were led by an even better campaigner, Aaron Burr. Burr put together a glittering slate, headed by former Governor Clinton, Horatio Gates, and one of the Livingstons. The Federalists had a slate of ordinary people: tradesmen, and a few professionals. Burr compiled dossiers on every voter in town, and he kept an open house for Republican electioneers: "Refreshments were always on the table and mattresses for temporary repose in the rooms." He sent German-speaking orators to campaign in German neighborhoods, and spent ten consecutive hours working one ward himself. For good measure, he joined Hamilton in defending Levi Weeks, who was acquitted. Robert R. Livingston, imitating Burr's methods, sent an "elegant chariot" to carry an old black man to the polls. This voter turned out to be a Federalist, but on the whole the Republicans' efforts paid off, as they swept the city. "We have beat you," Burr told a Federalist afterward, "by superior *Management*."[46] Burr's efforts to cultivate local politicians in western New York also helped produce a Republican swing there. As a result, twelve electoral votes that had gone to Adams in 1796 would now go to Jefferson.

They would also go to Aaron Burr. Burr had toyed with a vice presidential run in 1792, and made a serious effort in 1796, which had been undermined by the desertions of southern Republican electors.

This time, the Republicans had vowed to do what Hamilton would urge on the Federalists in his Adams letter—to stand behind both their candidates equally. If they did so, they would produce a tie, but that would be a problem for another day.

In the aftermath of the defeat in New York, Hamilton wrote John Jay, who had succeeded Clinton as governor, urging him to call a special session of the legislature, to change the election laws so that New York's presidential electors would be chosen by popular vote. This was a consistent position of Hamilton's, from his speech at the Constitutional Convention onward. His arguments on this occasion, however, make his letter to Jay the worst he ever wrote. "In times like these . . . it will not do to be overscrupulous. *It is easy to sacrifice the substantial interests of Society by a strict adherence to ordinary rules.*"[47] A lifetime's record shows this to be an anomaly, borne of shock and despair. Publius rejected Publius's suggestion.

Over the next eight months, Republican discipline held, the final tally giving Jefferson and Burr 73 votes each, with 65 for Adams and 64 for Pinckney. The Republicans' victory now gave them a crisis, for Aaron Burr made no move to signal that he was content to be vice president. His friends, such as Albert Gallatin, urged him to go to Washington, D.C., the brand-new capital. *"He must be on the spot himself."*[48] Federalists desperate to find some way of stopping Jefferson decided that Burr would be preferable. The Constitution prescribed (Article II, Section I) that tied presidential elections be settled by the House of Representatives, where the state delegations would vote as units. The Republicans controlled eight states, the Federalists six, with two evenly split. If the Federalists held firm for Burr, Jefferson could not win a majority of states. If some Republican congressmen could be persuaded to defect to Burr, Burr might win.

The object of these plots—grandson of Jonathan Edwards, son of Aaron Burr, Sr., the president of Princeton—had been a brave young officer in the Revolution, accompanying Benedict Arnold on his heroic winter attack on Quebec at the age of nineteen. Burr showed "perfect coolness and immobility under dangerous fire," a comrade wrote, though he seemed a "mere boy."[49] During the war, he met Mrs. Theodosia Prevost, a woman ten years his senior. Her husband was a

British officer, stationed in the West Indies; when he died, Aaron Burr married his widow. Burr seems truly to have loved her; when they were apart, they corresponded about new books—*The Social Contract, A Vindication of the Rights of Woman, The Decline and Fall of the Roman Empire.*

After the war, he moved to New York and became one of its most successful lawyers. Unlike Hamilton, Burr was no scholar; his forte was arguing a case before a jury. He had to be successful, for he spent money faster than he made it, and was always awaiting some investment bonanza that would make him rich.

Burr was of average height—five feet six—and slender. A Gilbert Stuart portrait, painted when he was thirty-six, shows a rather insipid face under a balding, egglike forehead—with, however, striking deep-set hazel eyes. Burr united politeness, charm, and a complete confidence in his social position. James Wilkinson, a veteran of the Quebec campaign, called him "the first gentleman in America." One New York Federalist wrote Hamilton that Burr had "an address not resistible by common clay."[50]

A man of his qualities, record, and talents was naturally drawn to politics, and after some hesitations, he aligned himself with Clinton and the Livingstons in New York, and with the Republicans nationally. His efforts for the Republican ticket in 1800 were not confined to his own state. His only child, also named Theodosia, married into a rich South Carolina family, and Burr kept track of developments there through local correspondents. At the same time, his gentlemanly mien and his lack of ideological dogmatism made many Federalists feel that he was someone with whom they could deal.

Still, the man had political liabilities. Burr's high living, and his huge debts, were matters of concern: since economy seemed to be out of the question, what else might he do to make ends meet? Burr was an adulterer in theory as well as practice—before and during his marriage, and after his wife (who was frail in health) died. His guide was another new book, Lord Chesterfield's *Letters to His Son.* Chesterfield's *Letters* were a terminus, reducing the idea of the gentleman to salon polish. Samuel Johnson said they taught "the morals of a whore, and the manners of a dancing master." "The indulgence you applaud in Chesterfield," Theodosia had written Aaron when they were courting, "is . . . reprehensible. Such lessons from so able a pen are dangerous to a young mind, and ought never to be read till the judgment and the heart are established in virtue. You have, undoubtedly, a mind superior to the contagion." Superior or inferior, Burr's mind accepted the contagion.[51] A man, like Hamilton, who had confessed that he had indulged this vice would be likely to resent a man who did not consider it to be one.

The lack of dogmatism that made Burr attractive to some Federalists caused Republicans and other Federalists to be suspicious of him. In February 1791, Senator Burr wrote a Federalist congressman that he had not "read with proper attention" Hamilton's proposal for a bank—a remarkable thing to say of the main issue then before the government. Burr was up on Rousseau, Gibbon, and Mary Wollstonecraft, but not on the Anglo-American politics that obsessed his peers. "Read the Abbé Mably's little book on the Constitution of the United States," he urged his wife in a letter. "This . . . will save me the trouble of reading it; and I shall receive it with much more emphasis per la bouche d'amour." His main interest in politics was politicking. Oliver Wolcott quoted a Virginian: "He has an unequalled talent for attaching men to his views, and forming combinations of which he is always the center." The first part of that judgment was wrong: it was always a question what Burr's views were. But he did want to array other men around himself. His approach to the law was similarly value free. "The law," he often said, "is whatever is successfully argued and plausibly maintained."[52]

A century later, an old man who had met an old Aaron Burr when he was young was asked about Burr's "rare attraction," and said it came from "his manner of listening. He seemed . . . to find so much more meaning in your words than you had intended; no flattery was more subtle."[53] Listening is a virtue of the judicious and the compassionate. But narcissists also do it surpassingly well. We associate Narcissus with beauty and self-regard, but the key to his myth is that it is about surfaces. Narcissus was captivated by his reflection because that was all he had. Narcissists must live through their interactions, because there is no one home. Burr's charm, attentiveness, and promiscuity; his ability to get schemes going, and his failure to follow them through; his lack of principle—all flow from his character. He was like a new refrigerator—bright, cold, and empty.

George Washington, the most un-Burr-like man in America, seems to have understood and disliked him immediately. Burr served only ten days on Washington's staff in 1776, yet for two decades the older man went out of his way to show his aversion. When Burr wanted to write a history of the war, President Washington told the secretary of state that he should not be allowed to read diplomatic correspondence. When Burr was proposed as minister to France, Washington refused to appoint "any person . . . in whose integrity he had not confidence." When President Adams wanted to make Burr a brigadier general in 1798, Washington admitted that he was "brave and able . . . the question is, whether he has not equal talents for intrigue."[54]

Hamilton's and Burr's interlocking careers and their points of resemblance have led many to discern some deep bond of attraction and repulsion between them. This is fanciful. Hamilton and Burr were lawyer-politicians in a town little bigger than modern Poughkeepsie. It was inevitable that they would work and socialize together. The resemblances—age, stature, veterans' status—were superficial; the differences—from reading (Plutarch vs. Chesterfield) to cast of mind (Hamilton wrote a plan for a national bank, Burr could not be bothered to study it)—were profound. They were not secret sharers, but obvious misfits, bound only by proximity and by their line of work.

Hamilton went through phases of believing (wrongly) that he could manipulate intriguers: hence his desire to promote Wilkinson. Hamilton also recommended making Burr a brigadier general in 1798. "He may be found a useful cooperator," Hamilton wrote Wolcott in the manner of a scientist considering a hypothesis; ". . . the case is worth the experiment." But he had always opposed Burr's efforts to attain offices that would give him an independent power base, such as a seat in the Senate, or the vice presidency. His view of Burr's leadership qualities was the same as Washington's. The possibility that Burr might become Washington's successor, with Federalist help, filled Hamilton with dismay. From December 1800 through January 1801, he sent a blizzard of letters to Federalist friends beseeching them to abandon the scheme. To

Gouverneur Morris, on Christmas Eve day: Burr "has no principle, public or private" and "will listen to no monitor but his ambition. . . . He is sanguine enough to hope every thing, daring enough to attempt every thing, wicked enough to scruple nothing." To James Bayard, a Delaware congressman on December 27: Burr is "a voluptuary by system—with habits of expense that can be satisfied by no fair expedients [i.e., he would have to sell himself to foreign patrons]. . . . Daring and energy must be allowed him; but these qualities, under the direction of the worst passions, are . . . objections, not recommendations."[55]

Hamilton did not only tear down Burr; he made the case for Jefferson. Here Hamilton had painted himself into a corner. Federalist polemics, many written by Hamilton, had been saying for almost a decade that Jefferson's years in France and his philosophical French friends were proof that he was not merely pro-French in his politics, but a vessel of revolutionary ideas. Hamilton's appeal to Jay to change New York's election laws had characterized Jefferson as an "atheist in religion." Many a Federalist electioneer had gone much further: the Reverend Jedidiah Morse, a Massachusetts minister, discerned a conspiracy of Republicans, French, and Illuminated Freemasons menacing the country. Meanwhile, Jefferson's surrogates had been attacking and insulting Hamilton for nine years. "If there be a man in the world I ought to hate," Hamilton admitted to Morris, "it is Jefferson. With Burr I have always been personally well."[56] But now he put all this aside. He trusted that Jefferson would do many wrong things; he did not trust Burr at all.

The Federalists, he wrote Wolcott in mid-December, should try to make a deal with Jefferson: let him keep the bank and the navy, and maintain neutrality, and they would acquiesce in his election. For all their history, Hamilton believed that Jefferson was a man who could make a bargain, and indeed the two had made one, on the funding system and the capital in 1790.

Hamilton made his final, grand appeal to Bayard in mid-January. Bayard occupied a key position, for he was Delaware's only representative in the House; since he controlled an entire state delegation, the deadlock lay in his hands. Hamilton ticked off all his old enemy's flaws:

Jefferson was "tinctured with fanaticism," "crafty," "not scrupulous," "not very mindful of truth," "a contemptible hypocrite." Like a man taking a bad medicine, he admitted some virtues: caution ("as likely as any man I know to temporize"), honesty in money matters, no hostility to presidential power ("he [is] solicitous to come into a Good Estate"). Then, in a passage marked *"very, very confidential,"* he laid into Burr one last time, writing that in 1798, when he had been major general, pushing for Burr to get a brigadier's slot, Burr had returned the favor by blaming him for not seizing the opportunity "to change the government. . . . when answered that this could not have been done without guilt, [Burr] replied, 'Les grandes âmes se soucient peu des petits morceaux' [Great souls don't bother about little scraps]."[57] Burr's phrase about *petits morceaux* resembled Hamilton's in his letter to Jay about ordinary rules, but there was no reason to think Burr's was anomalous.

Congress met in mid-February, and the deadlocked election was delivered to the House. After thirty-five ballots, Bayard announced that he would abstain on the thirty-sixth, making Jefferson president and Burr vice president. Though Jefferson ever after denied that he had made any deal such as Hamilton had outlined, he did all the things (at least initially) that Hamilton proposed. Hamilton had just turned forty-four; he would never hold public office again. He would die before the end of Jefferson's first term.

Chapter Seven

Words

SOME OF THE MOST dramatic changes President Jefferson made in political life concerned etiquette and appearance—riding on horseback instead of in a coach; wearing corduroy breeches; allowing his dinner guests at the White House to sit wherever they liked instead of seating them formally. As eloquently as any inaugural address, these gestures conveyed a message: the pomp of Federalism was gone; republican simplicity had been restored. Like all effective leaders, some of the founders were able, at their best, to make the significant gesture. Franklin wore a brown coat and long, undressed hair when he appeared at the French court to show the sophisticates what a simple Quaker he was. "People gathered around as he passed," wrote a dazzled Frenchman, "and said: 'Who is this old farmer who has such a noble air?'"[1] The greatest master of gesture was George Washington, whether he rode into battle to inspire courage, or sent a wine cooler to show confidence.

But dramatic moments come seldom (or perhaps they come regularly only to people with dramatic temperaments). Most of the founders' communicating was done through words. Of all the founders, the most energetic wordsmith was Hamilton. His official correspondence was voluminous; his state papers were long and comprehensive. His profession, the bar, required more public speaking than any other, except possibly the pulpit, and the arguments lawyers presented could last for hours at a stretch. From the age of fifteen until his death, he engaged in journalism, first as self-expression and polemic, then as a support to his official recommendations (Hamilton's rule for conducting a campaign was always to open a second front in the newspapers). His longest efforts were his contributions to *The Federalist,* and to the Camillus letters—about 100,000 and 70,000 words respectively. By way of comparison, this book is 78,000 words long. Hamilton wrote so much and so readily that people attributed pseudonymous pamphlets by other authors to him. Jefferson thought that, in addition to the Camillus letters, Hamilton wrote another series of pamphlets in defense of Jay's Treaty, which were in fact by James Kent and the future lexicographer Noah Webster. Jefferson biographer Dumas Malone blamed Hamilton for a series of anti-Jefferson pamphlets signed "Scourge," which were more abusive than Hamilton's own. Hamilton biographer John C. Miller wrongly credited him with a crude pro-Constitution blast, signed "Caesar," that appeared before Publius went to work. His actual productivity was impressive enough. Hamilton's grandson and biographer, Allan Maclane Hamilton, spoke of his grandfather's "power of prolific creation." Jefferson paid awed and dismayed tribute to his "indefatigableness." William Cobbett called himself Peter Porcupine, but the image of a bristling, ever-ready force had already been bestowed on Hamilton by a New York newspaper: he is "the political porcupine, armed at all points, and brandish[ing] a shaft to every opposer: a shaft powerful to repel and keen to wound."[2] Hamilton's public life was conducted in a torrent of words.

Hamilton's relationship with words was intimate, and inexhaustible. The words kept flashing from him, even when he was in private. Sometimes he talked to himself. In 1789, Philip Schuyler wrote his daughter with a funny story: a store-owner in Kinderhook, New York, had seen a man walking up and down in front of his store, "his lips moving rapidly as if he was in conversation with some person." When the man came inside to change a $50 bill, the owner refused, fearing that he had "lost his reason." "I have seen him before my door for half an hour, sometimes stopping, but always talking to himself, and if I had changed the money and he had lost it, I might have received blame." "Pray ask my Hamilton," Schuyler concluded, "if he can't guess who the Gentleman was."[3]

When there were people around, Hamilton talked to them. Before writing his defense of the constitutionality of the Bank of the United States, Hamilton paced in the garden of William Lewis, a Philadelphia lawyer, rehearsing the arguments aloud. While he was writing Washington's Farewell Address, he would read his work aloud to his wife, telling her that "you must be to me what Molière's old nurse was to him."[4] Molière used the old woman to test his laugh lines. The Farewell Address was not meant to be read aloud, and no one has ever found it funny. But for Hamilton, speech was a performance meant to persuade, and he was often rehearsing.

Words were his one tangible link with his family after it broke up: his mother's thirty-four books were the only possessions that Hamilton's in-laws were able to salvage from the auction of her estate. His skill in using words was one of the ways he had elevated himself, impressing the Reverend Hugh Knox and Nicholas Cruger, astonishing Dr. Myles Cooper, and establishing his acquaintance with John Jay. Although coolness, bravery, and energy won him a place on Washington's staff, and made him indispensable there, most of his time was spent helping to shape and direct the enormous flow of the commander-in-chief's official words. When he was courting Betsey, he urged her to read with an appeal that showed what words meant to him: "You excel most of your sex in all the amiable qualities, endeavor to excel them equally in the *splendid* ones [emphasis added]."[5] His favorite politician of antiquity was Demosthenes, who tried to stop Philip of Macedon with orations.

Words solidified Hamilton's accomplishments. Thirty-eight other men signed the Constitution; Hamilton made the strongest case for it at Poughkeepsie and in *The Federalist*. Arguments of Hamilton's found their way into opinions by Chief Justice John Marshall decades after Hamilton was dead. He not only recast America's finances and its economy, he explained what he was doing and why. Sometimes when he accomplished nothing, he left prophecies. The "Report on Manufactures" was a dead letter, but one that has been much read.

Hamilton was not the only founder to appear in print. Madison produced almost thirty of the *Federalist* papers, and other journalism during the 1780s and 1790s. Jefferson, more reticent, did publish his *Notes on Virginia;* the thoughts on race he expressed there dog him to this day. Adams, who was not reticent at all, published the *Discourses on Davila*, which began to dog him immediately. But only Benjamin Franklin published as often as Hamilton—not surprisingly, since he had been a printer by trade. Franklin also had the stylistic advantage of being, not one Franklin, but many, refracting his persona through a variety of genres, including advice, humor, and hoax. The Abbé Reynal, a French scholar, defended, in Franklin's presence, a howler he had included in a book on the New World by saying that he had the anecdote on "unquestionable authority." Franklin told him that his "authority" was a leg-pulling article that Franklin himself had written in one of his newspapers years earlier. "Very well, doctor," the philosopher replied, "I had rather relate your stories than other men's truths."[6] But Hamilton wrote in one tone, for one audience, for one purpose: seriously, to his fellow citizens, to persuade. The torrent of words flowed in only one direction.

Hamilton's singleness of focus was relevant to the Reynolds affair. After Hamilton had published the Reynolds pamphlet, his assailant James Callender dismissed the quoted letters of the Reynoldses as forgeries, arguing that their wild spelling was inconsistent with their forceful expression: Hamilton, said Callender, must have written the letters himself, throwing in gross blunders in an attempt to cover his tracks. The argument that good writers never spell badly is absurd: in one letter Abigail Adams wrote, in succession, "scaile," "scale," "skaill," and "scaill," finally asking, "[I]s it right now?"[7] But the strongest argument against Hamilton as forger is that he barely understood, and could never have created, the Reynoldses' emotional crosscurrents. Hamilton was an advocate and an arguer, not a novelist. All he could imagine was the future of a country.

Persuading people about public affairs was a much-admired intellectual activity, and one of the few that Americans did well. But there is a sense in which Hamilton's willingness to do so, repeatedly, in the common forum of the press was infra dig. His peers never said such a thing (though they criticized specific performances, such as the Reynolds pamphlet or the Adams letter). James Callender, the professional journalist, did say so, mocking Hamilton as "a threadbare lawyer, forgetting to earn daily subsistence for his family, that he may write 200 newspaper columns for nothing."[8] Callender could not respect any man who did what he did.

The historian Jacob Burckhardt called Pietro Aretino, the Renaissance blackmailer and pornographer, the "father of modern journalism."[9] (Aretino wrote a kind of newsletter, effusively praising those who paid him off, obscenely attacking those who did not.) Journalism has often risen above this level, without ever quite forsaking its disreputable roots. American journalists in the late eighteenth century were a lively combination of the best and the worst. Their best work is in the textbooks. At their worst, they were not only liars, but corrupt liars. When President Jefferson did not give Callender a postmastership after the election of 1800, he switched sides and became a Federalist, with consequences that still resonate—for it was Callender who first published the story of Sally Hemings. But even the journalists at the mudsill level were industrious, politically sophisticated, and occasionally eloquent.

The best of the professionals was undoubtedly Thomas Paine. After a miscellaneous and mediocre life in England, which included stints as a corset-maker, a privateer, a Methodist preacher, and an excise collector, Paine came to the Thirteen Colonies in 1774 and found himself as a writer. *Common Sense* was the great popular argument for declaring independence; "The American Crisis," which appeared on the eve of the battle of Trenton ("These are the times that try men's souls . . ."), was something more: the democratic equivalent of King Harry's speech on St. Crispin's Day, nobler for having been written for real life, not a play. Paine spent the late 1780s and the 1790s in England and France, where he turned to political philosophy (*The Rights of Man*) and theology (*The Age of Reason*). "Thomas Paine is in prison," wrote Gouverneur Morris from Paris at the height of the Terror, "where he amuses himself with publishing a pamphlet against Jesus Christ."[10] When Paine got out of jail, he published another pamphlet, against George Washington. These twin attacks severely crimped his reputation in America, and bad health and drink slowed him down. But in 1802, Paine returned to the United States, at President Jefferson's invitation, and delivered himself of a few more journalistic strokes.

Second in talent to Paine, and the best pen on the Federalist side, was William Cobbett. Cobbett had served as a sergeant major in the British army, resenting his officers, exposing corruption, and reading Paine. Fearing prosecution, he arrived in the United States in 1792, where his political sympathies underwent a complete reversal. Yankee Brit-bashing transformed him into a belated Tory, and Republican radical chic disgusted him. "At a dinner at Philadelphia . . . a *roasted pig* became the representative of Louis XVI and it being the anniversary of his murder, the pig's head was severed from his body, then carried round to each of the convives, who, after placing the liberty-cap upon [it], pronounced the word *tyrant,* and gave the poor little grunter's head a chop with his knife."[11] Cobbett's ideas were cut-rate Burke, without weight or gravity, but his tone was rollicking and vicious, and *Porcupine's Gazette* had at its peak 3,000 subscribers—a huge number. He "might do more good," Fisher Ames wrote admiringly but anxiously to Hamilton, "if directed by men of sense and experience."

The professional journalists and Hamilton had one trait in common—a high proportion of them were, like him, foreign-born. Paine and Cobbett were English; Callender was Scottish; William Duane, an editor of the Republican *Aurora,* and Matthew Lyon, a pamphleteering congressman from Vermont, were Irish. As in all times and places, the outsider was disproportionately disposed to comment on life. The professionals and Hamilton shared another trait. They yelled when they were hurt (and some of them were hurt badly: Callender and Lyon spent months in jail for violating the Sedition Act, and Cobbett was driven back to England by a politically inspired libel suit). But none of them believed in untrammeled freedom of expression. "There is a difference," Paine explained with his usual terseness, "between error and licentiousness."[12] Hamilton was harsh on what he considered journalistic licentiousness, though he actually defined it more narrowly than many of his contemporaries.

Few of the founders were great writers. Gouverneur Morris, who drafted the Constitution, was witty and cynical; the journals and letters of John Adams are sui generis. By far the best writers in a public capacity were Franklin and Jefferson. Franklin is perhaps the only founder who is now read by ordinary people with no middle-brow thought of showing off, for his essay on farting is advertised in supermarket tabloids, and some of his Poor Richard maxims are still current as bromides. Jefferson was the master of the single sentence. Time and again, like some harried quarterback deep in his own territory, he steps into the pocket—Tories, monarchists, clergymen swarming over his defensive linemen; Madison doing his earnest and ineffectual best to block; Washington sitting on the bench, remote and withholding; the crowd, a confused roar (the people, his mainstay, yet so often unaccountably misled)—and lofts a pass that floats for a hundred yards, and for centuries. These sentences have to be extracted from acres of lucid prattle, clear and flavorless as water, but the passage of time, and his own talent, make the job of editing him easy. Detractors may rail against the Declaration, abusing its philosophy, questioning its uniqueness. It doesn't matter: it rings like a bell. The Continental Congress rewrote it heavily, much to Jefferson's chagrin, who always preferred his original version. But none of Jefferson's editors and fellow delegates ever wrote anything as stirring, whereas Jefferson wrote many such things. Cut loose from their contexts and their meanings, his sentences travel under their own power. The phrase about the "wall of separation" between church and state has migrated into the First Amendment itself; the sentence about the blood-drinking tree of liberty was on Timothy McVeigh's T-shirt when he was arrested for the Oklahoma City bombing.

Hamilton enjoyed that gift once, in a shining passage on natural right from his teenage polemic with Samuel Seabury. Pennsylvania patriot John Dickinson had written a similar thought: "[T]he rights essential to happiness . . . are not annexed to us by parchments and seals. They are created in us by the decrees of Providence, which establish the laws of our nature. They are born with us; exist with us; and cannot be taken from us. . . ." Fifty years later, Jefferson expressed another similar thought, borrowing perhaps from Dickinson, perhaps from his old enemy: Americans "had no occasion to search into musty records, to hunt up royal parchments, or to investigate the laws and institutions of a semi-barbarous ancestry. We appealed to those of nature, and found them engraved on our hearts." Hamilton's version is superior to both:

"The sacred rights of mankind are not to be rummaged for among old parchments or musty records. They are written, as with a sunbeam, in the whole volume of human nature, by the hand of the Divinity itself, and can never be erased or obscured by mortal power."[13] *Rummaged* is wonderfully pungent; the extended metaphor of musty records and mortal erasers, set against nature's volume and God's hand, is an argument condensed into poetry; the sunbeam, a seeming throwaway, illuminates the whole.

He never hit that note again, because his mind was fundamentally interested in different things. Hamilton is not concise. He uses lively and active verbs, or adjectives formed from them; he typically has a bustling energy and momentum. But sentence by sentence, there are insertions, repetitions, little verbal accretions that make the whole somewhat monotonous and unshaped. There is rhythm, but no phrasing: too much eighteenth-century wind. Hamilton's favorite authors, from his boyhood, were Plutarch and Alexander Pope—not useful models. Plutarch, though charming, is garrulous, while Pope's genius, which is anything but garrulous, is so dependent on the structure of the heroic couplet that it offers little to prose writers.

Hamilton's unit of composition is the entire piece, which may run on for thousands of words. He thinks in arguments—and his arguments never merely answer the arguments of his opponents, but lay out a case of his own. Julius Goebel, Jr., the editor of his legal papers, described his notes for one case as "a cumulation of positive propositions so nicely articulated as to confront the opponents with a whole structure to be toppled."[14] Hamilton did not simply try to wear his enemies out with his energy; he sought to dismay them by constructing an impregnable fortress of demonstration. His method might be called "structural," if the word "structuralism" did not have a different, modern meaning. Other men could mint the battle cries, or the catchphrases. Hamilton wanted to find the principles, get answers, and outline a plan of action. He had time to learn only the first principles of the law, said Robert Troup; he wanted to inspect the foundations of every argument, said William Pierce. Having done so, he wanted to draw the conclusions and get going.

Hamilton's arguments, whether in a courtroom, a memo to Washington, or a newspaper article, expressed an assumption about the judge, the president, and the reader. He assumed they were as intelligent as he was. His thoughts could be their thoughts; they could understand his reasoning as well as he did. For a man so confident of his own abilities, he was not superior. He believed, naturally, that he knew everything worth knowing. But he was always willing to bring all he knew to the marketplace, and give it away.

Hamilton, of course, was familiar with other forms of persuasion. He traded horses like any other politician. And there were times, especially in the last years of his life, that were clouded by personal and political setbacks, when he argued that the Federalists had to learn to manipulate the people—through worthy impulses, to be sure, but nevertheless impulses different from those they themselves felt. Nothing came of these autumnal proposals, however. They were products of depression, and foreign to his nature. No matter what he advised in private, he never stopped churning out his columns.

What happened when his audiences ignored the advice so copiously offered? Sometimes Hamilton demonized his opponents. The stakes in the election of 1796, he wrote Troup, were "true liberty, property, order, religion and of course *heads*." But even that is a rather offhanded way of expressing a grim thought. Hamilton's first reaction when confronted with a failure to convince was puzzlement. He had "information on all points," wrote the Duc de Rochefoucauld-Liancourt, a French nobleman, but "he often wondered why others did not think and act as he did, the righteous necessities of the case seemingly being so apparent."[15] The key word is *wondered*. Some of us want to annihilate our enemies; some (perhaps even more aggressive) want to pray for them. Hamilton drew a blank. He had the answer; he would explain it, in 100,000 words if necessary; what was the problem? In May 1792, he wrote a long letter to Edward Carrington, trying to explain his break with James Madison. But their break had first manifested itself in February 1790, when Madison came out for discrimination between original and later holders of debt. Hamilton was inspecting the barn door long after the horse had gone.

In some instances he succumbed to despair, which he expressed by doubting his fitness for American life—or America's fitness for him. His complaints during the war about debt-repudiating and slave-owning politicians illustrate this mood. So does an outcry, five weeks after he retired as secretary of the treasury, when Congress failed to enact a recommendation of his that debt-holders who had not renewed their certificates be paid anyway. In an anguished letter to Rufus King, he called the move an "assassination of the national honor," and asked: "Am I, then, more an American than those who drew their first breath on American ground? . . . is there a constitutional defect in the American mind?"[16] Hamilton, and his enemies, conspired to ensure that his nationality would never quite be a settled question. But these arias of alienation mask a deeper anxiety, a darker fear. When he had given a problem his best words, and still failed to carry the day, he had nothing left to give. He was his arguments. Failure to persuade threatened his existence, as well as his citizenship.

Hamilton's characteristic mode of argument was opposed to bullying, especially the organized bullying of mobs. It was also opposed to intrigue. Adams thought him the greatest intriguer in America, but Hamilton was actually one of the least competent, his efforts at it either failing or succeeding disastrously (George Clinton would never have made the mistake of offending the Livingstons by giving "their" Senate seat to Rufus King). Hamilton, justifying the Adams letter, argued that, by not "declar[ing] the motives of our dislike . . . we have the air of mere caballers."[17] When Burr broadcast the letter to the world, Hamilton was not displeased: now everyone would have the opportunity to be persuaded by his arguments.

Hamilton was also opposed to lying—a seemingly simple and obvious preference, but what controversy, or newspaper, is entirely free of lies? In 1799, William Duane's *Aurora* printed a story that Hamilton had tried to buy the paper, using $6,000 given to him by the British ambassador out of a secret fund. Hamilton, as a major general in the army, was not covered by the Sedition Act; instead, the State of New York brought a libel action against the *Argus,* a New York City paper that had picked up the story. Hamilton offered to appear as a witness, "to prove that every part of it was false."[18] According to the common law of the day, however, truth was not a factor in libel cases; the only issue was whether a citizen had been exposed to the contempt of his fellows. The printer of the *Argus* was sentenced to four months in jail. Hamilton would encounter the common-law doctrine of libel again.

Hamilton's rhetorical style was also opposed to silence. Silence can be cunning, silence can be patience. In his old age, John Adams wrote that George Washington "possessed the gift of silence." That gift had passed both Adams and Hamilton by. Another founder who possessed it was Jefferson. In April 1795, Jefferson invited William Branch Giles to Monticello, with a warning that he would be "put . . . on very short allowance as to political aliment. Now and then a pious ejaculation for [European] republicans, returning with due despatch to clover, potatoes, wheat, &c."[19] Jefferson knew how to let things alone. The explosion over Jay's Treaty was only three months away; when it came, he would marvel over the "indefatigableness" of Hamilton's Camillus letters. But he would not be tempted to write any letters of his own. He was biding his time. This was a quality of Jefferson's which was foreign to Hamilton's nature.

His friend John Jay tried once to steer him in the direction of silence. In December 1792, nine months into the Newspaper War, Hamilton complained to Jay of "malicious intrigues to stab me in the dark . . . that distract and harass me." (An interesting slip of the pen, for the Newspaper War, though malicious, was carried on in the bright light of publicity; what Hamilton did not tell Jay was that he had just explained Maria Reynolds to Muhlenberg, Venable, and Monroe.) Jay, commenting on the public situation, gave him some good advice. "Your difficulties from persons and parties will by time be carried out of sight, *unless you prevent it*. . . . I think your reputation points to the expediency of memoirs" (emphasis added).[20] A man can write himself up, said Samuel Johnson, and he can write himself down. Let the daily attacks slide, Jay was telling him; there will be time to tell your story when you have retired. It was wasted advice.

There were also men who were silent because they had nothing to say. Since Aaron Burr thought of language as instrumental—the law, he said, was "whatever is boldly asserted and plausibly maintained"—there was no reason to commit words to paper. "Things written remain," he often warned his law clerks. "We cannot explain on paper," he wrote correspondents. Writing revealed your tracks, and restricted your room to maneuver. In person, Burr preferred to listen; when he spoke, he preferred to say nothing that could be pinned down. "It is remarkable," wrote a Virginia Republican, "that in all private conversations he more frequently agrees with us in principle than in the mode of giving them [*sic*] effect. . . ." "Perhaps no man's language," wrote a New England Federalist, "was ever more apparently explicit, & at the same time so covert & indefinite."[21]

There is a final form of persuasion that Hamilton's rhetoric excluded and, by excluding, limited his effectiveness. That is inspiration: the more than rational appeal that pulls, carries, enlivens those to whom it is made. (*Inspire* comes from the Latin words *in spirare*—"to breathe into.") Since our education system is built upon words, we tend to think of verbal examples: Paine's "American Crisis"; the sense conveyed by the opening of the Declaration of Independence that it is beaming universal truths; Patrick Henry's 1775 speech in Old St. John's Church at Richmond that ended with the cry "Give me liberty, or give me death." Hamilton's future friend, Edward Carrington, heard Henry through a window, and he told his wife that he wanted to be buried on the spot where he had heard those words, and he was. Inspiration can also come from the timely act: something as simple, and as hard, as being in the right place at the right time, and doing exactly the right thing.

The trouble with inspiration—the word or deed that binds a moment and a soul together, without argument or demonstration—is that it can be false. Sincerity is one of the easiest things to fake. Franklin, the Quaker at Versailles, was not a Quaker; he fought the Quakers in Pennsylvania politics, calling them "stiffrumps"; in Paris, he lived the opposite of a simple life, running up 100,000 pounds of unexplained expenses. (When Congress asked for an accounting, he told them, "Muzzle not the ox that treadeth out his master's grain.")[22] Franklin's insincerity can be defended: he did come from a society that was simpler than the French court, and wearing brown coats and long hair was a shorthand way of making the point. Still, his behavior was deceptive. Wayward inspirations, like Jefferson's floating incantations, can over time become more deceptive yet.

Inspiration can also become false through multiple attempts to recapture it. What was true when it was first said grows dim and worn through repetition; those who repeat it, forgetting what it once meant, apply it to anything and everything. Thus inspiration shades into flattery. The inspired leader can tell a man something he did not know about himself: that he is brave; that he is willing to die. The flatterer tells him what he has already heard, and wants to hear again. Inspiration stimulates virtue; flattery induces contentment. Hamilton was acutely aware of the dangers of flattery. He saw his enemies, from the Revolution to the election of 1800, as a parade of flatterers. Would the rule of law inconvenience us? Weaken it. Are taxes irksome? Don't levy them. Is the army expensive? Do without it. In a memo to Washington, defending himself against the charge that he wanted to erect a monarchy, he invoked those opposite poles in the magnetic storm of Roman history, Cato and Caesar. "The former frequently resisted, the latter always flattered, the follies of the people. Yet the former perished with the republic—the latter destroyed it."[23]

Plutarch's "Life of Phocion," which supplied Hamilton with one of his pseudonyms, contains a discussion of flattery and the problem of leadership. If "rulers be constantly opposite and cross to the tempers and inclinations of the people"—as Phocion was, as Hamilton was often accused of being—"they will be resented as arbitrary and harsh." On the other hand, "too much deference . . . to popular faults and errors, is full of danger." What does Plutarch recommend? "Human beings . . . are ready enough to serve well and submit to much, if they are not always ordered about and roughly handled, like slaves." If "a statesman gratifies his people that he may the more imperatively recall them to a sense of the common interest," then they can "be guided and governed upon the method that leads to safety."[24] Plutarch advises courtesy, and splitting the difference; show some respect, give some ground, and the people will do what they must.

But this does not state the whole problem. Here it is. There are three modes of leadership. The highest is inspiration: rare, sometimes false, but impossible to live without. Next is demonstration—honestly sharing all your reasons with all comers; explaining where they come from, and where they lead. Lowest is flattery, which either fools both the leader and his followers, or fools no one, but is indulged, because followers and leaders are too tired to think of anything else. Hamilton seldom rose to the highest level, and would not sink to the lowest. His greatest rivals, such as Jefferson, inhabited all three, especially the first and the third; hence their success.

It is not just Hamilton's problem.

Chapter Eight

R*ights*

WORDS WERE HAMILTON'S means. Rights were his ends, as they were the ends of everyone in late-eighteenth-century America. Rights talk was in the air; it was the air—a condition that still left wide latitude for discussing where rights came from and what they were.

The ultimate source of rights for all Americans was the order of things, divine and natural—the emphasis they gave to these qualifiers varying with their degree of religious orthodoxy. In truth, few strayed far from Christianity, and those who did generally concealed their steps. Even Thomas Paine, the future enemy of Jesus Christ, quoted the books of Judges and I Samuel in *Common Sense*. Hamilton was devout as a young man—Robert Troup remembered him praying at King's College—and the Divinity of "The Farmer Refuted" is a lively force: He writes, He has a hand. Jefferson's "Summary View of the Rights of British North America," written a year earlier, declared, "The God who gave us life gave us liberty at the same time: the hand of force may destroy, but cannot disjoin them."[1] This God is a shade more discarnate. He gives, but "force" has the hand.

Real debate arose over human expressions and definitions of rights. Hamilton did not share his countrymen's confidence in the Bill of Rights. The Constitution as originally passed did not have one, and in *The Federalist*, No. 84, Hamilton dismissed the bills of rights that existed in state constitutions as "aphorisms . . . which would sound much better in a treatise of ethics than in a constitution of government."[2] Given his own reservations about the document, amply expressed in Philadelphia, he placed only a provisional reliance on the Constitution itself.

Hamilton was less interested in enumerations of discrete prohibitions or entitlements than in structures of thought. (He approached rights in the same way that he approached arguing.) The sources of his structures of thought were the legal traditions he had first encountered at King's College, then used as a lawyer, writer, and statesman: the common law of England, and the laws of nature as expounded by seventeenth- and eighteenth-century European jurists.

Many of the founders were lawyers—including thirty-four of the delegates to the Constitutional Convention—and all American lawyers had been trained in the common law. English common law was an accumulation of rulings by judges, in thousands of cases over centuries, of what rulers and men could and could not do to each other. The common law evolved fitfully. New decisions might cancel old ones, and still newer ones might retrieve rulings that had been canceled. A king or a parliament, with a decree or a law, might make a sudden sweep of a whole thicket of precedent; then, like seedlings after a fire, the precedents sprouted again.

A milestone in the development of common law was passed early in Hamilton's life, with the publication, in 1765, of the first volume of Sir William Blackstone's *Commentaries.* Commenting on the laws was not a routine or a passive exercise, but an act of redefinition. One of Blackstone's most famous comments was his contradiction of an earlier commentator, Sir Edward Coke. In 1608, Coke had ruled that the common law could "control" and "void" acts of Parliament that were against common right or reason. But Blackstone declared that he knew of "no power that can control" Parliament, no matter what absurdities it might enact. (Impressed by Blackstone, Americans promptly shifted the ground of their complaints against British laws from arguing that they were unconstitutional to denying that Parliament had any authority to meddle in colonial affairs in the first place.) One American lawyer, Thomas Jefferson, who had been trained before Blackstone appeared, resented his dominance. Fretting about the orthodoxy of law professors at the University of Virginia, he complained that Coke had once been "the universal elementary book of law students, and a sounder Whig never wrote." But when "honeyed . . . Blackstone became the students' hornbook, from that moment," the legal profession "began to slide into toryism."[3]

The European writers on natural law were among the blizzard of authorities young Hamilton threw at Samuel Seabury, when he recommended to his perusal "Grotius, Puffendorf, Locke, Montesquieu, and Burlamaqui." Hugo Grotius, Samuel Pufendorf, and Jean Jacques Burlamaqui were almost as well known in their day as Locke and Montesquieu. Emmerich de Vattel was another representative of their school. They all tried to find some common legal principles for a Europe divided between Catholics and Protestants, and warring great powers. Perhaps not coincidentally, they came from smallish European states— Holland (Grotius), Saxony (Pufendorf), Switzerland (Burlamaqui and Vattel). Some of them had actual legal responsibilities: Grotius represented the Dutch East India Company in a dispute over whether it could legally capture a Portuguese ship on the high seas. An air of pedantry and futility clung to these writers even in the eighteenth century (it overwhelms them now). Laurence Sterne took a crack at Dutch scholarship when he wrote of a man who had never profited "by one single lecture upon Crackenthorp or Burgersdicius, or any Dutch logician or commentator." Jefferson, arguing against the Neutrality Proclamation of 1793, dismissed the lot. "Those who write treatises of natural law, can only declare what their own moral sense and reason dictate. . . . Where they agree their authority is strong; but where they differ (and they often differ), we must appeal to our own feelings and reason to decide between them."[4] When Hamilton invoked their names as a teenager, he was mostly bluffing, for he had not read them as thoroughly as he let on. But their arguments would crop up in his legal work; the margins of his brief in *Rutgers v. Waddington* are sown with references to Grotius and Vattel, as well as Coke.

What captivated him in both the exponents of the natural law and those of the common law was their dual focus, encompassing precedent and theory. The commentators and the jurists looked for principles of justice that would apply to specific cases. The commentators sought them in English laws or the decisions of English judges; the jurists sought them in natural law, as divined by their own reasonings and by earlier jurists. Their attempts were sometimes chaotic, sometimes comprehensive. In an argument during a libel suit in 1804, Hamilton memorably defined the tradition at its best. "What is . . . the great body of the common law? Natural law and natural reason applied to the purposes of Society."[5] The hand of the Divinity, it seemed, could write in some musty treatises and commentaries.

Hamilton's interest in such writers strikes us as bizarre, for we are more familiar with other modes of rights talk. There is fundamentalism—honoring some code, usually the Bill of Rights, in the manner of cargo cultists in the South Seas who worship the airstrips where the DC-6s once landed, though they have no idea where they came from or why. Alternatively, there is pure philosophy. If natural law is in the nature of things, then we can (following Jefferson) simply consult our feelings and our reason, assisted perhaps by philosophers who were too lofty to be bothered with lawsuits: academics, scientists, or writers (Locke was a physician, Machiavelli wrote plays). Finally, there is the rights talk that dismisses rights altogether, seeing (with Aaron Burr) every legal action from the Hague to night court as a power struggle. Hamilton paid more respect to the materials of his profession, and hoped for more from them.

Hamilton's preoccupations seem as idiosyncratic as his sources. He was as apt to think of the rights of government as of the rights of man. In 1783, in a caustic letter to John Dickinson, president of the state of Pennsylvania, who had let mutinous soldiers chase Congress out of Philadelphia, Hamilton declared, "The rights of government are as essential to be defended as the rights of individuals. The security of the one is inseparable from that of the other."[6] American history is filled with conflict over states' rights. Hamilton pondered the state's rights.

He believed the rights of government and the obligation to defend them arose from the nature of governing. Hamilton's defense of the constitutionality of the Bank of the United States in 1791 turned on the idea that all governments possess certain powers by definition. He cited a special case: if the United States conquered territory in war, it would hold jurisdiction over it, based on "the whole mass of the powers of the government" and "the nature of political society" itself, rather than any "powers specially enumerated" in the Constitution.[7] Here, yet again, is the Hamiltonian tone deafness. Drawing analogies from conquered territories was not the way to convince a man like Jefferson on a question of constitutional law. On the other hand, when President Jefferson bought the Louisiana Territory in 1803, he would administer it on the basis of just these assumptions about government power and political society.

When Hamilton turned to Jefferson's magnum opus, the Declaration of Independence, he found very Hamiltonian things in it. In the Gettysburg Address, Lincoln invoked a line from the second paragraph: "all men are created equal." In *Rutgers v. Waddington*, Hamilton invoked a line from the second-to-last paragraph: "[T]hese united colonies . . . have full power to levy war, conclude peace, contract alliances, establish commerce, and to do all other acts and things which independent states may of right do." "BY THE DECLARATION OF INDEPENDENCE," Hamilton told the court, ". . . the UNITED STATES assert their power to levy war, conclude peace and contract alliances. . . . Congress had then complete Sovereignty!!!" Hamilton conceded that the government established by the Articles of Confederation "abridg[ed] those *Powers*." He went on: "But *mutilating as it is* [the Confederation] leaves Congress the full and exclusive powers of WAR PEACE & TREATY."[8] Lincoln conned the Declaration for lessons on human nature and self-government. Hamilton turned to it to nail down a different starting point: that the United States was a government, and therefore had the responsibilities and (unless it explicitly forswore them) the powers of all governments.

The strong verb *mutilating* implies that Hamilton wished the powers of sovereignty had remained uncurbed: why else compare a constitution to an act of violence? Yet he did not mean to turn government loose in a void. In *Rutgers v. Waddington*, defining the powers of the American government was his first step in binding it by the law of nature. Congress had signed the Treaty of Paris; treaties obey the law of nations; the law of nations obeys the law of nature. But for Hamilton all these higher laws operated on, and through, governments.

Two specific applications of natural law that arose repeatedly throughout Hamilton's career concerned contracts and slavery. One way to gauge a man's thought is by reading the temperature of his speech. The positions Hamilton expressed on contracts and slavery could be so vehement that they have the air of touchstones, or irreducible axioms.

The contracts Hamilton most often dealt with were debts, public and private. Over and over during the war, he wrote that America's habit of repudiating its debts would bring "contempt" and "disgrace." In his writings on the funding system, he raised the stakes. Paying debts was commanded by "the immutable principles of moral obligation"; it was an aspect of "the order of Providence." Debts ought "to be held sacred and inviolable. . . . Without this there is an end of all distinct ideas of right and wrong. . . ."9 He acknowledged only two exceptional reasons for overriding debts: to avoid fatal national calamities; or, he added slyly, to maintain the special privileges of feudalism. But who, one can almost see him glance at his critics (probably Virginians), could be in favor of that?

In the Camillus letters, he took up the question of private debts, still owed to British creditors since the war. These too were "sacred obligation[s]," enjoined by the common law and the law of nations (he threw in a footnote citing Grotius). "But let it not be forgotten," he added, that he derived this principle "from a higher source, from the natural or necessary law of nature—from the eternal principles of morality and good faith."10 Hamilton talked about the morality of contracts more often than he talked about morality.

He took contracts so seriously that in 1797 he even put in a good word for land speculators, not his favorite class of investor. Throughout the 1790s, the old Southwest—what are now the states of Alabama and Mississippi—was a wild tract known as the Yazoo country, inhabited by Indians, coveted by Spain, and ruled, to the extent it was ruled at all, by characters like James McGillivray, a half-breed Scottish-Cherokee chieftain. In 1795, the State of Georgia sold 35 million acres of Yazoo land to four land companies. But in 1796, a new legislature, swept in on a tide of public disgust—all but one of the old legislators had profited personally from the deal—canceled the sale. In 1797, the land companies asked Hamilton for a legal opinion, and he answered that "the first principles of natural justice and social policy" prevented states from revoking their own contracts.[11] The matter was not settled until 1810 when the Yazoo claims finally came before the Supreme Court in the case of *Fletcher v. Peck*; Chief Justice John Marshall upheld Hamilton's judgment.

Hamilton could speak with equal bluntness on the subject of slavery. At times, it is true, he let the question slide, as did all of the founders. The bitterest denunciation of slavery at the Constitutional Convention was uttered by Gouverneur Morris. "Upon what principle," he asked, should slaves be counted in determining a state's representation in Congress? "When fairly explained [the proposal] comes to this: that the inhabitant of Georgia and S. Carolina who goes to the Coast of Africa, and in defiance of the most sacred laws of humanity tears away his fellow creatures from their dearest connections & damns them to the most cruel bondages, shall have more votes in a Govt. instituted for protection of the rights of mankind, than the Citizen of Pa. or N. Jersey who views with a laudable horror, so nefarious a practice."[12] Hamilton did not speak to this, or any other slavery-related question, at the convention. From his King's College polemics on, he often wrote, with a confidence that the nineteenth century would make fanciful, as if clashes between North and South were minor, or would soon dwindle away. His economic system, it is true, aimed to eliminate sectionalism, and there were moments when the hope did not seem quixotic: the southern states actually sent a small majority of Federalist representatives to the Congress elected in 1798, at the height of the war scare. Hamilton's most important patron, George Washington, and one of his best friends, John Laurens, were both southerners.

Not that opposition to slavery was universal in the North. In 1785, Hamilton and thirty-one other New Yorkers—among them Aaron Burr—organized the Society for Manumission of Slaves. Hamilton, as chairman of the Ways and Means Committee, reported a resolution that members of the society begin their work by freeing their own slaves. The resolution failed. The society did, however, successfully push to make slavery illegal in New York—a considerable achievement in a state where slavery was a real presence. "The moment you . . . enter N. York," Gouverneur Morris had declared at the Constitutional Convention, "the effects of the institution become visible"; in the rural villages around New York City—Brooklyn, Flatbush—the slave population was as high as thirty percent. Many biographies and history books state that Hamilton himself owned slaves, though Forrest McDonald has shown that the supposed evidence for this conclusion has been misinterpreted (e.g., references in family correspondence to "buying" a girl refer to the contracts of indentured servants). In June 1804, Angelica Church wrote pityingly that her sister and her beloved brother-in-law were to host a breakfast, ball, and dinner, and yet "they are without a saelev [slave]" to help them.[13]

When Hamilton and John Laurens proposed to raise a regiment of freed slaves during the war, Hamilton wrote Jay, then president of Congress, with premodern frankness. "I have frequently heard it" said, he began, that blacks were "too stupid" to be soldiers. But stupid soldiers could be better than smart ones, if they had good officers. "The king of Prussia . . . maintains this doctrine." What was good enough for central Europe was good enough for South Carolina. Hamilton went on: "[T]heir natural faculties are probably as good as ours. . . . The contempt we have been taught to entertain for the blacks, makes us fancy many things that are founded neither in reason nor experience." He ended by fingering the source of that contempt: "an unwillingness to part with property of so valuable a kind, will furnish a thousand arguments" against black soldiers, or black freedom.[14] Lincoln would make Jefferson the grandfather of emancipation, for writing that all men were created equal, and rightly so. But the racist fantasies that disfigure the *Notes on Virginia*—that black faces show no emotion, that black artists show no talent, that blacks prefer to mate with whites even as orangutans prefer to mate with blacks—look cracked and shabby next to the plain talk of the colonel from St. Croix.

Slavery crossed Hamilton's desk again as a matter of policy during the debate over Jay's Treaty. Jay had been instructed to demand that

Britain return slaves liberated from rebel owners during the war. Britain's purposes had been primarily tactical, and only incidentally and inconsistently humanitarian: Sir Guy Carleton sent liberated slaves to Nova Scotia and freedom, while Lord Cornwallis shipped them to the Caribbean in exchange for supplies. In 1795, Americans had outstanding claims against the British for 2,000 slaves, worth $400,000. Hamilton advised President Washington that returning men to slavery would be "an odious thing, speaking in the language of the law of nations." In the Camillus letters, he went further: "In the interpretation of treaties, things *odious* or *immoral* are not to be presumed. The abandonment of Negroes . . . to fall again under the yoke of their masters, and into slavery, is as *odious* and *immoral* a thing as can be conceived."[15] A word like *odious* hardly needs italics; he italicized it anyway.

Did Hamilton see any link between the morality of contracts and the immorality of slavery, apart from the rhetoric he bestowed on them? In the case of Jay's Treaty, there was an incidental connection: reenslaving blacks, he wrote, would "impose . . . an act of perfidy on one of the contracting parties"—the British, who had promised liberty in return for loyalty. "The obligations which Great Britain had contracted towards the Negroes" made it impossible for America legally to demand their return. A moral contract trumped an immoral bond. More generally, slavery was the ultimate negation of contracts—the state in which a man lost the power to make his own arrangements. Only the contract that bound him had validity, and he had no role in making it. In his ironic acknowledgment of feudalism as a special case under which contracts might be superseded, Hamilton compared feudalism to slavery: the feudal privileges "which once oppressed all Europe, and still oppress too great a part of it . . . make absolute slaves of a part of the community, and rendered" most of the rest "not much more eligible."[16] Special privileges were the mark of despots and slave-owners. Contracts were the handiwork of free men.

Hamilton was disposed to take slavery and contracts seriously because of the circumstances of his upbringing. He came from islands where slaves outnumbered freemen twelve to one. Even his mother, when she was down on her luck, had owned slaves. Some combination of temperament, principle, and marginality caused him to dislike the institution rather than support it. But he could not ignore it. Nor could he ignore contracts. The islands were both dependent and isolated. Their necessities, to say nothing of their riches, were generated by exchanges with people hundreds of miles distant whom the islanders never saw. Contracts were their lifeblood. They were young Hamilton's livelihood, as he toiled for Nicholas Cruger in Christiansted. Slavery characterized a world that held nothing for him; contracts characterized that part of it which freed him. No wonder when he wrote about them he reached for words like *odious* and *sacred*.

Locke defined the rights of man as lives, liberties, and property—the formula that Jefferson, in the Declaration of Independence, amended to life, liberty, and the pursuit of happiness. Historians have argued ever since whether Jefferson meant his famous change to be a simple restatement, or a venture into new territory. If it was the latter, then Congress was either equally venturesome, or inattentive, because they let the phrase pass without comment. Indeed, the long second sentence of the Declaration (beginning "We hold these truths"), which describes human nature, the ends of government, and the conditions under which revolutions may legitimately occur, suffered only one minor editorial change. Congress tore the Declaration's particulars and its peroration to shreds; they left its philosophy unscathed, because it was common property. Yet despite their broad consensus, the founders actually held a range of opinions on the pursuits of property and of happiness—different views of the process, different visions of an acceptable result—differences reflecting their life experience.

In 1785, Jefferson wrote Madison from Fontainebleau, the king's residence in hunting season. While out walking, he had met a poor woman laborer; heard her hard life story; and given her the equivalent of a shilling, at which she burst into tears of gratitude. This poignant episode set off in Jefferson a "train of reflections" on the grossly unequal distribution of land and wealth in France, which ended with this thought: "The earth is given as a common stock for man to labor and live on. If for the encouragement of industry we allow it to be appropriated, we must take care that other employment be provided to those excluded from the appropriation. If we do not, the fundamental right to labor the earth returns to the unemployed."[17] He suggested that inequality in land could be lessened by abolishing primogeniture (under which entire estates passed to only one heir, the eldest son), and by progressive taxation of land.

Two years later, in New York City, the recipient of this letter addressed the question of property rights in *The Federalist*, No. 10. There Madison wrote that, of the many sources of faction, the "most common and durable" was the "unequal distribution of property." Would he start worrying about the old woman and her lack of shillings? No: he argued that inequality exists because government "protect[ed] different and unequal faculties of acquiring property." Indeed, the protection of these faculties was government's "first object."[18] Politics could be stabilized by playing factions off against each other, but factions based on inequality could never be abolished, because inequality was natural.

The two Virginians were not in fact that far apart. The landless laborers that appalled Jefferson were peculiar to France—products of the feudalist monopolies that Hamilton would write about. Primogeniture had just been abolished in Virginia, thanks to Jefferson, and he never again proposed progressive taxation. Jefferson and Madison did not think the economic inequality that existed in America was inherently bad, and Madison believed he had a solution for the political problems it caused. (Slavery might have upset the neatness of their calculations, but they did not consider it.)

Another way in which they agreed, particularly in contrast to Hamilton, was that their discussions of "labor" and "faculties" were notably static. Jefferson thought that laboring was an end of man—something men do, and have a right to do. He also thought that the reward of property encourages industry. But so long as feudalism was not in the way, he was not curious about the effects of labor or industry on the industrious. Madison also assumed that men work, and that they brought to their work different capacities and talents: hence the different rewards they earned. But he too probed no further. He wrote of faculties almost as givens, like programming or genes. Some people will get rich, some won't; he left it at that, and called in the referee.

Naturally, Jefferson and Madison thought so, given their backgrounds as rich powerful men raised by rich powerful men. Born on third base, they had a short trip to home plate. They had to have faculties of the highest order to become great men, but it was guaranteed that whatever faculties the sons of Virginia aristocrats possessed would have free play. Their station in life did not determine their ideas or their character, but it did fix the plane on which they moved. Hamilton turned out to have faculties equally great, if not greater. Yet, as the son of a ne'er-do-well, then of a single mother, then of no one, he knew he might easily have languished in obscurity, or fallen below mediocrity. That is why Hamilton's thoughts about labor and industry were so much more detailed, dynamic, and earnest. He knew from his own life that opportunities did not merely display men's faculties, but shaped them, and that the vigor of a man's nature could be lost in the absence of congenial pursuits. Rights talk could not stop with hypothetical qualities men had at birth. It had to account for the "spirit of enterprise" that helped men make themselves. The goal of a statesman was to ensure that that spirit had the widest possible range of objects. Hamilton, who wrote of "the busy nature of man," knew that a man's business developed his nature.

Jefferson and Madison thought about the problem of human development when they thought about education. Jefferson, in particular, thought about education often: writing letters of pedagogical advice to his children and nephews; drawing up public education laws for the state of Virginia; helping Washington with a plan for a national university; throwing himself, with Madison's help, into the University of Virginia, building the buildings, designing the curriculum, overseeing its affairs, and finally leaving instructions that these efforts be commemorated on his tombstone. Hamilton was also concerned with education, in a less monumental way. He became a trustee of his alma mater after the war, when it changed its name from King's College to Columbia, and he was a trustee and namesake of the Hamilton Oneida Academy, founded deep in upstate New York to educate whites and Indians together (Jefferson sent the school some shade trees). The Reverend Samuel Kirkland, the academy's founder, believed that the differences between the races were "not so much owing to nature as to education"[19]—a sentiment more in accord with Hamilton's letter on black soldiers than with the *Notes on Virginia.* Ironically, the school's most famous graduate, long after it became Hamilton College, was Ezra Pound, a great admirer of Jefferson, among others.

School ends; work does not. Hamilton believed in property as firmly as any disciple of John Locke. He had no intention of handing it out to anyone for nothing. He wanted women and children to work; he wanted the poor to work; he wanted Americans to work. "We labor less now than any civilized nation of Europe," he had complained to Robert Morris when he was on Washington's staff, "and a habit of labor in the people is as essential to the health and vigor of their minds and bodies, as it is conducive to the welfare of the state."[20] Work helped America, but it helped Americans too. They had selves to make.

Chapter Nine

Passions

RIGHTS SPRING FROM the law of nature, and words were the primary medium in which Hamilton's peers expressed and debated them. Words laid down the law. But there was a third force in their political world, natural but not always lawful: the passions.

In 1797, when Hamilton had just turned forty, he wrote a letter to his uncle, William Hamilton, Laird of the Grange, the family seat in Scotland. It was the first time the American Hamilton had communicated with his Scottish relatives, and he gave a thumbnail sketch of himself: his "steady and laborious exertion" at King's College; his service in the Revolution ("I . . . engaged in some interesting operations"); his success as a lawyer ("a very lucrative course of practice"). He spent two paragraphs on his six years as secretary of the treasury, and while he did mention that he had managed to introduce "order in the finances," he mostly wrote of the difficulties and the attractions of the job (since he had quit two years earlier, the difficulties were foremost in his mind). The problems of his tenure were caused by "passions, not very worthy," but "common to human nature, and which act with peculiar force in republics"; he mentioned "jealousy of power," and the "spirit of faction." The gratifications of public service included not only "the opportunity of doing good," but also "the love of fame, if that passion was to be the spring of action."[1] If that passion was not to be the spring of action, why mention it? So the very act of discounting his motive drew attention to it.

Some passions were bad—the passions of Hamilton's enemies fi-

nally made his job no longer worth doing. But some could be good—
the love of fame spurred him to take it in the first place. This was no
discovery of Hamilton or the founders, for like philosophers for thousands of years, they sought ways to sift the passions, encouraging some,
neutralizing others. Sometimes they resemble engineers, blithely tin-
kering with the engines of humanity. Ambition, Madison declared in
The Federalist, No. 51, must be made to counteract ambition. "I do not
know that passion is ever to be reasoned down," wrote Fisher Ames;
"but other passions could be reasoned up to resist the prevailing one."
"The true politician," wrote Hamilton in an unpublished essay on the
funding system, "will seek . . . to lead [man] to the development of his
energies according to the scope of his passions."[2] Such adjustments are
never as easy as they sound, however. The passions *are* energies. They
know only themselves, and have a way of careening around the most
well-designed systems.

Each founder had his own characteristic language of passion, and
his own special objects. The tone of Jefferson's emotions is typically
vivid, but detached. Before he wrote his flirtatious letter to Angelica
Church, he wrote a much longer one to Maria Cosway, a woman with
whom he was seriously infatuated. This is the famous dialogue of the
Head and the Heart, which the Heart finally wins. But the form of the
letter to Maria—four thousand words of laboriously written whimsy
(literally: he had broken his right wrist while picnicking with her)—
makes it a not very convincing victory. As minister to France, Jefferson
had a ringside seat on one of the most tumultuous events of his lifetime,
apart from actual battles: the start of the French Revolution. His reports on it, like his comments on Shays's Rebellion across the sea, can
seem almost eerily aloof. One letter to Paine contains this odd image:
the National Assembly showed "a *coolness*, wisdom and resolution to set
fire to the four corners of the kingdom" rather than back down (emphasis added).[3] Did the old world end in fire, or in ice? For Jefferson, it
ended in icy fire.

The passion in Washington's heart was violent anger. Hamilton
saw glimpses of it: in their argument at the top of the staircase; at the
battle of Monmouth (if Hamilton did not actually witness the explo-

sive encounter with Charles Lee, he saw the commander-in-chief often throughout that day, during which "trace[s] of displeasure" clung to him). Hamilton saw another eruption at one of the daily cabinet meetings during the Genet crisis. Knox read to the group an antiadministration satire in Freneau's *National Gazette,* which ended with a fantasy of Washington going to the guillotine. The president, noted Jefferson in his journal, "got into one of those violent passions where he cannot command himself." Hamilton, perhaps because he had seen the spectacle before, felt no need to make a note of it. Washington mostly controlled his temper, but he never expunged it from his character. Although "thousands" of other men "have learned to restrain their passions," said Gouverneur Morris in his eulogy for Washington, "few among them had to contend with passions so violent."[4]

Hamilton did not have a violent temper. The foolish aggressiveness of such work as the open letter to Adams came from pride and stubbornness rather than rage. He had, rather, an all-pervading ardor. He loved his ideas, his work, and his friends. One evening when Hamilton and other New York lawyers were riding the circuit along with Judge James Kent, Kent retired early, feeling ill. Later that night, Kent overheard Hamilton come into his room to put an extra blanket on him: "Sleep warm, little judge, and get well. What should we do if anything should happen to you?" He was not an "indifferent mortal," Hamilton confessed to the Poughkeepsie convention. His ardor had a partly physical basis in his high-strung temperament. His intensity undermined his health, even as it contributed to what Adams called his "effervescence." McHenry (who had been a surgeon) fretted about him during the Revolution, telling him to cut down on milk, and on wine. "The great Paracelsus," he warned, "trusted to [a] pill to destroy the effects of intemperance, but he died (if I forget not) about the age of 30 notwithstanding his pill."[5] Schuyler told his daughter in 1799 to make sure that her husband did not overwork himself, and that he ride every day.

One passion often found in financiers is the love of money. Robert Morris, Hamilton's predecessor under the Articles of Confederation, and William Duer, Hamilton's assistant, loved money so well, and so recklessly, that they both went to debtors' prison. Certainly, Hamilton assumed acquisitiveness in others, while his enemies assumed it in him: James Callender charged that greed, not lust, bound him to the Reynoldses, while Commodore Nicholson whispered that he had stolen 100,000 pounds on the job. "Had a long discourse in the Committee Room" on Hamilton's speculations, wrote Senator Maclay in his diary. "No Body can prove these things but every body knows them." Every body was mistaken, however. Despite relentless congressional investigations, Hamilton was never found to have mishandled, or pocketed, a dime of public money. His friends, particularly McHenry and Troup, urged him to make money in private life—Betsey "has as much merit as your Treasurer as you have as Treasurer of the wealth of the United States," McHenry chided him—and while he boasted to his Scottish uncle of his lucrative practice, his periods of public service, the distractions of journalism, and his own scruples kept his income as a lawyer below what it might have been. Hamilton hopefully put his income at $12,000 a year; Ames guessed it was $6,000 to $10,000. He preemptively gave up his veteran's benefits while debating the issue in Congress in the early 1780s, lest he seem self-interested, and after returning to private life in 1795, he turned down an offer from Troup to assist some British land speculators because a British business connection might spoil his prospects for future public office. "There must be some *public fools* who sacrifice private to public interest," he told Troup, and "my *vanity* whispers I ought to be one" of them.[6] The italics suggest a degree of preening that is self-conscious, even self-mocking. Hamilton knew that the alternative to Troup's offer was not the poorhouse. Had he lived to his biblical span, he would have left his large family in comfort, if never wealthy. Still, it was true that other people's money was always more interesting to him than his own.

One passion that Hamilton notoriously felt was lust. He was not the only founder to succumb to it: Franklin had an illegitimate son, and Gouverneur Morris, despite a peg-leg which he acquired after a carriage accident, managed while living in Paris to detach a mistress from Talleyrand. But Hamilton was the only founder to admit it in any detail (Franklin in his posthumous *Autobiography* mentioned that he had "intrigues with low women," though his illegitimate son is simply omitted). Even now, in an era of gossip as reporting and confession as a spectator sport, the Reynolds pamphlet remains the frankest admission of adultery by any major American politician. The press rewarded his candor by never letting him forget it. The "frosts of America are incapable of cooling your blood," one paper wrote. He had made his house a "rendezvous of . . . whoredom," wrote another. During the New York Assembly elections of 1800—three years after the scandal broke—a Republican paper snidely described Hamilton campaigning to disheartened Federalists: "[H]e talks of perseverance, and (God bless the mark) of virtue!" Still later, the Reynolds affair drew from John Adams a masterpiece of vituperation: Hamilton's ambitions, he thought, had their source in "a superabundance of secretions which he could not find whores enough to draw off."[7] Even now, in an era of talk radio and TV talk shows, this is unsurpassed.

Hamilton on more than one occasion used sexual imagery to condemn his opponents. In his letter to Edward Carrington, he deplored Jefferson's "womanish attachment to France," and "womanish resentment against Great Britain." During the Genet crisis, he wrote in an article that, while a "virtuous Citizen . . . will regard his own country as a wife," there were Americans who "have a passion for a foreign mistress; as violent as it is irregular; and who, in the paroxisms of their love" are "too ready to sacrifice the real welfare of the . . . family, to their partiality for the object of their tenderness." These metaphors yield their full jolt when they are put in the chronology of the Reynolds affair. Hamilton wrote about womanish emotions to Carrington as he was trying to bring the affair to an end, despite Maria's pleas (and his own susceptibility to them). The article contrasting marital and extramarital love appeared a few months after the accusatory congressmen had appeared in his office. Hamilton knew what he was writing about—better than Carrington or his Philadelphia newspaper readers suspected. Even after he had exposed himself in the Reynolds pamphlet, he continued to treat sexual subjects. One of his charges against France during the war crisis of 1798 was that the Revolution had enacted a divorce law "which makes it as easy for a husband to get rid of his wife, and a wife of her husband, as to discard a worn-out habit."[8] There is something both painful and gallant about a man who had been unfaithful to his wife defending the institution of marriage; he would not let his conduct drive him from his principles.

During the eighteenth century, the word "licentious" meant what it means now—lacking sexual restraint. But it also described those not bound by any laws. (Probably the word has come to focus on sexual anarchy because sexual laws are the most fun to break.) Hamilton was always more alarmed by licentiousness in its second, now uncommon meaning. Long before the French Revolution got around to changing the divorce laws, he was writing Washington about the "licentiousness and disorder" it had shown in its early stages. He had worried about licentiousness in the early stages of the American Revolution, when he wrote John Jay about the patriotic manhandling of James Rivington: when "the passions of men are worked up to an uncommon pitch," they "seem to grow giddy and are apt . . . to run into anarchy."[9]

On one occasion, Hamilton looked for license in the wrong place. During the Newspaper War, writing as "Catullus" (not the poet, but a Roman politician), he took a swing at Jefferson, whose "vizor of Stoicism" and "plain garb of Quaker simplicity" concealed an "Epicurean" and a "voluptuary."[10] Both features of this indictment—the supposed pretense, and the supposed reality—show how wildly Hamilton was swinging. Jefferson never pretended to live the simple life; he was a connoisseur of wine, food, and music, and an avid collector of books, knickknacks and *objets d'art*. When the capital moved from New York City, Jefferson furnished his Philadelphia house with ninety-eight cases of imported furniture, statuary, and wine; Hamilton in his capacity as treasury secretary let it all in duty free, except for the wine and 145 rolls of wallpaper. On the other hand, Jefferson's most furtive passion (for Sally Hemings) stayed unproven so long in part because of his ability to detach himself from it. Hence his bright confidence in so many things that alarmed Hamilton; he could calmly envision a revolution every twenty years, or even half the earth desolated, because he could not really *see* either. Defended against their power, he did not fear the passions, except those of anglomen and monocrats.

Hamilton, more ardent, was more aware of passion's dark side. In his "Letter from Phocion," he warned of "the furious and dark passions of the human mind"—not the minds of remote villains but of the New Yorkers he was addressing. In *The Federalist*, No. 6, he told New Yorkers and Americans that men are "ambitious, vindictive, and rapacious." Collectively, they love power; individually, they are prey to all manner of "attachments" and "enmities," and to prove it he called a roll of destructive historical figures, beginning with Pericles, who were driven by private grudges and affections. Last on the list was Daniel Shays ("a *desperate debtor*"). It had happened in America; it could happen again. "Is it not time to awake from the deceitful dream of a golden age" and see "that we, as well as the other inhabitants of the globe, are yet remote from the happy empire of perfect wisdom . . . ?" In his letter on Rivington, Hamilton had told Jay, with all the seriousness of an eighteen-year-old, that his analysis of popular passions had been confirmed by "reading, and by my own experience."[11] But Jefferson was at least as well read as he was, and had ample political experience. Hamilton had different experience of his heart. And of the hearts of his parents—adulterers and deserters both. He was spared two dark passions, greed and rage. But he knew enough of one form of licentiousness to fear the other.

A passion that all the founders looked on with mistrust was ambition. They distrusted it even though they all, by definition, felt it. (If they had been content to stay at home, they would not have been founders.) Yet they believed that any one among them, if he loved his own glory too much, could bring the republic down.

The founders had an almost dismayingly austere example of ambition successfully applied and properly curbed in the career of George Washington. Fisher Ames's account of Washington's earnest and abashed demeanor as he read his First Inaugural Address captured in a nutshell what most of the founders felt about him most of the time. Ames, who was on his way to becoming the best orator of his generation, watched the performance like a critic on opening night. Why was it so moving? Gradually, the answer dawned on him: *He really means this.* "It seemed to me an allegory in which virtue was personified, and addressing those whom she would make her votaries."[12] The founders watched Washington walk the tightrope of ambition with fear, and anxiety: afraid that he might slip into self-aggrandizement; afraid that, if he did slip, they might not mind (who would make a better home-grown king?). His success forced them all to live up to their ideals.

The ambitions of lesser mortals were more problematic. To cope with them, the founders devised checks and balances: Madison's *Federalist*, No. 51, laid out a scheme of "opposite and rival interests," like the equal and opposite reactions of a physics textbook. They scanned each other with eagle eyes, watching for the moment when unseemly ambition might raise its head. When Jefferson left Washington's cabinet, Adams wrote his son John Quincy that Jefferson hoped "to get a reputation of an humble, modest, meek man, wholly without ambition or vanity. He may even have deceived himself into" thinking that he was one. But "ambition," the father warned, "is wonderfully adroit in concealing itself from its owner."[13]

The founders' model of uncurbed ambition came from the ancient world: Julius Caesar. Madison took such careful notes at the Constitutional Convention because he had found, in his researches, that the origins of governments were so scantily described. But there was no need to take notes about the end of the Roman Republic, or Caesar's role in it, for they had been immortalized by Plutarch and Shakespeare. The founders watched for portents of a similar end to their own venture. Since Caesar had been most famous as a general, the most obvious form for a successor to take would be the man on horseback. In August 1779, Major Henry (Light-Horse Harry) Lee, an impetuous cavalry officer, drove the British out of an important outpost on the New Jersey shore of New York Bay. Lee was "an officer of great capacity," Hamilton wrote John Laurens, but added that he had "a little spice of the Julius Caesar. . . . If he had not . . . he would be a very clever fellow." (Lee had proposed the previous year to decapitate deserters, and was told by Washington not to do it, but had gone ahead and done it anyway.) Eight years later, Hamilton wrote in *The Federalist*, No. 21, that it was a lucky thing the "malcontents" of Massachusetts had been led by a Shays instead of a Caesar.[14]

But Caesar had been most dangerous as a politician, concealing his ambition as he gratified it, aping republican forms and sentiments while he made his way to the top. "When that the poor have cried, Caesar hath wept;/Ambition should be made of sterner stuff." It was, but it wore a human face. In his long August 1792 defense of his measures submitted to Washington, Hamilton saw Caesarism in the populist and libertarian rhetoric of his critics. "It has been aptly observed, that *Cato* was the Tory, *Caesar* the Whig of his day.... When a man, unprincipled in private life, desperate in his fortune, bold in his temper, possessed of considerable talents, [and] having the advantage of military habits" joins "in the cry of danger to liberty . . . it may justly be suspected that his object is to throw things into confusion, that he may 'ride the storm and direct the whirlwind.'"[15]

Hamilton had a specific man in mind. It was not Jefferson, but Aaron Burr, who was then considering a run for vice president. Jefferson, much as Hamilton disliked him, was not desperate in his fortune, and had no military habits. Burr was a bold, talented colonel, perennially in debt, and unapologetically, if discreetly, licentious. "If we have an embryo-Caesar in the United States," Hamilton wrote another correspondent a month after his memo to Washington, "'tis Burr."[16] He held the same opinion eight, and twelve, years later.

Hamilton's critics tried to pin the Caesar label on him. For many years, a pair of 1787 New York newspaper articles signed "Caesar" were routinely assigned to Hamilton. The New York Caesar wrote to rebut a series of attacks on the Constitution by George Clinton, signed "Cato." But there was not much in Caesar's roughshod style or arguments that recalled Hamilton (or even the historical, ingratiating Caesar). "I am not one of those who gain an influence by cajoling the unthinking mass (tho' I pity their delusions).... I despise the trick of such dirty policy.... For my part, I am not much attached to the *majesty of the multitude.* . . ." The letters might better have been signed "Coriolanus." In fact, they were written by one John Lamb. Days later, the Constitution acquired a better defender in "Publius."[17]

The strongest link between Hamilton and Caesar was made by Thomas Jefferson. In 1811, he wrote a letter describing the dinner in Philadelphia twenty years earlier at which Adams and Hamilton had praised the British system, but added this detail. "The room being hung around with a collection of the portraits of remarkable men, among them . . . Bacon, Newton and Locke, Hamilton asked me who they were. I told him they were my trinity of the three greatest men the world had ever produced. . . ." For Jefferson to call these three the "greatest" was a revaluation of a widely accepted scale of human achievement, formulated, ironically enough, by one of his three idols— the seventeenth-century scientist and philosopher, Sir Francis Bacon. Bacon had placed founders of states at the pinnacle of fame; Jefferson was supplanting them with philosophers. Since he had claims to both roles, his choice was a fair test of his inclinations. Hamilton, Jefferson went on, "paused for some time: 'the greatest man,' said he, 'that ever lived, was Julius Caesar.'"[18]

This would have been as troubling to Jefferson as Hamilton's praise of corruption—if Hamilton actually said it. Hamilton's 1791 praise of Caesar is bracketed by hostile references, public and private, from 1779 to 1792. In a verbose life, he made no other endorsement of Caesar's greatness. Jefferson did not record the comment in his journals, only in a letter two decades later, when he was sixty-eight years old. Perhaps Hamilton, with his flair for annoying his colleague, had praised Caesar. If so, it ran counter to the mass of his judgments.[19]

It also ran counter to Washington's estimate of him. When Adams balked at appointing Hamilton second-in-command of the army in 1798, the commander-in-chief sent the president a sketch of his former aide. "By some, he is considered as an ambitious man, and therefore a dangerous one. That he is ambitious I shall readily grant; but it is of that laudable kind which prompts a man to excel in whatever he takes in hand."[20] America's preeminent master of ambition had judged Hamilton's character and saw in it no threat to the republic.

One other passion, like ambition, that could be laudable or destructive, bulked large in Hamilton's life and times—the passion for honor. Nations and individuals had honor that they were obliged to defend. Hamilton urged the United States to uphold its honor by paying its debts, following the rule of law, and avoiding the weakness that invites depredations. He upheld his own by serving in the army, discharging his financial duties honestly, and defending his record, even at the expense of exposing an affair or assailing a president. There was another forum, however, in which honor could be challenged and defended, besides the courts, the marketplace, or the newspapers, and that was the dueling ground.[21]

When we think of dueling in America, we think of cowboys or would-be cavaliers: *High Noon* or John Randolph of Virginia dueling Henry Clay of Kentucky. Randolph had compared Clay to a mackerel by moonlight—he shone and he stank. Clay challenged, they fought, and Thomas Hart Benton of Missouri called it "the last high-toned duel that I have witnessed, and among the highest toned I have ever witnessed," which was "due to the noble character of the seconds as well as to the generous and heroic spirit of the principals."[22] But like most of what we think we know about dueling, these stereotypes are misconceptions. Dueling was a practice, and an issue, for the founders too.

Duels were originally a degeneration of the judicial combat: the battle between principles or their champions that showed God's judgment. When dueling took hold in England in the seventeenth century, justice and God had dropped out of the equation. The laws did not recognize the practice (the English legal commentators equated deaths in duels with murders), and while Providence could be said to determine the outcome, it was a remote and fickle Providence, compounded of chance and human will.

Many of the founders deplored dueling, by word and example. Franklin attacked the "murderous practice" in typical fashion, with two arguments and a joke. "How can such miserable worms as we are entertain so much pride, as to [suppose], that every offense against our imagined honor, merits death?" In dueling, "every one . . . makes himself judge in his own cause—condemns the offender without a jury—and undertakes to himself to be the executioner." This argument addresses another misconception, this one romantic, that duels were well-regulated affairs of honor. There were written codes—one of the most popular in the English-speaking world had been drawn up in Ireland in 1777—and for each duel, the seconds drew up rules to cover details, such as the weapons and the commands. But the crucial decision—

whether to shoot to kill—depended solely on the vengefulness of the principals. Then came Franklin's punchline. "A gentleman in a coffee house desired another to sit further from him.—'Why so?'—'Because, Sir, you smell.'—'That, Sir, is an affront, and you must fight me.'—'I will fight you if you insist, but I don't see how that will mend the matter; for if you kill me, I shall smell too; and if I kill you, you will smell, if possible, more than you do at present.'"[23]

When he was a young man, Washington avoided a duel, an incident that was seized upon by his moralizing biographer, Parson Weems. Washington had fallen into a political argument with a man named Payne who, though he was shorter, managed to knock him down with a club. The next day Washington "went to a tavern, and wrote a polite note to Mr. Payne, whom he requested to meet him. Mr. Payne took it for a challenge, and repaired to the tavern, not without expecting to see a pair of pistols produced." Instead, there was "a decanter of wine and glasses on the table," and Washington apologized for quarreling, and shook hands.[24] For many years this story was doubted, simply because Weems had told it. But historians have concluded that, unlike the story of the cherry tree, it actually happened.

As an even younger man, Aaron Burr gave a paper in his college literary club against dueling. "I have courage to fight with feeble man," he read, "but I am afraid to sin against Almighty God."[25]

But despite these sentiments, there were numerous duels in the founding period, particularly in the army. The rarest and most valuable signature of any signer of the Declaration of Independence is that of Button Gwinnett. He produced so few because he died in 1777 in a duel with a fellow officer in the Georgia militia. Both the Conway Cabal and the court-martial of Charles Lee generated duels. Conway was called out and shot through the jaw ("I have stopped the damned rascal's lying tongue," his opponent boasted);[26] Lee was challenged by three officers, including John Laurens. Some of these contestants had imbibed notions of honor prevailing in the foreign armies in which they had served (Conway and Lee were Europeans). But the others, like Laurens, were all-American. The decisive factor was that they were officers, accustomed to command and to violence, and hence susceptible to dueling. Though Washington had chosen not to duel Payne, he also chose not to forbid his officers from dueling each other.

Laurens's second in his duel with Lee was Hamilton. When the first shots resulted in a wound to Lee, the seconds and the principals had a talk. Laurens said he was there because "General Lee had spoken of General Washington in the grossest and most opprobrious terms." Lee "said every man had a right to give his sentiments freely of military characters." But he denied ever abusing Washington "in the terms mentioned . . . because he had always esteemed General Washington as a man" and "because such abuse would be incompatible with the character he would ever wish to sustain as a gentleman." In fact, Lee thought, and often said, that Washington was an untutored rube, while one of Lee's aides, emulating his chief, called Hamilton a "son of a bitch." But the exchange of sentiments satisfied Lee and Laurens, and their seconds wrote that the two gentlemen had shown the "politeness, generosity, coolness, and firmness that ought to characterize a transaction of this nature."[27]

The war ended, but dueling did not. In 1797, George Thacher, a congressman from Massachusetts, was challenged by a congressman from North Carolina. Thacher turned the challenge aside. But a year later, Brockholst Livingston, of the New York clan, killed a Federalist in a duel across the Hudson in Weehawken, New Jersey. The fatal result did not diminish Livingston's reputation, for President Jefferson appointed him to the Supreme Court. Dueling followed regional lines, though not the simple line of South versus North. New Englanders could dismiss challenges without losing caste. Ames wrote of the Thacher affair as a scrape with peculiar foreigners, much as Bostonians a century later would write of encounters with French waiters or Italian touts. In New York, dueling was illegal, which is why New York City duelists crossed the river to New Jersey, which also prohibited it but penalized it less severely. But New Yorkers took it as seriously as southerners.

In 1787, one of Hamilton's clients asked him to be a second, but Hamilton advised him to "be content with *enough* for more ought not to be expected." Hamilton nevertheless came close to dueling himself several times in the 1790s: with James Monroe; with one of the Livingstons; and with Aedanus Burke, a South Carolina congressman who took offense at his eulogy for Nathanael Greene (Hamilton had called the militia a "mimicry of soldiership," and Burke, a militia veteran, resented the staff officer's scorn).[28] But each quarrel had been composed short of the dueling ground. One of Hamilton's in-laws was not so adept. In 1799, Angelica's husband, John Church, went to Weehawken to fight Aaron Burr, in a quarrel arising from a deal between New York State and a Dutch land company. Burr on one side, and Hamilton, Schuyler, and Church on the other had each tried to help the speculators by lobbying the legislature. When Burr got his deal through, Church accused him of bribing the lawmakers, hence the duel. Burr misfired, Church nicked a button on Burr's coat. The two men declared themselves satisfied, and sailed home.

Hamilton gave his mature opinion of affairs of honor in his last major argument before a court, in February 1804. Duels, he declared, were forbidden "on the principle of natural justice, that no man shall be the avenger of his own wrongs, especially by a deed, alike interdicted by the laws of God and of man."[29] What had seemed polite, generous, cool, and firm when he was twenty-one, now seemed, when he was forty-seven, prohibited by nature, God, and man. But he had had more experience of dueling before making this statement.

All the passions—greed, licentiousness, ambition, and honor carried to excess—elevated the self above its proper role in a republic. Men in the grip of them broke laws, contracts, and vows, and threatened homes, states, and the peace of society. But the passions also commandeered selves, and made men their instruments. A true politician should not encourage passions that impede the development of man's energies. But passions need little encouragement, and they were not always amenable to the founders' recommendations.

Chapter Ten

Death

FOR HAMILTON, the Jefferson administration was a looking-glass world. His old opponent in the cabinet was president; his collaborator-turned-opponent, James Madison, was secretary of state; and Albert Gallatin, the "Swiss incendiary" whom he had thought of arresting during the Whiskey Rebellion, held his old job as secretary of the treasury. Yet Jefferson's inauguration, the first to be held in Washington, D.C., was notably pacific. The new president foresaw an end of partisanship itself. "We are all republicans— we are all federalists," he declared. Hamilton, for his part, welcomed Jefferson's inaugural address as a "retraction of past misapprehensions."[1] But in case conflict should arise again, Hamilton founded a newspaper, the *New York Evening Post*.

Among the notable Federalist editors of the past decade, John Fenno of the *Gazette of the United States* had died, William Cobbett had been forced to return to England, and Noah Webster, an Adams loyalist, had called Hamilton, after his Adams letter, "the evil genius of this country." So for the first editor of his paper, Hamilton picked a thirty-five-year-old lawyer and writer, William Coleman. Coleman had been born in a Boston poorhouse, had studied law with Aaron Burr, and had written a pamphlet on the Levi Weeks murder trial. As editor of the *Evening Post*, Coleman had a measure of independence, sometimes taking positions that Hamilton disagreed with. But most of the editorials on important topics came from Hamilton directly. Coleman described the process: "He appoints a time when I may see him . . . as soon as I see him he begins in a deliberate manner to dictate and I to note down in shorthand; when he stops, my article is completed." Editing the *Evening Post* was a rough-and-tumble assignment: Coleman fought a duel, with the city's harbormaster, whom he killed. Afterward, he "got out the paper in good style, although half an hour late." Many leading Federalists were skeptical of newspapers, as they were becoming skeptical (having lost) of politics itself. Ames compared newspapers to thermometers: they "show what the weather is, but will not make it better." Hamilton had higher hopes for the *Evening Post*. "It is the *Press* which has corrupted our political morals—and it is to the *Press* we must look for . . . regeneration."[2] The paper started publication in November 1801.

In its eighth issue, it reported a duel involving Hamilton's eldest son, Philip, who was nineteen years old. Of all the Hamilton children, Philip had the paternal temperament, if not the talents. When he was fifteen, he boasted to his father of a speech he had given at Columbia as an exercise in rhetoric. His professor "had no objection to my speaking," though he had "blotted out" the "most animated" sentence. ". . . you may recollect it—*'Americans, you have fought the battles of mankind; you have enkindled that sacred fire of freedom which is now,'* and so forth." When Philip graduated from college, he studied law, according to a regimen dictated by his father. "RULES FOR MR. PHILIP HAMILTON From the first of April to the first of October he is to rise not later than six o'clock; the rest of the year not later than seven. If earlier, he will deserve commendation. Ten will be his hour of going to bed throughout the year. From the time he is dressed in the morning till nine o'clock (the time for breakfast excepted) he is to read law. At nine he goes to the office, and continues there till dinnertime. . . . After dinner he reads law at home till five o'clock. . . . From twelve on Saturday he is at liberty to amuse himself."[3]

One evening for amusement, Philip and a friend went to see a play, *The West Indian,* a melodrama set in the Caribbean. In the next box they spotted George Eacker, a young Republican politician, who had given a Fourth of July speech that year accusing Alexander Hamilton of wanting to use the army to suppress Republicans. The charge, a staple of Republican polemic, had been old hat when Eacker made it, and was by then four months older. Nevertheless, young Hamilton and his friend went into Eacker's box and made jeering remarks about the orator. Eacker declared that he would "not be insulted by a set of rascals."[4] The discussion continued outside the theater, and in a tavern, where the two Federalist wits demanded to know who Eacker meant to call rascals. Eacker replied, both of them, and challenges followed. Philip told his uncle, John Church, who tried to negotiate a settlement, in vain. Eacker met Philip's friend first, at Weehawken, where they exchanged four shots, without injury, and declared themselves satisfied. The next day, Eacker met Philip, who had borrowed his uncle's pistols for the interview, the same set that Church had used in his duel with Burr two years earlier. Eacker's first shot struck Philip above the right hip, and lodged in his left arm.

Hamilton was taken back to New York to the Churches' house, and "the news spread like a conflagration," as one of his Columbia classmates wrote. "On a Bed without curtains lay poor Phil, pale and languid, his rolling, distorted eyeballs darting forth the flashes of delirium—on one side of him on the same bed—lay his agonized father—on the other his distracted mother. . . . returning Home I quickened my pace almost unconsciously, hoping to escape the image as well as the reality of what I had witnessed!"[5] Philip lingered for fourteen hours, then died.

The *Evening Post* reported that Hamilton had been "murdered in a duel," and called for "strong and pointed legislative interference" with "this horrid custom. . . . Fashion has placed it upon a footing which nothing short of this can control." It also wrote that Philip, conscious that he had given the first provocation, had resolved to hold his fire. The Republican press came to Eacker's defense, and pointed out, reasonably enough, that if Philip was conscious of "Being in fault," he should have apologized. The Irish Code Duello indeed prohibited "dumb shooting or firing in the air. . . . The challenger ought not to have challenged without receiving offense; and the challenged ought, if he gave offense, to have made apology before he came on the ground: therefore, *children's play* must be dishonorable. . . ."[6]

The blow struck another young Hamilton: Angelica, the second oldest, who had just turned seventeen. She could not accept what had happened; for the rest of her life (and she lived to be seventy-three), she spoke of her dead brother as if he were still alive. Mrs. Hamilton, who was two months pregnant, gave birth to her last son the following June: his parents named him Philip.

Hamilton was crushed. "Never did I see a man so completely overwhelmed with grief," wrote Troup. "My loss is indeed great," Hamilton wrote Benjamin Rush, a Philadelphia Republican who had sent his condolences. "But why should I repine? It was the will of heaven, and he is now out of the reach of the seductions and calamities of a world full of folly, full of vice, full of danger. . . ."[7] It was heaven's will, in the sense that all things are, but that will operates through natural and human circumstances, and one of these had been Hamilton's career— which had supplied the subject of Philip's quarrel with Eacker. This was reason to repine.

There was a heavier reason for Hamilton's grief. The *Evening Post* implied that Philip's "numerous relations" had not known of the duel beforehand (though Church clearly had). The classmate who described Philip's deathbed wrote a different story: "General Hamilton heard of [the duel] and commanded his Son when on the ground to reserve his fire 'till after Mr. Eacker had shot and then to discharge his pistol in the air."[8] Killing men in duels was immoral, though dueling, it seems, was not. This was terrible advice to have given. James Hamilton, Sr., had been a bad father and an irresponsible man, yet he had never given lethal advice to his sons. How much better a father, for all his solicitude, had Alexander been?

The remaining years of Hamilton's life were never entirely free of the pall of depression. There would be periods of light and activity, but his life, as he turned forty-five, had entered another season. "What can I do better than withdraw from the scene?" he wrote Gouverneur Morris in February 1802. "Every day proves to me more and more, that this American world was not for me."[9] Morris and Hamilton had been corresponding about Federalist politics, and Hamilton, disagreeing with him, had made his familiar complaint about his countrymen. But the phrase now had a deeper shade. He was complaining less about America than the world—the world of folly, vice, and danger.

. . .

Partisanship, as Hamilton had foreseen, returned, and the election of 1802 was as squalid as that of 1800. Federalist journalism had received a new recruit—James Callender, who joined the staff of the *Richmond Recorder*, the better to torment his new enemy, President Jefferson, in his home state. Callender now wrote that Jefferson had subsidized him during the 1790s, which was true, and that Jefferson had a slave mistress, Sally Hemings, a story the American id embraced, even before genetic testing, not caring whether it was true. Federalist hacks and versifiers went wild.

> *What though she by the glands secretes;*
> *Must I stand shil-I shall-I?*
> *Tuck'd up between a pair of sheets*
> *There's no perfume like Sally.*

Such ditties (one was written pseudonymously by John Quincy Adams) managed to be anti-Jefferson, implicitly antislavery, and grossly racist all at the same time. The *New York Evening Post* spared its readers the poems, but reprinted Callender's original stories, including the Sally Hemings scoop. The latter drew from Hamilton a disclaimer in his own paper, deploring "all personalities, not immediately connected with public considerations."[10] Callender had forced Hamilton to expose his sins, and Hamilton was not going to encourage him to traduce his enemy.

These thrashings had no effect politically. Jefferson had cut taxes, and commerce flourished in a temporary worldwide peace. Buoyed by popular esteem, the president struck back. His first step was to muzzle the Federalist press. The evil of the Sedition Act and the sufferings of its victims had been major Republican themes in the election of 1800, but state sedition laws met with Jefferson's approval, so long as they were enforced by Jeffersonians. In a letter to the governor of Pennsylvania, after fretting that "licentiousness" would deprive journalism of "all credit," Jefferson suggested that "a few prosecutions of the most prominent offenders would have a wholesome effect in restoring the integrity of the presses. Not a general prosecution, for that would look like persecution, but a selected one. . . ."[11] Jefferson also moved to purge the judiciary, which Adams, in his last act as president, had packed with Federalists, and to cut back the navy (Paine would explain that America's harbors could be adequately defended by rowed gunboats).

Disheartened by these policies, and by their own failure, northern Federalists—there was hardly any other kind left—sunk into a depression of their own. A final blow for them was Jefferson's greatest success, the Louisiana Purchase in 1803. The Purchase eliminated the threat of a Napoleonic army on America's borders, and opened half a continent. Hamilton admitted, in the *Evening Post*, that Louisiana was "an important acquisition," though he thought seizing it would have been cheaper than buying it, and judged that the land to the west of the Mississippi would be "a wilderness . . . for many years, if not centuries to come." His fellow Federalists were incensed rather than grudging, for they saw the Purchase as a field for carving out new Republican states. "The otters would as soon obey" American laws and customs, wrote Ames, as the "*Gallo-Hispano-Indian* . . . savages and adventurers" the nation had acquired. Republicans already dominated the South, and the larger middle states. With the states made from the Louisiana Purchase, they would, or so the Federalists believed, enjoy a permanent margin in Congress and the Electoral College. The leading voice of Federalist dismay was Timothy Pickering, newly elected a senator from Massachusetts. Pickering's solution was secession—"a new confederacy" of New England and New York, "exempt from the corrupt and corrupting influence and oppression of the aristocratic Democrats of the South." One of Pickering's Federalist colleagues, shocked by his train of thought, asked him if disunion "was not the object which General Washington most pathetically warned" against in the Farewell Address. "Yes," Pickering answered, "the fear of it was a ghost that for a long time haunted the imagination of that old gentleman."[12]

A third depressed politician was Vice President Burr, whose national career effectively ended before it began. Burr's reticence during the election deadlock of early 1801 had banished whatever disposition Jefferson had to trust him. The president instead allied himself in New York with George Clinton, who had been reelected to his seventh and last term as governor, and with the Livingstons (Jefferson avoided Hamilton's mistake of 1789 by promptly naming Robert R. Livingston minister to France). Burr found himself cut out of federal patronage in his own state. In 1802, a new Republican journalist in New York City, an Englishman with the wonderfully appropriate name of James Cheetham, began attacking Burr, seemingly out of the blue. In fact, Cheetham had been corresponding secretly about Burr with the president ("I must pray you, after reading this to destroy it," Jefferson wrote, since a "certain description of persons are so industrious in misconstruing . . . every word from my pen"). Burr finally confronted Jefferson at the White House, asking why his assailant held the contract for publishing federal laws in New York. Jefferson responded that the contracts were assigned by the secretary of state, "without any reference to me," and said he had ignored Cheetham's attacks "as the passing wind." Burr knew he was a marked man.[13]

Hamilton worked through his depression in several ways. In the spring of 1802, he sent James Bayard, his correspondent during the election crisis, a proposal for a new national organization, the Christian Constitutional Society. The Federalists, he wrote, had "erred in relying so much on the rectitude and utility of their measures." Instead, they needed to "take hold of, and carry along with us, some strong feelings of the mind" in order to "cultivat[e] . . . popular favor." The strong feelings he proposed were those evoked by the Constitution, and Christianity. These "good passions" might overcome the "vicious" ones encouraged by Republicanism.[14]

There is a calculating, instrumental tone to Hamilton's treatments of religion in the late 1790s, from his attacks on French atheism, to his discussion in the Farewell Address of religion and morality as "props" sustaining society. (Washington's own words on Providence—as in his First Inaugural—though doctrinally reticent, are, by comparison, awed and earnest.) His proposal for a Christian Constitutional Society dovetails with this tone. It is certainly a discouraging retreat from his earlier frankness. Yet it also suggests that he had come up against a limitation of his worldview. Hamilton had been a pious boy, at King's College, and on St. Croix, under the influence of the Reverend Hugh Knox. Philip's death brought a return of his devotion, in a melancholy mood. In later years, his sane, surviving children remembered him reading the Bible to them and praying with them. The Christian Constitutional Society never materialized, and the Federalists continued their long decline, broken only by temporary benefits from Republican mistakes.

He threw himself into building a house in northern Manhattan, nine miles from town. He had bought the property, about thirty acres, in 1800. He borrowed $5,000 from Lewis LeGuen, the client for whom he had won the $120,000 settlement. The builder was Ezra Weeks, brother of Levi. John McComb, who also worked on New York's present City Hall, was the architect. Hamilton called the house the Grange, after the family seat in Scotland. The bay windows had sweeping views of the Harlem River to the east and the Hudson to the west. (The house now stands wedged between a church and a tenement, and has no views at all.) James Kent, who stayed there once in a storm, wrote that "the second storey . . . rocked like a cradle" in the wind. Hamilton put thirteen gum trees in a circle on the lawn, but, as one of his children recalled, he planted them too closely, and they "languished and died." In December 1802, Hamilton wrote Charles Pinckney from the Grange asking for melon seeds and Carolina paroquets for Angelica—"she is very fond of birds." He added: "*As farmers,* a new source of sympathy has arisen between us." This was joshing. The Grange was not a working farm, still less an estate like Pinckney's or Schuyler's or Gouverneur Morris's. It was a country house, and a retreat. Elsewhere in the letter, he put it plainly. "A garden, you know, is a very useful refuge of a disappointed politician."[15]

Hamilton may have been a disappointed politician and a disappointed man, but he was still the best lawyer in New York, and early in 1804 he argued *The People* v. *Croswell,* the last important trial of his career. The case arose from Jefferson's desire for "a few prosecutions" of Federalist journalists. Ambrose Spencer, the state attorney general, settled on Harry Croswell, publisher of the *Wasp,* a small weekly sheet in the town of Hudson, thirty miles south of Albany. (Spencer was a recent convert to the Republican party, and a frequent target of the *Wasp*—extra motives for zeal.) During the campaign of 1802, the *Wasp* had accused President Jefferson of "hostility" to the Constitution, and of paying James Callender for "grossly slandering" leading Federalists. In January 1803, Croswell was indicted for seditious libel. "The torrents of slander which pour from the press opposed to government," said Spencer, "must be checked."[16]

Croswell's lawyers filed numerous motions for delay, one on the grounds that they wished to summon Callender himself to testify. But in July, Callender was found dead in three feet of water in the James River (the coroner's jury ruled that he had drowned accidentally while drunk). Spencer was prepared to argue that Callender's testimony was irrelevant in any case, for under the common law of libel, truth was not a defense. All that had to be proved was that a seditious libel—a statement bringing a public figure into public contempt—had been printed. Croswell was convicted, but his lawyers moved for a new trial—a motion heard by the State Supreme Court, sitting in Albany in February 1804.

Hamilton had by then joined Croswell's defense team (Coleman had been covering the case in the *New York Evening Post*). Hamilton made his concluding argument over two days, during which he spoke for six hours; the courtroom was packed, in large part with lawmakers, for the legislature was sitting in Albany, though it did little business when Hamilton performed.

It was in this speech that Hamilton defined the common law as "natural law . . . applied to the purposes of Society," and, in passing, condemned dueling. He contrasted the current common law of libel with older, better precedents—"extraneous bodies grafted on the old trunk"—and with the Sedition Act, which had admitted truth as a defense. But the main line of his argument examined libel as a legal and political fact. He agreed that there were libels that should be illegal, whether they were true or false, such as those that "disturb[ed] the peace of families" (his own family, for instance?). But political leaders, in their political capacities, had to be open to critics, however harsh, who told the truth. "At all times men are disposed to forward principles to support themselves. . . . such is the natural Progress of the Passions." But "we have been careful that when one party comes in, it shall not be able to break down and bear away the others. . . . To watch the progress of such endeavors is the office of a free press. To give us early alarm and put us on our guard against the encroachments of power. . . . To make the people exercise their own functions." He concluded: "Never can tyranny be introduced into this country by arms; these can never get rid of a popular spirit of enquiry. . . . It is to be subverted only by a pretence of adhering to all the forms of law, and yet by breaking down the substance of our liberties. By devoting a wretched, but honest man as the victim of a nominal trial." Madison in *The Federalist* had sought to defend freedom through checks and balances. For Hamilton, at the end of his career as all through it, the bulwark of freedom was words—his, Croswell's—and the people's willingness to weigh them. James Kent, who was one of the four judges hearing the case, called Hamilton's argument "a master Piece of Pathetic, impassioned & sublime Eloquence. . . . I never heard him so great."[17]

Hamilton's eloquence went for nought, as far as the case at hand: the judges split evenly, on party lines, and the motion for a new trial failed. The legislature however passed a new law of libel, conforming to Hamilton's arguments, in April 1805. Hamilton was not available for congratulation.

. . .

Eighteen-four was yet another election year, and Jefferson's enemies had to consider what, if anything, they could do. In February, the Republican party caucus in Congress ratified the hopeless meeting Aaron Burr had had at the White House by choosing, as the party's vice presidential candidate, George Clinton (who had let it be known that he would look on the vice presidency as a "respectable retirement").[18] By this vote, Burr was formally an outcast from his party. Before that happened, he had dined in Washington with half-a-dozen disappointed spirits in the Federalist party, including Timothy Pickering.

The Federalists who came to dinner, all New Englanders, told Burr that the United States "would soon form two distinct & separate governments." One of them remembered Burr agreeing that this would happen—though he later realized that Burr had not committed himself as to whether it should happen. If it did happen, the New England Federalists wanted New York to secede with them. Whatever his thoughts on the union, Burr wanted Federalist support in New York for his next political move—running for governor. If Clinton had taken Burr's place, perhaps Burr could take Clinton's—but given Jefferson's hostility to him, he could only do it as a fusion candidate, combining his personal following and the state's Federalists. In February, a Federalist meeting at Lewis's City Tavern in Albany showed strong sentiment for Burr's candidacy. Burr's "views," wrote a Federalist secessionist hopefully, "must extend beyond the office of Governor of New York. He has the spirit of ambition and revenge to gratify. . . ."[19]

The spirit of ambition had sunk in Hamilton, but he still distrusted Aaron Burr as a politician. In Albany to defend Harry Croswell, he attended the meeting at the tavern in order to attack Burr. Federalists, he argued, had long believed that Burr was "a man of irregular and unsatiable ambition."[20] One Federalist, at least, had long believed it. Why should Burr have changed? If he had not changed, how would a man of his character fit with their principles? Burr had two spies under a bed in an adjoining room who heard everything that was said.

Hamilton also rejected Timothy Pickering's plots. John Quincy Adams, the other Federalist senator from Massachusetts, though not a secessionist, happened to call on Rufus King in New York in March. When he arrived at King's, who should be leaving but Pickering. King then told Adams that his colleague had been talking up the northern confederacy—"and he has also been this day talking of it with General Hamilton." King added, "I disapprove entirely of the project; and so I am happy to tell you does General Hamilton."[21]

New York voted for governor in April. Burr ran as the Federalist; the regular Republicans ran Morgan Lewis, a decent hack and a Livingston in-law. Though Burr did well in New York City—Coleman, his former clerk, endorsed him in the *Evening Post*—he lost overall, by a vote of 30,829 to 22,139—the greatest defeat in any New York governor's race so far. New York would not be joining the northern confederacy anytime soon; Pickering, nothing daunted, planned a meeting of secessionists in Boston for the fall.

Pickering could look ahead because he was a man of convictions, albeit fanatical ones. If the Union was a devil's bargain with a "corrupt and corrupting" South, then it still deserved to be broken up, however many reverses the incorruptible experienced. Burr had no such resources. He was not a vindictive man, but his situation was bleak. He had toyed with the secessionists to keep himself in play, without success. His bills could be evaded as long as he held office; soon they would come due. Assuming (as narcissists always do) that he had no responsibility for his predicament, there were two men who had brought him to this pass: Jefferson and Hamilton. Only one of them had made a habit of expressing his opposition openly.

In late June, Hamilton received a note from Burr asking him to explain certain statements. They were neither recent nor clear. Two items had appeared in an Albany newspaper in April, recounting a dinner conversation about the governor's race. The writer quoted Hamilton as saying all the usual things about Burr, then added that he had uttered "a still more despicable opinion."[22]

It would dignify the mummeries that followed to describe them in detail. Letters were exchanged. Burr found Hamilton's evasive; Hamilton found Burr's puzzling. In a note to his second, William P. Van Ness, Burr complained that Hamilton had for years been making "base slanders," which Burr declined to "particularize." Burr felt he had "exercised forbearance till it approached to humiliation," but enough was enough. Hamilton wanted to know exactly what Burr objected to—which opinion? more despicable than what?—then gave his second, Nathaniel Pendleton, a statement offering to "disclaim and disavow . . . any expression tending to impeach the honor of Col. Burr."[23] But by then, the machinery of dueling had gone too far.

Hamilton was granted brief delays to put his affairs in order. He made a will, which was sanguine as to his assets, and wrote something like an apology for building the Grange. "Men who have been so much harassed in the busy world as myself . . . look forward to a comfortable retirement." He calculated that if he continued to earn $12,000 a year during the period of his "full energy," while lowering his expenses to $4,000 a year, he could pay off his house and other debts. He also expected the Grange's value to increase because of "the progressive rise of property on this island."[24] He visited the law office of Egbert Benson, whom he had argued against in *Rutgers v. Waddington,* and rather obviously left a note in a volume of Pliny. It turned out to be an assignment of authorship for *The Federalist Papers.* He claimed too many for himself; Madison's counterclaim, years later, was also too generous. The work outlives the authors, and the argument.

He wrote two letters to his wife, who, since only a handful of gentlemen had been told of the affair, had no idea what was unfolding. In one, he explained that he would have avoided "the interview" if possible. "But it was not possible, without sacrifices which would have rendered me unworthy of your esteem." As he had in the Reynolds pamphlet, he was binding her to his view of his "name." In the other letter, he explained what that view now entailed. "The scruples of a Christian have determined me to expose my own life to any extent, rather than subject myself to the guilt of taking the life of another. This much increases my hazards, and redoubles my pangs for you. But you had rather I should die innocent than live guilty. . . . Adieu, my darling, darling wife." He attended the Fourth of July banquet of the Society of the Cincinnati, the organization of Revolutionary War officers which, since the death of Washington, he had headed. As the evening wore on, he stood on the table and sang favorite soldiers' songs, including "The Drum."[25]

> 'Twas in the merry month of May
>> When bees from flower to flower did hum.
> Soldiers through the town marched gay,
>> The village flew to the sound of the drum.
>
> The clergyman sat in his study within
> Devising new ways to battle with sin:
> A knock was heard at the parsonage door,
> And the Sergeant's sword clanged on the floor.
>
> "We're going to war, and when we die
> We'll want a man of God nearby,
>> So bring your Bible and follow the drum."

Colonel Burr also came, did not sing, and left early. The interview was set for the morning of July 11, at Weehawken, where Philip had been killed. Hamilton borrowed John Church's pistols, the same which Philip had used.

Each particular of the duel—Hamilton's failure to explain himself; Burr's exasperation; the caliber and construction of the pistols; Hamilton's expressed intention of wasting his shot; Burr's evident intention of not wasting his—has been seized on by some historian, biographer, journalist, or partisan of one of the duelists, as unusual, and therefore requiring special explanation (which, if supplied, will explain the event, and the participants, usually in some revisionist fashion). But the premise that generates these exercises is faulty. There is no rule or pattern of dueling that some duel did not violate. For all its sheen of rhetoric and punctilio, dueling was an arbitrary system—as arbitrary as the law often is, or as Burr thought it necessarily was, with the difference that it was more often lethal. It was chance and wrath disguised as order. No wonder that many of the founders, including Hamilton by this point in his life, deplored it.

Why then did Hamilton go through with it? Many of his supporters, and a few of his enemies, prompted by some "explanatory . . . remarks" that he left, along with his will and his letters to Betsey, have assumed a political explanation. "The ability to be in future useful," Hamilton wrote, "whether in resisting mischief or in effecting good, in those crises of our public affairs which seem likely to happen . . . imposed on me (as I thought) a peculiar necessity not to decline the call." The "crises" he had in mind could only refer to the double maneuvers of the winter and spring—Burr's appeal to the Federalists, Pickering's appeal for a northern confederacy—which he had opposed, and which he could be counted on to oppose again when the secessionists caucused in Boston in the fall. Enemies of Hamilton hold that he wanted to be the military leader of the confederacy himself (an unlikely ambition for a man who had put down two rebellions in Pennsylvania and who despised the revolution in France: one revolution had been enough for his lifetime). The more likely view is that, in order to prevent Burr from seizing such a role, he believed that he must meet his challenge on the field of honor. Hamilton's credibility as a supporter of the Union and a critic of Burr required him to face Burr's fire. The night before the duel, Hamilton wrote a note to Theodore Sedgwick, a Massachusetts congressman. "[D]ismemberment of our empire will be a clear sacrifice of great positive advantages . . . administering no relief to our real *disease,* which is *democracy,* the poison of which, by a subdivision, will only be the more concentrated in each part. . . ."[26] How much more concentrated, if one of the parts was led by a Caesarean figure like Aaron Burr?

This is a reasonable explanation of Hamilton's frame of mind, though the frame of mind was not reasonable. The secessionists were, to a man, New Englanders, and New England was the region of the country where dueling had no hold. Who among the die-hards of Massachusetts and Connecticut would be impressed by an interview in New Jersey? Who would be scandalized by Hamilton's declining to participate?

The larger cause of his actions was the somber coloring of his life for almost three years. John Randolph shrewdly observed of the Hamilton-Burr correspondence when it was published that "it reminded me of a sinking fox pressed by a vigorous old hound" (if he had added that the hound was desperate, the comparison would have been perfect). Hamilton could think about the law and the press with all his old clearness, but he could not think clearly about himself. Or perhaps, unbeknown to himself, he was thinking very clearly. He had written Betsey that, by reserving his fire, he might "live innocent" rather than "die guilty."[27] He would follow the advice he had given their son Philip. If it was innocent advice then, it would be innocent still; if guilty, it would be doubly so, though he would pay the penalty.

New Yorkers have written about the hazes of the Hudson since Washington Irving, and experience them still. The morning of the eleventh was muggy. The principals and their seconds left their homes at five o'clock. Burr and Van Ness arrived at Weehawken first. Dr. David Hosack, a physician and botanist, stayed with the boatmen out of sight, in case he was needed. The regulations of the interview, as agreed by the seconds, required that the pistol barrels be no longer than 11 inches. Church's pistols had 9-inch barrels, and were .544-caliber—enormous by modern standards, though dueling pistols tended to have large bores. Pendleton asked Hamilton if he wanted the hairspring set (a hairspring is a mechanism that would give the trigger a much lighter touch). He said, "Not this time."[28] The distance agreed upon between the two men was ten paces—about twenty feet. At the command "Present," the two pistols went off almost simultaneously. As with many important events in Hamilton's life, there is a disputed account. Van Ness afterward claimed that Hamilton fired first, though Pendleton maintained that Burr had, and that Hamilton's shot was a convulsive contraction. (The letters to Betsey support Pendleton; Van Ness's version was typical of postduel damage control.) Hamilton's bullet went high and wide, shearing off the branch of a cedar tree. Burr's pierced Hamilton's abdomen.

The vice president moved as if to help his stricken foe, but Dr. Hosack and the boatmen were coming up, so Van Ness hustled him off (if there was a trial, the doctor had to be able to swear truthfully that he had not seen the victor on the field). Dr. Hosack found Hamilton half-sitting in Pendleton's arms. "His countenance of death I shall never forget." "This is a mortal wound, Doctor," Hamilton said, then fainted. They hurried him to the boat, hoping that the river air, muggy as it was, would revive him. When he opened his eyes, he happened to see his pistol in the boat. "Take care of that pistol," he said, "it may go off and do harm." He was taken to the house of a friend in Greenwich Village.

Although Dr. Hosack administered laudanum, the patient's pain was "almost intolerable. I had not the shadow of a hope of his recovery," but other doctors were called to confirm the diagnosis. (Dr. Hosack later explored the wound and found that the bullet had passed through the liver and the diaphragm, and lodged in the spine. "The vertebra in which it was lodged was considerably splintered. . . .") The Right Reverend Benjamin Moore, Episcopal bishop of New York, and president of Columbia, was also summoned, for Hamilton wished to take communion. But the bishop did not want to give it too hastily to a duelist. He came back again in the afternoon and asked Hamilton to consider "the delicate and trying situation in which I was placed."[29] They considered the bishop's situation together, and also Hamilton's. The dying man abjured dueling, confessed his faith in God's mercy through Christ, and forgave Burr.

Betsey was first told that her husband was suffering from spasms. "No one dare tell her the truth," Oliver Wolcott, who happened to be in town, wrote his wife; "—it is feared she would become frantic." Wolcott was not calm himself. "Thus has perished one of the greatest men of this or any age. I am as well as could be expected, considering how my mind is agitated." When Betsey learned the truth, she did become frantic; Hamilton calmed her by repeating, *"Remember, my Eliza, you are a Christian."*[30] He fell silent once, when his children, from Angelica to two-year-old Philip, were brought in to see him. Once again, a Hamilton father was abandoning his family. He lingered for more than thirty hours, and died on the afternoon of the twelfth.

The next day Wolcott, the assistant, the admirer, the man of no genius, wrote his wife another letter in which he allowed himself to be angry. "Nothing can present a more humiliating idea of the imperfection of human nature than the scene we have witnessed." What good was Hamilton's "respect for justice in comparatively small matters," shown by his preduel preparations, when he had "disregard[ed] its obligations on points of the first importance"? Wolcott knew the political argument for the duel: he had alluded to it in his first letter, and he did not buy it. ". . . it proves, that on certain points, the most enlightened men are governed by the most unsound reasons."[31]

Burr, who lived in Greenwich Village, had sent a note to the death house, asking after Hamilton's health. As the mood in the city turned ugly, he began to think of his own. (The Republican press, which had never had a good word to say for Hamilton, now wailed for him as a martyr, the better to defame Burr.) The vice president went to Philadelphia, where he dallied with an old flame. "If any male friend of yours should be dying of ennui," he wrote his daughter, "recommend him to engage in a duel and a courtship at the same time."[32] He moved on to South Carolina, where he stayed with his son-in-law, and with Pierce Butler, one of Hamilton's colleagues at the Constitutional Convention.

Opinion in the South was, on the whole, favorable to him; some Virginia Republicans gave a banquet in his honor.

Hamilton's notable peers reacted in character: Jefferson included him in a list of "remarkable deaths lately" in a letter to a European friend, and made no other comment. Adams had several reactions: he called it an end fit for a "caitiff," or a cowardly wretch, but he also exclaimed, "No one wished to be rid of him in that way!" Fisher Ames managed a sentence that was both well-crafted and moving. "My heart . . . grows liquid as I write, and I could pour it out like water." A professional peer offered this tribute: "In my defense, and that of the American press," wrote Harry Croswell, "this greatest of men made his mightiest effort."[33]

New York City declared the day of the funeral, July 14, an official day of mourning, which was appropriate: the funeral procession, which took the coffin from the Churches' house on what is now Park Place, and made a near-circle of town until it arrived at Trinity Church, passed within sight of many places important in both Hamilton's and the city's history: St. Paul's Chapel, the old Federal Hall, Hanover Square, the Battery—speeches, trials, riots, gunfire. The procession itself had a military cast, which was less appropriate. It was led by his riderless horse, with boots and spurs reversed; soldiers and drummers accompanied it; the foreign ships in the harbor, French as well as British, fired minute guns. Hamilton had his glory and his achievements as an officer, but they were only a portion of him.

The eulogy was delivered by Gouverneur Morris, who did not effectively complete the portrait. Morris had known Hamilton for almost thirty years, and had seen much of him during his years at the Grange. But Morris brought conflicting emotions to the task. He wrote in his diary before the funeral that Hamilton "was on Principle opposed to republican and attached to monarchical government." No more than Morris himself, who said at Philadelphia that America had better strike a bargain with a king while it could make a good one, though Hamilton had expressed his doubts more pungently even than Morris. Morris held that against Hamilton too: "He was indiscreet, vain and opinionated." In the eulogy, this became, "he bore" his heart "as it were in his hand." The speech as a whole was rhetorical and diffuse, though on the day it was given the city was so stunned and seething, Morris hardly needed to say anything. Afterward, Morris imagined himself as Mark Anthony: "How easy it would have been to make them, for a moment, absolutely mad!"[34]

Biography ends with death, but when a man is killed in middle age, it is tempting to imagine what he might have done had he lived out his natural life span. Hamilton would have opposed the secessionists—the Boston meeting was canceled after he was killed—but the movement probably would have collapsed under the weight of Burr's frivolity and Pickering's seriousness without him. In an era of Republican dominance, public office could never have returned to him, even if he had sought it. His best work probably would have been done as a lawyer; the landmark cases of the next decades that used his arguments—*Fletcher* v. *Peck, McCullough* v. *Maryland*—might have been argued by him in person.

It is possible to look beyond the action to see what became of his contemporaries. Philip Schuyler died of age, grief, and gout three months after his son-in-law; his affairs were scarcely in better shape than Hamilton's, and Betsey got little from him. She had to sell the Grange, and apply to Congress for the veteran's benefits her husband had forsworn. Her children, except for Angelica, had decent, middling lives. Betsey wore mourning until she died, age ninety-seven, in 1854.

Thanks to a renewed world war and his own embargo, Jefferson's second term was as disastrous as his first had been brilliant. James Madison succeeded him, presiding over two terms that were even worse. In 1811, the charter of the Bank of the United States expired. Madison and Gallatin by then favored renewal, but the Senate was tied, and Vice President George Clinton voted against the bank, with the result that when the United States a year later declared war on Britain, it had no funds to sustain it. Military failure revived the secession movement; only peace, and the battle of New Orleans, retrieved the debacle.

Aaron Burr, after laying aside his office, turned his eyes west. He floated down the Ohio to the Mississippi with a party of armed men, intending to attack Mexico, or to split off the western United States—historians still do not know which. Undoubtedly, he did not know himself. He was turned in by his chief coconspirator, James Wilkinson. Acquitted of treason, he lived for a time in Europe, wearing his duel like the medal of some select order. Was Hamilton a gentleman? he was once asked, and answered, "Sir, I met him."[35] Returning to New York, he married a rich widow, a former prostitute, who lived in a house about a mile from the Grange. When he began running through her money, she divorced him.

In their long retirement, Thomas Jefferson and John Adams reestablished their friendship, and in an exchange of immortal letters, looked back on 1776, and arranged themselves for futurity. They died on the same day, July 4, 1826. Adams's last words were about Jefferson; Jefferson's were about the Fourth.

Of all the great Virginians, James Monroe had the most successful presidency, in part because his party had by then adopted much of the Federalist program. When Monroe was an old man, he paid a call on Mrs. Hamilton. A nephew was with her when his card came in. "Her voice sank, and she spoke very low, as she always did when she was angry. 'What has that man come to see me for?' escaped from her. 'Why, Aunt Hamilton,' said I, 'don't you know, it's Mr. Monroe, and he's been President, and he is visiting here now in the neighborhood, and has been very much made of, and invited everywhere, and so—I suppose he has come to call and pay his respects to you.'" She said she would see him.

Monroe, who made a little speech about forgiving and forgetting, deserves credit. He alone of his circle made an effort to bridge the personal gap, and he had much to bridge, given his role in the Reynolds affair. He does not deserve much credit, though, for he was saying nothing substantive, only trying to soothe himself, and perhaps an old woman.

For decades, she had said little; before she died, she would burn her letters. Now she spoke. "Mr. Monroe, if you have come to tell me that you repent, that you are sorry, *very* sorry, for the misrepresentations and the slanders, and the stories you circulated against my dear husband, if you have come to say this, I understand it. But, otherwise, no lapse of time, no nearness to the grave, makes any difference." By slanders, she did not mean stories about her husband's whoring, which were true, but stories about his corruption, which were false. In life, he had insisted on holding himself, and her, to his view of his public duties, however painful (as during the Reynolds affair) or obviously wrong (as before the duel). She was upholding their choice now. Monroe left.[36]

That was a message in the history of the Hamilton family. There was another, important to the history of Hamilton's country. Hamilton left a multitude of messages, in papers, speeches, articles, and letters; he had trouble making them short. But Gouverneur Morris managed an epitome in his eulogy. It was the one thing the eulogy got right, but it was the most important thing Hamilton had to say. It came at the point of the speech when Morris touched on Hamilton's death—the moment he imagined he could have driven the crowd mad.[37] "On this last scene," he said, "I must not dwell. It might excite emotions too strong for better judgment." He urged them to be orderly, and unlike Mark Anthony, he urged them sincerely. "Suffer not your indignation to lead to any act which might again offend the insulted majesty of the law." The message went beyond one audience, and one passion. It expressed Hamilton's methods as a politician, and his hopes for his fellow citizens. It was the best he had to offer. "From his lips, though with my voice—for his voice you will hear no more—let me entreat you to respect yourself."

Notes

Hamilton's papers are available in Harold C. Syrett et al., eds., *The Papers of Alexander Hamilton* (New York: Columbia University Press, 1961–87)—hereafter cited as *PAH*—and Julius Goebel, Jr., ed., *The Law Practice of Alexander Hamilton* (New York: Columbia University Press, 1964–81)—hereafter cited as *LP.* Also valuable is Allan Maclane Hamilton, *The Intimate Life of Alexander Hamilton* (New York: Charles Scribner's Sons, 1910), a collection of letters and anecdotes (cited as *IL*).

Hamilton is less well served outside libraries. *The Federalist Papers* can be found in every bookstore, along with Forrest McDonald's *Alexander Hamilton: A Biography* (New York: W. W. Norton & Co., 1979), an excellent book, especially strong on his policies and his intellectual influences. But there is little else by or about him. Michael Lind's *Hamilton's Republic* (New York: Free Press, 1997) contains brief selections from the "Report on Manufactures" and the Pacificus letters. John Steele Gordon's *Hamilton's Blessing* (New York: Walker & Co., 1997) is a history of the national debt, which begins with Hamilton. Richard Morris's *Alexander Hamilton and the Founding of the Nation* (New York: Dial Press, 1957), a one-volume anthology of his writings, can still be found in secondhand shops. There is no equivalent in print.

I have modernized most punctuation and spelling, except in cases where it is interesting or important: Hamilton at age twelve, Lafayette's franglais, and the letters of Mr. and Mrs. Reynolds.

Introduction

1. Fisher Ames, *The Works of Fisher Ames*, as published by Seth Ames, edited and enlarged by W. B. Allen (Indianapolis: Liberty Classics, 1983), p. 1386; John C. Miller, *Alexander Hamilton: Portrait in Paradox* (New York: Harper & Bros., 1959), p. 502.

2. Max Farrand, *The Records of the Federal Convention* (New Haven, Conn.: Yale University Press, 1937), app. A, p. 89; *PAH*, V: 348.

3. Robert A. Hendrickson, *The Rise and Fall of Alexander Hamilton* (New York: Van Nostrand Reinhold Co., 1981), p. 10.

4. Miller, p. 523.

5. Aristotle, *Politics*, b. I, chap. 11.

6. Paul Rahe, *Republics Ancient and Modern* (Chapel Hill: University of North Carolina Press, 1994), III: 313.

7. Miller, p. 358; Ezra Pound, *The Cantos* (New York: New Directions Publishing, 1975), p. 350.

8. Dumas Malone, *Jefferson and the Rights of Man* (Boston: Little, Brown & Co., 1951), p. xxii; Thomas Jefferson, *The Life and Selected Writings*, ed. Adrienne Koch and William Peden (New York: Modern Library, 1944), p. 521; Conor Cruise O'Brien, *The Long Affair* (Chicago: University of Chicago Press, 1996), p. 150.

9. *PAH*, XXVI: 309; James Madison, *Debates in the Federal Convention of 1787*, ed. James McClellan and M. E. Bradford, (Richmond, Va.: James River Press, 1989), p. 40; Ames, p. 1364; Hendrickson, p. 615.

10. Joseph J. Ellis, *American Sphinx* (New York: Alfred A. Knopf, 1997), p. 61.

11. *PAH*, I: 441; XXV: 544.

12. Forrest McDonald, *Alexander Hamilton: A Biography* (New York: W. W. Norton & Co., 1979), p. 314.

13. *Plutarch's Lives*, trans. John Dryden, ed. Arthur Hugh Clough (New York: Modern Library, 1992), I: 325.

1: St. Croix/Manhattan

1. Bryan Edwards, *The History, Civil and Commercial, of the British Colonies in the West Indies* (London: John Stockdale, 1793), p. 8.

2. Jill Tattersall, *Fabled Feasts of the Caribbean* (Island Legends, 1993), p. 25; F. R. Angier et al., *The Making of the West Indies* (Trinidad: Longman Caribbean, 1960), p. 107.

3. Saul K. Padover, ed., *The Washington Papers* (New York: Harper & Bros., 1955), p. 29.

4. Florence Lewisohn, *St. Croix Under Seven Flags* (Hollywood, Fla.: Dukane Press, 1970), p. 98; Edwards, pp. 433, 435.

5. *IL*, p. 9.

6. *PAH*, XXV: 89.

7. Francis Jennings, *Benjamin Franklin, Politician* (New York: W. W. Norton & Co., 1996), p. 183; Hendrickson, p. 9; McDonald, p. 7.

8. Harold Larson, "Alexander Hamilton: The Fact and Fiction of His Early Years," *William and Mary Quarterly* 9 (April 1952): 148.

9. Hendrickson, pp. 12, 8.

10. *PAH*, III: 617; XIV: 536–37; XXV: 89.

11. *Ibid.*, I: 4.

12. Lewisohn, p. 107; Lito Valls, *What a Pistarckle! A Dictionary of Virgin Islands English Creole* (St. John, U.S.V.I.: L. Valls, 1981), pp. 80, 86, 125.

13. *PAH*, III: 18, 30.

14. *Ibid.*, I: 35–38.

15. Hendrickson, p. 29.

16. Nathan Schachner, ed., "Alexander Hamilton Viewed by His Friends: The Narratives of Robert Troup and Hercules Mulligan," *William and Mary Quarterly* 4 (April 1947): 209.

17. Bayard Still, *Mirror for Gotham* (New York: New York University Press, 1956), p. 21.

18. *Ibid.*, pp. 34–35, 27, 24.

19. *Ibid.*, pp. 39, 37.

20. Michael Kammer, *Colonial New York—A History* (New York: Charles Scribner's Sons, 1975), pp. 360, 343.

21. Schachner, p. 211.

22. Miller, p. 9.

23. *PAH*, I: 86, 150, 93–94, 122, 53, 156.

24. Schachner, p. 214.

25. *Ibid.*, p. 219.

26. *PAH*, I: 177.

27. Schachner, p. 210.

28. Washington Irving, *George Washington: A Biography*, ed. Charles Heider (New York: Da Capo Press, 1994), p. 370.

2: War

1. Hendrickson, pp. 62, 84.

2. Milton Lomask, *Aaron Burr* (New York: Farrar, Straus & Giroux, 1979), p. 216.

3. James Thomas Flexner, *George Washington* (Boston: Little, Brown & Co., 1965–72), I: 343.

4. *PAH*, I: 301.

5. *Ibid.*, I: 220–21.

6. Flexner, II: 200.

7. *PAH*, I: 354, 352; Hendrickson, p. 79.

8. Hendrickson, pp. 82–83, 79.

9. Preston Russell, "The Conway Cabal," *American Heritage Magazine*, February–March 1995, pp. 89, 87; *PAH*, I: 428.

10. Joseph Plumb Martin, *Private Yankee Doodle*, ed. George F. Scheer (Conshohocken, Pa.: Eastern Acorn Press, 1991), p. 127; *PAH*, I: 522; Martin, p. 127; Flexner, II: 305.

11. *PAH*, I: 512–13.

12. Hendrickson, p. 98.

13. *PAH*, II: 421.

14. Martin, p. 204.

15. *PAH*, II: 441–42.

16. Clare Brandt, *The Man in the Mirror: A Life of Benedict Arnold* (New York: Random House, 1994), p. 228; Hendrickson, p. 132.

17. *PAH*, II: 466–67.

18. *Ibid.*, I: 540–41.

19. *PAH*, I: 569.

20. Miller, p. 37; *PAH*, II: 169.

21. *IL*, pp. 246, 263; Miller, p. 22; *PAH*, II: 35, 169.

22. *PAH*, III: 121; II: 167.

23. *Ibid.*, III: 103; I: 391.

24. *Ibid.*, I: 379, 384–85.

25. *Ibid.*, II: 402, 408, 414, 404, 416–17, 635.

26. Hendrickson, p. 62; Maria Sadtler Horner, "A Washington Affair of Honor, 1779," *Pennsylvania Magazine of History and Biography*, 65, no. 3 (July 1941): 370; *PAH*, II: 31; Hendrickson, p. 22.

27. Hendrickson, p. 111.

28. *IL*, pp. 107, 76, 259.

29. Miller, p. 465.

30. Miller, p. 64; *IL*, p. 105; Hendrickson, p. 116.

31. Lomask, p. 128.

32. *IL*, pp. 125, 257.

33. *PAH*, II: 564, 566. The last judgment appears only in a nineteenth-century edition of Hamilton's works by his son, John Church Hamilton, and the editors of *PAH* question its authenticity.

34. *IL*, p. 261; *PAH*, II: 637.
35. Flexner, II: 456; Hendrickson, p. 149.

3: Laws

1. *PAH*, IV: 192; IX: 560–61.
2. *Ibid.*, III: 472.
3. Rahe, *Republics Ancient and Modern* (Chapel Hill: University of North Carolina Press, 1994), p. 128; Miller, p. 85; William Maclay, *The Diary of William Maclay*, ed. Kenneth R. Bowling and Helen E. Veit (Baltimore: Johns Hopkins University Press, 1988), p. 207; *IL*, p. 35; Ames, p. 568.
4. Farrand, p. 94.
5. Ames, p. 628.
6. *PAH*, III: 106; II: 671; Miller, p. 86.
7. Miller, p. 90; *PAH*, III: 246; Hendrickson, p. 169.
8. Miller, p. 94.
9. *PAH*, III: 306, 472.
10. *LP*, pp. 8, 51–52.
11. Schachner, p. 215; Richard B. Morris, ed., *Alexander Hamilton and the Founding of the Nation* (New York: The Dial Press, 1957).
12. *PAH*, III: 431; *LP*, p. 216.
13. *Plutarch's Lives*, II: 250; *LP*, p. 216.
14. *PAH*, III: 512.
15. *LP*, p. 302.
16. *Ibid.*, pp. 373, 383.
17. *Ibid.*, p. 417.
18. *Ibid.*, pp. 312, 314.
19. Hendrickson, p. 195; *PAH*, III: 688–89.
20. George Washington, *Writings*, ed. John Rhodehamel (New York: Library of America, 1997), p. 609.
21. Lomask, p. 130; *PAH*, V: 277.
22. Farrand, pp. 89, 88, 93.
23. Madison, p. 119.
24. *PAH*, III: 145; Madison, p. 135.
25. *PAH*, X: 428; Madison, p. 135.
26. Madison, p. 127.
27. *Ibid.*, p. 131; *PAH*, II: 404; Richard B. Morris, ed., *Alexander Hamilton and the Founding of the Nation* (New York: Dial Press, 1957), p. 155.

28. Madison, pp. 132, 135.

29. Madison, pp. 132, 135; McDonald, p. 105.

30. Plato, *Republic,* 563e; Morris, p. 156; Madison, p. 134.

31. Madison, pp. 47, 177, 76.

32. *PAH,* II: 404; Madison, pp. 134, 128–29, 170–71.

33. Forrest McDonald, *Novus Ordo Seclorum* (Lawrence, Kans.: University Press of Kansas, 1985), p. 181; *PAH,* IV: 224; Farrand, p. 85.

34. Morris, p. 158; Madison, p. 558.

35. *PAH,* XXVI: 148.

36. Madison, p. 621.

37. *Plutarch's Lives,* I: 135.

38. Alexander Hamilton, James Madison, and John Jay, *The Federalist Papers* (New York: New American Library, 1961), pp. 342, 83, 64–66, 92, 160.

39. *Ibid.,* p. 285.

40. *Ibid.,* p. 322.

41. *Ibid.,* pp. 87, 89, 91, 80, 168.

42. *Ibid.,* pp. 208, 468, 423, 414; Alexander Pope, "Essay on Man," Epistle III, lines 304–5.

43. *II,* p. 82.

44. Maclay, p. 76; Washington, p. 692.

45. *PAH,* IV: 649; V: 2.

46. Miller, p. 211; *PAH,* V: 124, 97, 95.

47. Henry Cabot Lodge, *Alexander Hamilton* (Boston: Houghton Mifflin Co., 1910), pp. 74–75.

48. Miller, p. 213; Hendrickson, p. 240.

4: Treasury Secretary

1. *PAH,* V: 336.

2. Ames, p. 568; Maclay, pp. 13, 23, 683, 11, 8.

3. Ames, pp. 638, 729.

4. *PAH,* IV: 276.

5. Miller, p. 225.

6. *PAH,* V: 351; Ellis, pp. 77, 93.

7. Ellis, p. 79; Jefferson, pp. 436, 423; *The Federalist Papers,* p. 513; Jefferson, p. 452.

8. Maclay, p. 275.

9. Jefferson, pp. 460–61.

10. Simon Schama, *Citizens* (New York: Alfred A. Knopf, 1989), p. 89.

11. John Brewer, *The Sinews of Power* (London: Unwin Hyman, 1989), p. 89.

12. Thomas Paine, *Collected Writings*, ed. Eric Foner (New York: Library of America, 1995), p. 113.

13. Jonathan Swift, *Gulliver's Travels and Other Writings* (New York: Bantam Books, 1986), p. 77.

14. Stanley Elkins and Eric McKitrick, *The Age of Federalism* (New York: Oxford University Press, 1993), p. 628; *PAH,* V: 433, 439, 373.

15. *PAH,* V: 465, 526.

16. W. B. Allen, ed., *George Washington: A Collection* (Indianapolis: Liberty Classics, 1988), p. 412.

17. *PAH,* VI: 68, 69, 75, 79, 99, 70.

18. Maclay, pp. 183–84; Hendrickson, p. 276; Ames, p. 835.

19. Ames, pp. 733, 726; Maclay, p. 191.

20. Maclay, p. 239.

21. Elkins and McKitrick, p. 155.

22. *Ibid.,* p. 160.

23. Ames, p. 841; *IL,* p. 315.

24. *PAH,* VII: 307, 314, 315–16, 331, 322.

25. McDonald, *Alexander Hamilton: A Biography,* p. 201.

26. *PAH,* VIII: 98, 100–101, 124.

27. Flexner, III: 289, 287; Miller, p. 282.

28. Miller, p. 282.

29. *PAH,* X: 249, 251, 260, 253, 270.

30. William Wordsworth, "Lines Composed a Few Miles Above Tintern Abbey," lines 109–11; *PAH,* X: 255–56.

31. *PAH,* X: 301.

32. William Carlos Williams, *Paterson* (New York: New Directions Publishing, 1963), p. 245.

33. *PAH,* X: 293.

34. *IL,* p. 473; *PAH,* XXI: 226–27, 250.

35. *PAH,* IX: 7; XXI: 252.

36. *PAH,* XXI: 262; *IL,* p. 474.

37. *PAH,* X: 379, 376.

38. *Ibid.,* X: 520, 557.

39. *Ibid.,* XXI: 256.

40. *Ibid.,* XXI: 252.

5: Fighting

1. Hendrickson, p. 355.

2. Ames, p. 879.

3. John Steele Gordon, *Hamilton's Blessing* (New York: Walker & Co., 1997), p. 28; McDonald, *Novus Ordo Seclorum*, p. 131; Gordon, p. 35; Maclay, p. 346.

4. Maclay, pp. 345–46.

5. Rahe, p. 137; Maclay, p. 330.

6. *PAH*, XII: 480.

7. Jefferson, p. 126.

8. Malone, p. 357.

9. *PAH*, VIII: 478.

10. Hendrickson, p. 339.

11. *PAH*, IX: 75.

12. *Ibid.*, X: 126; Elkins and McKitrick, p. 278.

13. Elkins and McKitrick, p. 284.

14. *PAH*, XI: 444.

15. *Ibid.*, XII: 252.

16. Jefferson, p. 521.

17. *IL*, p. 475.

18. *PAH*, XXI: 258.

19. *Ibid.*, XXI: 136.

20. Hendrickson, p. 379.

21. Don E. Fehrenbacher, ed., *Abraham Lincoln: A Documentary Portrait Through His Speeches and Writings* (New York: New American Library, 1964), p. 42.

22. Paine, p. 370; *PAH*, V: 425; *IL*, p. 300.

23. Elkins and McKitrick, p. 125.

24. Jefferson, p. 522; *The Federalist Papers*, p. 87.

25. O'Brien, p. 146; *PAH*, XXI: 238.

26. John Keane, *Tom Paine* (Boston: Little, Brown & Co., 1995), p. 381.

27. Elkins and McKitrick, p. 343.

28. *PAH*, XV: 85, 106.

29. Elkins and McKitrick, p. 362.

30. *PAH*, XI: 97; XII: 312.

31. Elkins and McKitrick, p. 475.

32. *PAH*, XVII: 17–18; Elkins and McKitrick, p. 479.

33. *PAH*, XVII: 148, 160.

34. *Ibid.*, XVII: 255; Miller, p. 411.

35. *IL*, pp. 259, 74.

36. *PAH*, X: 515.

37. *The Complete Novels of Jane Austen* (New York: Vintage Books, 1976), II: 592; Ames, p. 1194.

38. Hendrickson, p. 399.

39. *Ibid.*, p. 431.

40. *PAH*, XVIII: 451–52.

41. *Plutarch's Lives:* I.: 178, 185; *PAH*, XIX: 478; *PAH*, XVIII: 499; *PAH*, XIX: 91.

42. *PAH*, XVIII: 525; Elkins and McKitrick, p. 435; Ames, p. 1130.

43. Miller, p. 424; Hendrickson, pp. 435–36; Lodge, p. 187.

44. Hendrickson, p. 438.

45. *PAH*, XVIII: 506.

46. *The Federalist Papers*, p. 72.

6: Losing

1. *PAH*, XX: 175.

2. Washington, p. 964.

3. *Ibid.*, pp. 966, 965, 942; Morris, p. 509; Washington, p. 965.

4. *Ibid.*, pp. 966, 976.

5. *IL*, p. 111.

6. Matthew Spalding and Patrick J. Garrity, *A Sacred Union of Citizens* (Lanham, Md.: Rowman & Littlefield, 1996), p. 197.

7. Elkins and McKitrick, p. 528.

8. *PAH*, XVIII: 275; Miller, p. 563; John Ferling, *John Adams* (New York: Henry Holt & Co., 1992), p. 394; Elkins and McKitrick, p. 886.

9. Ferling, p. 150.

10. Hendrickson, p. 511.

11. Miller, p. 481; Ames, p. 1385.

12. *PAH*, XII: 501–2.

13. Hendrickson, p. 469; Fawn Brodie, *Thomas Jefferson: An Intimate History* (New York: Bantam Books, 1974), p. 422.

14. *PAH*, XXI: 132.

15. *Ibid.*, XXI: 134.

16. *Ibid.*, XXI: 243.

17. *Ibid.*, XXI: 244–45, 243–44, 267.

18. *Ibid.*, XXI: 139; Lomask, p. 208; *PAH*, XXI: 163.

19. *Ibid.*, XXI: 214–15.

20. Washington, p. 971; *PAH*, XXI: 244.

21. *PAH*, XX: 422.

22. *Ibid.*, XXI: 22, 99; Elkins and McKitrick, p. 562.

23. *PAH*, XXII: 345; *IL*, p. 255.

24. Elkins and McKitrick, pp. 571, 573.

25. *PAH*, XXI: 345.

26. Ames, p. 1302; Hendrickson, pp. 495.

27. *PAH*, XXI: 365–66, 436.

28. *Ibid.*, XXI: 386.

29. Ames, p. 1273; William Cobbett, *Peter Porcupine in America*, ed. David Wilson (Ithaca, N.Y.: Cornell University Press, 1994), pp. 253–56; Elkins and McKitrick, p. 700.

30. *PAH*, XXI: 495, 522; Brodie, p. 424.

31. McDonald, *Alexander Hamilton: A Biography*, p. 341; Hendrickson, p. 490; Ferling, p. 361.

32. *PAH*, XXIV: 340; XXIII: 240, 122; *IL*, pp. 328ff.

33. *PAH*, XXII: 154–55.

34. *PAH*, XXIII: 192.

35. Elkins and McKitrick, p. 720; *The Federalist Papers*, p. 298; Henry Adams, *John Randolph*, ed. Robert McColley (Armonk, N.Y.: M. E. Sharpe, 1996), p. 34.

36. *PAH*, XXIII: 600, 604; XXII: 453.

37. *PAH*, XXII: 552.

38. Ames, p. 1386; Ferling, p. 412.

39. Elkins and McKitrick, p. 619; *PAH*, XXII: 493.

40. Miller, p. 502.

41. *PAH*, XXIV: 155.

42. Ames, p. 1359; Ferling, p. 394.

43. *PAH*, XXV: 186, 190, 192, 233–34.

44. Elkins and McKitrick, p. 739; Ames, p. 1381.

45. Lomask, p. 244.

46. *Ibid.*, pp. 244–46.

47. *PAH*, XXIV: 465.

48. Lomask, p. 287.

49. *Ibid.*, p. 114.

50. Henry Adams, *History of the United States During the Administrations of Thomas Jefferson* (New York: New American Library, 1986), p. 580.

51. *Boswell's Life of Johnson* (Oxford: Clarendon Press, 1934), vol. I, p. 266; Lomask, p. 69.

52. Lomask, pp. 98, 190, 87.

53. *IL*, p. 376.

54. Lomask, pp. 183, 215.

55. *PAH*, XXI: 521–22; XXV: 272, 276.

56. *Ibid.*, XXIV: 465; XXV: 275.

57. *Ibid.*, XXV: 319–20, 323. Early editions of the letter to Bayard give the last word of Burr's French quotation as *moraux*, "morals"; *PAH* reads *morceaux*, "morsels," which makes the statement even more contemptuous. The confusion arises from mistaking a handwritten "a" for "ce."

7: Words

1. Schama, p. 44.
2. *IL*, p. 62; McDonald, *Alexander Hamilton: A Biography*, p. 317; Hendrickson, p. 244.
3. *IL*, pp. 42–43.
4. *Ibid.*, p. 111.
5. *Ibid.*, p. 128.
6. Jefferson, p. 180.
7. Ferling, p. 404.
8. Hendrickson, p. 469.
9. Jacob Burckhardt, *The Civilization of the Renaissance in Italy* (New York: Harper & Row, 1958), I: 171.
10. Keane, p. 403.
11. Cobbett, p. 199.
12. Paine, p. 430.
13. Benson Bobrick, *Angel in the Whirlwind* (New York: Simon & Schuster, 1997), p. 201; Rahe, p. 261; *PAH*, I: 122.
14. *LP*, p. 3.
15. *IL*, p. 37.
16. *PAH*, XVIII: 278.
17. Miller, p. 520.
18. *Ibid.*, p. 488.
19. Page Smith, *John Adams* (Garden City, N.Y.: Doubleday & Co., 1962), p. 1084; O'Brien, p. 219.
20. *PAH*, XII: 338, 384.
21. Lomask, pp. 87, 189, 190, 341.
22. Jennings, p. 47; Bobrick, p. 362.
23. *PAH*, XII: 252.
24. *Plutarch's Lives*, II: 246.

8: Rights

1. Jefferson, p. 311.
2. *The Federalist Papers*, p. 513.
3. *LP*, p. 284; Jefferson, p. 726.
4. Laurence Sterne, *Tristram Shandy*, p. 54; Jefferson, p. 319.
5. *LP*, p. 830.
6. *PAH*, III: 451–52.
7. *Ibid.*, VIII: 100.

8. *LP,* p. 374.

9. *PAH,* I: 440; VI: 69, 436.

10. *Ibid.,* XIX: 245, 342.

11. Miller, pp. 547–48.

12. Madison, p. 392.

13. *Ibid.;* McDonald, *Alexander Hamilton: A Biography,* p. 373; Hendrickson, p. 3.

14. *PAH,* II: 17–18. In the sentence on natural faculties, Hamilton originally wrote that those of blacks were "perhaps" as good as whites', but crossed it out and boosted it to "probably."

15. *PAH,* XVIII: 415, 519.

16. *Ibid.,* XI: 472.

17. Jefferson, pp. 388–90.

18. *The Federalist Papers,* p. 78.

19. Miller, p. 279.

20. *PAH,* II: 635.

9: Passions

1. *PAH,* XXI: 77–78.

2. Ames, p. 1042; *PAH,* XIX: 59–60.

3. Jefferson, p. 478.

4. Flexner, II: 306; Richard Brookhiser, *Founding Father* (New York: Free Press, 1996), pp. 5–6.

5. *IL,* p. 46; Hendrickson, pp. 239, 104.

6. Maclay, p. 383; *IL,* p. 106; *PAH,* XVIII: 329.

7. Jennings, p. 206; Miller, p. 463; Lomask, pp. 244, 258.

8. *PAH,* XI: 439; *PAH,* XIV: 267; *PAH,* XXI: 404.

9. *PAH,* VII: 51; I: 176–77.

10. *PAH,* XII: 504.

11. *The Federalist Papers,* pp. 54, 56, 59; *PAH,* I: 177.

12. Ames, p. 568.

13. *The Federalist Papers,* p. 322; Smith, p. 846.

14. *PAH,* II: 168; *The Federalist Papers,* p. 140.

15. *PAH,* XII: 252.

16. *Ibid.,* XII: 480.

17. Morris, p. 134.

18. Jefferson, p. 609.

19. See Thomas P. Govan, "Alexander Hamilton and Julius Caesar: A Note on the Use of Historical Evidence," *William and Mary Quarterly* 32 (1975): 475–80.

20. Washington, p. 1013.

21. For American dueling of the period, see Joanne Freeman, "Dueling as Politics: Reinterpreting the Burr-Hamilton Duel," *William and Mary Quarterly* 53 (April 1996): 289–318; and Hamilton Cochran, *American Duels and Hostile Encounters* (Philadelphia: Chilton Books, 1963). Cochran prints the 1777 Code Duello in an appendix. Merrill Lindsay, "Pistols Shed Light on Famous Duel," *Smithsonian*, November 1976, pp. 94–98, gives the relevant statistics on John Church's pistols; though, like much modern writing on dueling, it is marred by the weird failure to recognize that dueling pistols were accurate at the ranges used, that a good shot could aim to kill, and that the deaths that frequently resulted from interviews were therefore not accidental.

22. Adams, *John Randolph*, p. 2.

23. Cochran, p. 8.

24. Mason Weems, *A History of the Life and Death, Virtues and Exploits of General George Washington* (Cleveland: World Publishing Co., 1965), p. 313.

25. Lomask, p. 29.

26. Bobrick, p. 306.

27. *PAH*, I: 603–4; *IL*, p. 280.

28. *PAH*, IV: 228; V: 350.

29. *LP*, p. 814.

10: Death

1. Jefferson, p. 322; *PAH*, XXV: 365.

2. Hendrickson, p. xi; *IL*, p. 72; Ames, p. 1390.

3. *IL*, pp. 216–17; *PAH*, XXV: 288–89.

4. "The Duels Between ———— Price and Philip Hamilton, and George I. Eacker," *Historical Magazine* II, 2nd series (October 1867), p. 198.

5. *Ibid.*, pp. 203–4.

6. *Ibid.*, pp. 193, 201; Cochran, p. 291.

7. Miller, p. 549; *PAH*, XXV: 584.

8. "The Duels," p. 203.

9. *PAH*, XXV: 544.

10. Brodie, pp. 472–73; Hendrickson, p. 574.

11. Hendrickson, p. 577.

12. *PAH*, XXVI: 129, 133; Ames, p. 1468; Henry Adams, ed., *Documents Relating to New England Federalism* (Boston: Little Brown & Co., 1905), pp. 338, 106.

13. Lomask, pp. 316, 335.

14. *PAH*, XXV: 606.

15. *IL*, p. 351; *PAH*, XXVI: 71.

16. *LP,* pp. 777, 782.

17. *Ibid.,* pp. 822, 820, 822, 836, 831, 839.

18. Lomask, p. 332.

19. *Ibid.,* pp. 340–41.

20. *PAH,* XXVI: 189.

21. Adams, *Documents,* p. 148.

22. Harold C. Syrett and Jean G. Cooke, *Interview in Weehawken* (Middletown, Conn.: Wesleyan University Press, 1960), p. 48.

23. *Ibid.,* pp. 68, 85.

24. *Ibid.,* p. 124.

25. *PAH,* XXVI: 293, 308; *IL,* p. 47. Schuyler Hamilton, another grandson, claimed that Hamilton sang "How Stands the Glass Around?", a sentimental eighteenth-century soldier's song, and not "The Drum." An article in the *William and Mary Quarterly* 22 ("What Was Hamilton's 'Favorite Song'?", April 1955, pp. 298–307) makes this case, with unwarranted confidence. I cannot find a description of the range of Hamilton's voice. Allan Maclane Hamilton, evidently relying on family tradition, called it "rich" (*IL,* p. 47), which is probably how a nonmusical person would describe a bass-baritone voice. A tenor might elicit "sweet."

26. *PAH,* XXVI: 309,

27. Adams, *John Randolph,* p. 84.

28. Syrett and Cooke, p. 152.

29. *Ibid.,* pp. 160–63, 145.

30. *IL,* p. 405; Syrett and Cooke, p. 164.

31. *IL,* pp. 407–8.

32. Lomask, p. 357.

33. Hendrickson, p. 619; Cochran, p. 185; *IL,* p. 422; Ames, p. 513; Hendrickson, p. 619.

34. Hendrickson, pp. 615–17.

35. *IL,* p. 427.

36. *Ibid.,* pp. 116–17.

37. Hendrickson, p. 617.

Index